FOREWORD BY GOVE[

THIRTEEN BALLOTS

THE MANUFACTURED SCANDAL THAT OVERTURNED AN ELECTION

Elizabeth B. Harris Psalm 62

*Mark Harris
Lamentation 3:22-23*

ELIZABETH HARRIS

EPILOGUE BY DR. MARK HARRIS

outskirts
press

TABLE OF CONTENTS

FOREWORD

"POLITICS IS A full contact sport, played without pads or protective equipment. If you can't stand the sight of your own blood, don't get in the game." That's the advice I've shared with countless people who are considering stepping into the arena, based on my own experience of how rough the experience can be. When I shared that counsel with Mark and Beth Harris when we met in New York for an extended dinner, I had no idea they would truly shed more blood than most folks ever have in simply seeking to serve God and the country in the public square. I liked them from the moment I first met them, and through the years, I've come to love them and cherish them as dear friends. Beth details the excruciating ordeal they have endured through various campaigns. It's a story of hope and seeming success and then the tragedy of betrayal, corruption, and self-dealing from not only the opposition party, but from those they had trusted on their own team.

The beauty is that they emerged from the brutal process still faithful to God, dedicated to country, and without an understandable cynicism that most people would have been left with.

Beth takes you on the riveting journey with her and Mark as they experience the nastiest political trickery imaginable. I am genuinely sorry that Mark is not in Congress right now. He's one of the smartest, most disciplined, and articulate political figures I've met in the past 30 years. It's not just that North Carolina could use him—the country needs him!

If you are trying to persuade someone to run for office and want to tell them how easy it will be, you probably don't want them to read this book. But if you are a friend who wants the best people to run for office, you DO want to read it and share it with all."

Mike Huckabee

INTRODUCTION

Mary Chapman, Harris for Congress Volunteer

THOUGH MY FRIENDSHIP with Beth and Mark Harris was founded based on a common mission to get Mark elected to Congress in North Carolina's Ninth District in 2018, that friendship was cemented in adversity. Before and after the Democrats achieved their goal of getting a new election for the Ninth District, Mark and Beth were largely battered in the press as the media portrayed Mark as a "cheater" and suborner of "voter fraud."

The Democrats vowed to win a new election after claiming "hundreds or thousands" of votes were taken from Mark's opponent Dan McCready. Republicans who did not know Mark and Beth suspected what the media fed them: that Mark and/or his people cheated. Republican leadership in North Carolina, which had failed to support Mark when his election was not certified, largely abandoned him. Those close to Mark and Beth who knew that he was innocent, were stunned, angry, disappointed, and left with the specter of a new primary as well as a new general election for the Ninth District House seat. Democrat candidate Dan McCready, who had never protested the outcome of the November 2018 election, and who conceded to Mark the day after the election, would run again.

Among his many writings, George Washington wrote that "religion and morality" are "indispensible supports to a republic." The 18th century use of the word "religion" meant Christianity in Colonial

America. It is clear to this writer that Washington's "religion and morality" are largely abandoned in 21st Century America. Thus the former supports that sustained the Republic have been toppled. The Republic is fragile. The majority of Americans no longer possess the moral character and civic virtues Washington spoke about. Likewise, the integrity of the free press has been largely compromised. They have been replaced with the Machiavellian sentiment "the end justifies the means." It has become the norm for to smear and demonize those with whom you disagree because in today's world, narrative becomes reality.

This book is the story of what happened to Mark Harris. Truly Republicans naively play checkers, while the far left plays chess. It is we who love God, Life, Liberty, and America who must awaken and act. It is we who trust God who must repent and believe the Gospel, and know that God redeems all of our stories for His glory and our good. Mark and Beth Harris believe that.

But the hour is late. Our political institutions, which were set up to complement a Republican form of government, are largely in ruins and being weaponized to bring about democratic socialism, a destroyer of markets and liberty. Duties constitutionally assigned to our elected Representatives are being systematically reassigned to partisan appointed commissions, unelected bureaucrats, and judges. The administrative state, or in the common vernacular, "the Deep State," has far too much control over our lives. When we surrender our representation through apathy and ignorance, we willingly return to the condition our forefathers revolted against—our elected representatives rendered powerless, our money and personal property confiscated by a tyrannical State, our civil liberties trampled. Arise in hope, America! Trust in God!

THIRTEEN BALLOTS

NOVEMBER 27, 2018. I leaned my head on the window of a charter bus. It had been a busy day of orientation activities for new members of Congress and their spouses. I was headed back to the hotel with the busload of other spouses. My phone buzzed. A text popped up from my friend Mary: "They're going to try to steal the election." My husband Mark's campaign for the Ninth Congressional District seat had been long and hard, but nothing like what was about to hit us. Everything so many of us had worked for was about to be snatched away.

CHAPTER 1

LEAP OF FAITH

I'VE BEEN MARRIED to Mark Harris for thirty-three years. That's a long time. That's more years than I lived in my entire life before I married him. I can read his eyes in almost any situation. Like many married couples, we are opposites in many ways. Mark is decisive and determined. He is a people person and a networker. He is the guy who always returns phone calls. To solve a problem, he will find a friend with experience in that area and call for advice. I'm deliberate, analytical, and slow to make decisions. If I want to know something, I will find an expert's book on the subject. I am averse to risk. Together Mark and I make a great team.

I've never known anyone with a stronger work ethic than Mark Harris. He is the embodiment of old-school American values like thrift, hard work, and living within your means. Mark had a paper route in his hometown of Winston-Salem, North Carolina. He had to deliver twice a day back then, morning and evening. His mom and dad helped him pick up his papers, roll and bag them, and get them on front porches before Mark went to school and his dad went to work. In the afternoons, his mom helped him accomplish the routine once again.

Once he was able to drive, he worked at Lottie's Shoe Store after school. He also attended church every time the doors opened while in high school. Mark's political interest formed early, and his engagement in that arena won him a seat at Boys' State, and then at Boys' Nation in Washington, DC. He and the other North Carolina Boys' Nation representatives took a picture on the Capitol steps with North Carolina Senator Jesse Helms in their Boys' Nation polo shirts. That is one of Mark's treasured photos. He also volunteered for Ronald Reagan's 1980 campaign, even though at fourteen, Mark was too young to vote. Another treasured memento is his invitation for Reagan's first inauguration in 1981. Mark attended, joining a charter bus of Winston-Salem Republicans and chaperoned by a neighbor who had also volunteered. As he tells the story, he was so far back in the crowd at the inauguration all he could really see was Nancy Reagan's red hat.

My family talked about political issues around the breakfast and dinner tables, but my high school life was full of artistic pursuits: piano, dance, drama, band. I was kind of the classic band kid. Music is the reason my path intersected with Mark's while we were students at Appalachian State University. Mark isn't all that artistically inclined, but God has blessed him with an incredible singing voice. Frankly, it used to make me mad that he had all that natural ability while I longed to have singing talent. Virginia Harris, Mark's mother, was a music teacher and choir director who often sang publicly in Winston-Salem. While at Meredith College, Virginia auditioned for, and won, a place on a rather elite ensemble that sang at the White House.

Virginia wanted Mark to audition for a singing team sponsored by the Baptist Student Union at Appalachian State. As it happened, the year before Mark arrived on campus, I was the pianist for the group and had been chosen as the student leader for it. The first time I saw Mark was the day he walked in for his audition. I sat behind a table with the "adult" judges. The minute he opened his mouth and sang the first note, we knew he belonged on the team musically.

An interview followed, just to make sure we weren't going to saddle ourselves with someone who would make life difficult for the team. I had prepared a question to weed out anyone with a bad attitude toward a female leader. I was being sneaky. I asked, "What would you say or do if your mother asked you not to serve on the team?"

Travel was involved on a lot of weekends, with rehearsals two nights a week. It was quite conceivable that a mom who knew her child was a weak student might discourage jumping in. If a potential ensemble member became abrasive or talked about standing up to his/her mom, I would know I had a hothead on my hands.

I asked my sneaky question. Mark instantaneously responded, "My mom was the one who wanted me to audition."

I tried to get at the heart of the matter. "But hypothetically, what if she didn't want you to do it."

"That's impossible. She wants me to."

"But hypothetically."

"It's impossible. She wants me to."

Mark had the art of the tricky interview nailed by age eighteen.

He made the team and I was already on the team, and the rest is history.

Mark and I took very different paths to arrive at the Baptist Student Union that day. Mark and I both grew up going to North Carolina Baptist Churches in the 1960s and 1970s. After a conversation with some neighborhood boys, Mark asked his parents about the gospel at age ten. They did what most parents of their generations did: they made an appointment to speak with the pastor. Pastor Foy Martin explained to Mark that all have sinned, and that sin carries the penalty of death. Coming to faith in Christ is to believe that Jesus died for our sins and then rose from the dead. We follow Christ publicly by baptism. After that conversation, Mark was ready to be baptized.

I grew up going to "Sunday morning" church, and sporadically to other church activities. My parents were teachers. My dad also coached multiple sports and worked a second job on the weekends as a park ranger at Kings Mountain National Military Park. My parents were the salt of the earth, but they didn't fit the political definition of evangelical Christians. At age twelve, after a lot of people had been asking me about when I was going to join the church, I did so, with a neighbor. We were both baptized.

Unfortunately, that experience didn't have a lot of meaning for me. In high school, I attended church only the minimum that my parents required. In the late 1970s and 1980s, youth culture in general was anti-authoritarian and smug in the way that stupid people who have had life really easy can be smug. It was the era of flippant attitudes toward abortion and high school partying.

God protected me during this time. I never took drugs, and my very steady high school boyfriend determined sex was not for us due to a bad experience in a previous relationship that taught him high school students were too young for that. My path to the Baptist Student Union was through a more radical conversion experience right after high school.

Mark and I began dating at App State. In the summer of 1986, he gave me a diamond and we set the wedding for the following summer, June 1987. Mark is the youngest of five children and never gave his parents an ounce of trouble. As a result, he had a lot of freedom to keep his own hours and make his own decisions. His parents did make one request. They wanted each of their children to finish college before marriage. This request probably stemmed from his dad's own disrupted school experiences due to World War II.

Mark's father, Everette Harris, enlisted in the Army Air Corps during World War II just after high school. In 1944, his plane, the *Eight Ball*, was shot down while on a mission to bomb German oil refineries. Everette didn't talk about the war much in his later years, but he did tell one very funny story about bailing out of the plane. The crew had been trained to jump out of the plane and count to ten before pulling their parachute chords. As the *Eight Ball* plunged downward, Everette said he jumped out, closed his eyes, counted "one, five, ten" and pulled the cord. I can still see Everette telling that story sitting at in a recliner at Sunset Beach, while Virginia and the grandchildren worked a big puzzle on a card table. Everette worked in manufacturing, and that one-week beach vacation with family was priceless to him. He always started laughing right after he told that story, and then sometimes tears would fill his eyes right after that. Tears also filled his eyes when it was time for everyone to pack up and head home after that week of vacation.

The Germans captured Everette and he remained in a POW camp until 1945. As the Allies closed in, Hitler ordered the wholesale slaughter of POWs in Everette's camp. It seems that the guards were too afraid to carry out that evil order, knowing the Allies would bring them to justice. Instead, they marched Everette and his fellow soldiers out of the camp. Along the way, the march became chaotic. Everette and a couple of other guys were able to escape and make their way to the Allied lines. After recuperating at Camp Lucky Strike, Everette got to return home.

After the war, Everette started at North Carolina State University on the GI Bill, but dropped out after he and Virginia married. Everette never got to finish his college education. Like most of the dads of the Greatest Generation, Everette wanted more for his kids than he had. Mark wanted to respect his parents' wishes and finish college before we married. We planned that we would marry in June 1987 after Mark's graduation in May. Mark would start law school in the fall of 1987, and I would teach. We would postpone having children until he finished law school. But God's plans are not our plans.

Two weeks before we were to be married, Mark came to the school where I was teaching in Winston-Salem. He was troubled. Since childhood, Mark had one vision for his life. He would become an attorney and be politically active. He had already been accepted into law school. At class change, I stepped into the hall to monitor the students and there stood Mark. He couldn't shake off the feeling that God was calling him to ministry. He wanted to enter seminary instead of law school. Would I be supportive of that? It would mean a radically different lifestyle than the one he had expected to provide when he had given me a diamond and asked me to marry him.

Mark has said many times how grateful he is for my reaction as we stood in a tiled hallway surrounded by metal school lockers. I threw my arms around him and hugged him. That would be great, I asserted.

Inwardly, I was relieved. Mark and I had visited one meeting of the College Democrats while at Appalachian State, and the "meeting" was basically a drunken party. I was completely turned off. I had registered as a Democrat because my parents were Democrats, but I was also becoming more and more aware of the pro-life movement and the horrors of abortion. The Republican Party was the party that respected life. Soon I would change my registration and join the Grand Old Party.

The hardest part of Mark's decision not to start law school was telling his family. They had known him longer than I had. They knew he was the weird little kid who actually watched the Watergate hearings, spellbound. I tried to be wise and not be too vocal. We could both tell that his parents were mostly concerned that Baptist churches can chew up their pastors and spit them out. Like all parents, they also wanted Mark to be financially comfortable.

Being blessedly young and dumb, I wasn't the least bit worried about any of it. Mark stuck to his guns. He took a leap of faith. He made plans to enroll in Southeastern Baptist Seminary in January 1988. God also had other plans for when we would start our family. Although we had planned to wait awhile, God sent us Laura ten months after we married. She is our only daughter, and we are so thankful she is in the world!

I became a full-time working mother. I was grateful for that experience when Mark ran for office. I never want to forget the women who are working full time because they have to, like I was. I was the provider of our medical insurance. I know what it is to cry when you drop your baby off at daycare. I know what it is to feel guilty because you stayed a little late at work to catch up. I know the exhaustion and the concerns many women face when their financial options are limited.

In 1989 Mark wanted to take another leap of faith. He felt led to pastor Center Grove Baptist Church in Clemmons, North Carolina while still a seminary student. I was hesitant. I was teaching full-time, we had a baby, and had just bought a house. To me the church seemed out in the middle of nowhere, and the parsonage run-down. He, however, was so excited about it I couldn't refuse to consider it.

Ten years later, the church had experienced tremendous growth, relocated to a more visible location, and I had developed priceless friendships that would carry me through all of my adult life. I was able to be a stay-at-home mom for a few years and then return to work part-time on my terms in a much better situation, because we accepted the pastorate of Center Grove Baptist. Mark's leap of faith turned out to be one of the best experiences of our lives.

While at Center Grove, the Republican mayor of Clemmons invited Mark and me to attend a dinner called the "Lincoln Day" dinner. It was held to honor Abraham Lincoln's birthday. The feel was so very different from that Young Democrats alcohol-soaked party at App State. It was a casual fried-chicken dinner. Everyone was welcoming, and there was generally a very family-friendly atmosphere. We were busy, however, and never really engaged politically other than voting and promoting the pro-life position during our years at Center Grove. Still, I look back on that dinner as a very positive introduction to the Republican Party.

During our time at Center Grove, I paid my first-ever visit to the nation's capital, Washington, DC. Mark's family had taken him and his siblings there once when they were young, and he had attended Reagan's inauguration, of course. My family just always seemed too busy at home to do much educational travel. The world was also a much larger place back then. People didn't routinely fly here and there, and a five-hour drive seemed a great distance.

My first trip to Washington wasn't to tour the capital, but rather to protest. James Dobson and other Christian leaders called for a million citizens to meet on the National Mall to rally for life. We attended the March for Life 1990 with another young couple from our church. It was incredible to join with between 500,000 and 750,000 citizens. I was so excited and happy. Now the media and politicians would have to notice those of us who were pro-life. We were too many to ignore.

We got in our little car to return home and turned on the car radio, anxious to hear news reports. We were astounded when the rally was barely mentioned, then the station cut to Raleigh, our state capital, where they gave forty pro-abortion protestors several minutes of on-air time to state their position. The media coverage of March for Life 1990 was so biased that someone made a documentary called *To Tell the Truth*. I bought it, and I still have it on VHS. I can't bring myself to throw the tape away. This was my first taste of true political activism, and my first taste of media bias.

When it was time to leave Clemmons and the ministry of Center Grove and move to Augusta, Georgia I trusted Mark, and once again, although it was hard to move, I felt certain that it was the right decision. It was another big leap of faith. We left Center Grove in December 1999. As we stood on a bridge over the Savannah River with our three children (ages seven, ten, and eleven) and watched fireworks shoot over the water to welcome the new millennium, I was excited about our future in Augusta.

During our years in Augusta came the most difficult leap of faith I had ever made. Our oldest son, John, qualified for a program called TIP run by Duke University. Part of the program included taking the SAT college admission test. When our son took the SAT as a 7th-grader, he achieved a very high score, and elite schools from around the country began filling our mailbox with their promotional materials. One of those schools was McCallie, an all-boys boarding school in Chattanooga, Tennessee.

My first reaction to those school brochures was to throw them all away. There was no way my child was leaving me before college. But someone urged Mark not to throw away the McCallie material. One thing led to another, and we found ourselves on a visit to McCallie. Mark asked me simply to be open as we visited the campus. The visit impressed me. The school was nothing like I had imagined. The school emphasized developing the whole person, not just elite academics.

Attendance at a worship service in the student's faith tradition was mandatory. The school also specialized in challenging young men, and its goal was to turn boys into men who embraced "Honor, truth, duty," the school's motto.

After our visit, our son John found himself on a scholarship week-end visit to McCallie. The school was terribly expensive, but with scholarship and financial aid it was feasible that John could attend. Mark felt that the final decision had to belong to John. I waited a week or two on edge. I really didn't want my son to go off to school at age fourteen. But that's what he ultimately did, and today I know that decision was the right one.

Five and a half years later, when we again moved to come to First Baptist Church of Charlotte, North Carolina, I had no hesitation. Over the years, I had learned a few things about Mark and his leaps of faith. They weren't really crazy. He was capable of developing a plan to execute his ideas. Most of all, he valued my input. I can truly say that he has never made a decision to make a change in our lives until I was fully on board with it. I was trying to let God teach me not to jump so quickly to "no," which was my immediate instinct toward anything that was going to change my world.

When Mark assumed the role of senior pastor at First Baptist Church Charlotte in 2005, he quickly got involved in denominational life at the state level. He turned forty in 2006 and was proving himself a seasoned leader after nearly twenty years in ministry.

By fall of 2011, Mark was serving as First Vice President of the North Carolina Baptist State Convention. In early fall of 2011, Raleigh attorney Tami Fitzgerald requested a meeting with Mark. Fitzgerald is the executive director of North Carolina Values Coalition. Fitzgerald knew that it was likely that delegates to the convention's annual meeting in November would elect Mark as the president of the North Carolina Baptist State Convention.

Mark had been willing to take the lead on a dispute within the convention regarding Myers Park Baptist Church in Charlotte. The church's ordination of gay and lesbian members to leadership clearly violated the theological tenets put forth in *The Baptist Faith and Message 2000*, the national convention's most recent doctrinal document. One of the Baptists' cherished traditions is church autonomy, so churches could determine their own interpretations of Scripture on such matters. They could, however, be designated "cooperating" or "non-cooperating" at both national and state levels. Eventually Myers Park was removed from "cooperating" status in the North Carolina Baptist Convention for its refusal to accept Scripture on the matter of marriage and sexual behavior.

Fitzgerald, also a Baptist, recognized that Mark was willing to be out front on controversial issues. She also realized that he would have a natural platform with which to connect with pastors and churches.

Fitzgerald told Mark that North Carolina's May 8, 2012 primary would include a referendum on gay marriage. Technically known as Amendment One, the primary ballot presented voters with a "yes" or "no" vote on adding an amendment to the North Carolina Constitution that defined marriage as the legal union of one man and one woman. Certain conservative North Carolina legislators, among them the late physician Dr. Jim Forrester, had been trying for years to give voters the opportunity to decide how they wanted marriage defined. After 2010, when the North Carolina General Assembly flipped to a Republican majority, the referendum was approved.

The proponents of the amendment needed help on two fronts: fundraising and networking with voters. Fitzgerald wanted Mark to join Vote for Marriage North Carolina, an advocacy organization for the marriage amendment. Mark accepted Fitzgerald's offer to join Vote for Marriage North Carolina as a charter member. At the North Carolina Baptist State Convention Annual meeting in November 2011, Mark was elected president. At the same meeting, the 4,200 churches of the North Carolina Baptist Convention passed a resolution supporting Amendment One.

By December 2011, Mark had put together five regional meetings of one hundred key pastors from North Carolina Baptist Churches from across the state. In the ensuing months, Mark traveled the state making sure the evangelical community understood the amendment and garnering support for it at the grassroots level. He was shocked at how few in the evangelical community actually voted. I sometimes traveled with him, but often I did not. One night he returned home and told me a story that stuck with both of us. He had been connecting with voters and met an elderly woman. I believe she was at least eighty years old and identified as a church-going Baptist. She assured Mark she would vote on May 8, *although she had never voted before in her life.* How many more Baptists were out there like her? Why weren't they voting? How could these voters be engaged? These questions burdened Mark.

The Obama Administration dispatched Secretary of Health and Human Services Director Kathleen Sibelius to Charlotte and Raleigh to speak against Amendment One. Obama, who had claimed in August of 2008 at the Civil Forum sponsored by California megachurch pastor Rick Warren that he supported traditional marriage, did not personally come to North Carolina, but signaled his opposition of the amendment through Sibelius.

On May 8, 2012 Obama won the Democratic presidential primary in North Carolina. Mitt Romney won the Republican primary. Both Obama and Romney were already the presumptive nominees for their respective parties, so their victories were unsurprising. What was a surprise was the 61% passage of Amendment One. Most pundits had placed its odds of passage at 50-50 going into the May 8th election. North Carolina's rural voters overwhelmingly passed Amendment One affirming traditional marriage. Bladen County, the center of the controversy in the Ninth District in 2018, passed it with 83% of the vote.

The Left was embarrassed. North Carolina was supposed to be the Democrats' purple southern gem. Barack Obama won the state in 2008. Urban Charlotte and Raleigh were growing by leaps and bounds, driven by migration out of the northeast and into the friendlier tax climate of the sunny south. Charlotte gained national prominence with its selection as the site for the 2012 Democratic National Convention.

The day after North Carolinians affirmed their overwhelming belief that marriage should be defined as the union of one man and one woman, President Obama publicly reversed his earlier position on marriage, claiming that he had completed a year of soul-searching and that his views had evolved. In an interview with Robin Roberts of ABC, Obama affirmed his "personal" support of gay marriage.[1]

Following his relatively high-profile involvement with the Marriage Amendment, Mark received invitations to many events. He spoke at the Watchmen on the Wall conference held by the Family Research Council in Washington, DC just a couple of weeks after the successful passage of the Marriage Amendment. Although Mark was a speaker at the conference, he has always said that he took away much more than he gave. He was awakened to the fact that in early America, pastors led the way for liberty. He began to catch a vision for the role a pastor could play in impacting the culture, including the political arena.

In August we both were privileged to attend a conference put on by the Alliance Defending Freedom in Naples, Florida. There we took a deep dive into the rationale behind how Judeo-Christian morality has influenced law and how those moral standards benefit society. We had little idea how significant North Carolina's 61% passage of the Marriage Amendment had been in the eyes of politically engaged evangelicals until we arrived in Naples.

The ADF conference was held in a beautiful hotel and kicked off with a fancy banquet. We had gotten settled in our hotel room following a sweaty flight to Florida, showered, and dressed in our best, just happy to be there. We were stunned when we came into the ballroom and found that we had been seated at the very front, at a table with the president of Alliance Defending Freedom. Mark's hard work traveling the state had gained him some much-deserved recognition.

Although I had been peripherally involved in the promotion of the Marriage Amendment through Mark's involvement, in 2012 my mind was at home. Our oldest child had finished college and launched into life as a young professional with an apartment in Charlotte. Laura was having fun, and I loved it. I delighted in hearing about game nights, girlfriend trips, and the antics of kindergarteners. Our second child and older son John graduated from UNC-Chapel Hill on Mother's Day, 2012. In the days leading up to the May 8, 2012 primary I was busy finalizing party plans. Just before graduation, John proposed to his long-time girlfriend. We would be having a wedding in 2013! There would be much to do in the exciting months ahead. Our younger son, Matthew, was majoring in business at Wake Forest University. Since his childhood, Matthew had been a huge Wake fan, and being accepted there was a dream come true for him. He also had a scholarship and financial aid package that included a job in the athletic department. Matthew is my athletic child, and so this job was icing on the cake.

Mark's participation in Vote for Marriage North Carolina reignited his political interest. Mark decided to put feelers out for a run for the Senate seat held by Democrat Kay Hagan, who would be up for re-election in 2014. A Draft Mark Harris committee was formed in 2013, to good feedback and support. Mark decided to take a sabbatical due him at First Baptist Charlotte, as well as an unpaid leave of absence, to step into the 2014 race. He launched his campaign in 2013. It was our biggest leap of faith yet.

CHAPTER 2

SWING STATE

BETWEEN 2010 AND the time we stepped into the 2014 Senate race, North Carolina experienced a sea change in its political landscape. In 2008, helped by idealistic youth on North Carolina's many college campuses, Barack Obama won North Carolina. But Obama-era court rulings imposing drastic social change against the will of the people became a bridge too far even for North Carolina's reliable rural Democrats.

My dad was an example of just such a Democrat. Obama dismissed people like my dad, who as a teacher, coach, and school administrator was a leader on the front lines of school integration in the 1970s with his characteristic kindness and good cheer. At the same time, Dad enjoyed hunting and attended church with his Bible in his hand most Sundays. Obama, like his party's successor Hillary Clinton, embraced only the coastal elites and played the games of an insider very well. North Carolina's reliable older conservative Democrats began to change parties in the Obama era. In rural Bladen County, which had supported the Marriage Amendment with an overwhelming 83% vote, the Democrat Party lost nearly 20% of its members between 2010 and 2018.

September 4-6 2012, in Charlotte, the Democratic National Convention nominated Barack Obama to a second term. We hosted a conservative Democrat Councilman from New York City named

Fernando Cabrera in our home during the days preceding the DNC. Cabrera could not have been elected without being a Democrat in his district, but he was a pastor and had actually been taken to jail for some of his stances. For us living in Charlotte at the time, these stories of a pastor being hauled off to jail seemed far-off and surreal. Cabrera was in Charlotte for the Democratic National Convention to try to be a voice of reason to slow down the takeover of the Democrat Party by the radical left. During the convention, Charlotteans saw leftist groups up close for the first time. Occupy Wall Street camped out in Marshall Park, right behind First Baptist Church, where Mark was the pastor.

First Baptist held prayer each Sunday morning for several weeks leading up to the convention. Those willing to get up a little earlier and meet to pray came to the church and walked around uptown, especially around the perimeter area for the convention. We prayed for peace and safety for the convention while it was meeting in Charlotte.

While the convention was an exciting opportunity for the city, there were dark moments as well. Many in Charlotte were very uncomfortable with the removal of any mention of God and the lack of support for Israel in the Democrat Party Platform finalized at the convention. While it was later asserted that booing which occurred during the debate over the party's platform was directed at leadership over a procedural matter, it appeared at a glance that the convention was booing the word "God," which caused a furor in church-going Charlotte. The 2012 Democrat Convention was a high-profile event in North Carolina, but in the end, it left more conservative Democrats feeling alienated from the party of their fathers.

In the 2010 Obama-care backlash, Republicans captured a majority in the North Carolina legislature, an unprecedented political revolution with huge consequences. The Republican-majority North Carolina General Assembly redrew our Congressional Districts after the 2010 census, which is their constitutionally assigned duty. Court challenges to North Carolina's new districts mounted. Racially charged allegations were leveled against the North Carolina legislature as the

2012 election loomed.

Going into the general election of 2012, North Carolina was considered one of nine true swing states.[1] Obama had carried North Carolina in 2008, but political reporters recognized that college students were largely responsible for his narrow win.[2] Most pundits thought the presidential election would be close here. No one saw the red wave coming.

In the November 2012 general election, North Carolina reversed itself and chose Mitt Romney over Barack Obama. Worse for North Carolina Democrats, a former Mayor of Charlotte, Republican Pat McCrory, defeated Democrat Walter Dalton handily to become governor in 2012, garnering 54.62% of the vote. McCrory was the first Republican governor elected since James G. Martin rode in on Ronald Reagan's coattails in 1984. McCrory was an affable and comfortable candidate. He focused mainly on economic and transportation issues but did not actively oppose the social conservatives in his party. North Carolina also elected a Republican lieutenant governor, Dan Forest.

North Carolina's congressional delegation shifted to majority Republican in 2012 as well. Conservative Democrat Heath Shuler, who had unsuccessfully challenged Nancy Pelosi's leadership, decided not to run, and Republican Mark Meadows won the Shuler seat in western North Carolina. Prior to Shuler's win, however, the seat had been Republican, even under the old district maps drawn by Democrats. In rural eastern North Carolina, Conservative Democrat Mike McIntyre held on to his seat in a redrawn district that favored Republicans. Redistricting wasn't solely responsible for the flip of North Carolina's congressional delegation to majority Republican. Nonetheless, the court challenges continued.

Republicans not only maintained their majority in the North Carolina legislature, which they had established in 2010 for the first time in over one hundred years, but turned it into a veto-proof supermajority in 2012. When the new North Carolina legislators took office in January 2013, the GOP immediately went to work to chip away at the pillars of North Carolina Democrats' power: straight-ticket voting and early voting.

In 2013, House Bill 589 was passed by the North Carolina General Assembly and signed into law by Republican Governor Pat McCrory. It took several months to get the 56-page bill through, with passage coming just a few days before the end of the 2013 legislative session. The new law made sweeping changes in voting procedures in North Carolina. It required photo ID to vote and created a standard absentee-ballot request form, replacing the old method whereby a voter simply wrote a request and sent it to his or her local elections board. A voter would have to include either his North Carolina driver's license number or the last four digits of his Social Security number on the absentee ballot request form to prevent fraud. This absentee-ballot request form could now be downloaded from the State Board of Elections website and legally reproduced under the new law. House Bill 589 also eliminated straight-party voting and reduced early voting hours.

Why would Republicans target straight-party voting and early voting? Straight-party voting enabled down-ballot candidates to escape the phenomenon known as "voter roll-off," the tendency of people to vote only for the top few races on their ballots and quit. Straight-party voting also served to entrench one party in power in certain locales. Ending straight-party voting would enable conservative Democrats to change parties and still have some hope of winning their elections. Without straight-party voting, each race would be voted individually. Presidential races were already voted individually and indicated North Carolina voters were aligning with Republicans more and more.

In essence, straight-party voting made the political party's activities more significant and the candidate's activities less so. With the elimination of straight-party voting, candidates were responsible for themselves and their own grassroots efforts to a much greater degree, a fact that would have far-reaching implications for us. Before 2013, each political party simply had to get its voters to the polls and have them cast one vote, or two in presidential years. The focus was on getting voters to the polls, and early voting provided the opportunity to do just that.

Each day of early voting is an opportunity for a paid "hauler" to bring voters to the polls for hours on end. Hauling with straight-party voting was especially effective, as the party could pay the hauler and trips to the polls were over quickly, allowing more voters to get to the polls in a day. While there is nothing illegal about hauling as long as the voter is not given any type of compensation for making the trip to the polls, many Republicans thought the practice unethical, or at least offensive to their sensibilities. Other Republicans embraced the practice but seemed less successful at it than their Democrat counterparts. Politically, a reduction in early voting hours translated to a reduction in the number of voters who could be hauled into the polls. Third-party groups that worked to Get Out the Vote (GOTV) for candidates would be less successful if early voting hours were reduced.

The North Carolina Chapter of the NAACP and the League of Women Voters immediately challenged House Bill 589 in court. The court battle over H.B. 589 pitted two elected officials against one another in a battle that would foreshadow their 2016 fight for the governor's seat. North Carolina's Democrat Attorney General Roy Cooper refused to defend House Bill 589 in court. Governor McCrory, along with Speaker of the North Carolina House Thom Tillis, had to hire a private law firm to defend the new law. Tillis and McCrory hired the Raleigh law firm Ogletree Deakins, where the North Carolina State Board of Elections Executive Director Kim Strach's husband is a shareholder. Ogletree Deakins raked in more than one million dollars in legal fees defending House Bill 589.

When a federal appeals court stayed portions of the new law prior to the 2014 election, Strach openly condemned the decision. Members of the appointed board that oversees the state elections agency raised questions about potential conflicts of interest and the arrogance shown by Strach in criticizing a court of law. According to Democrat board member Dr. Maja Striker, her concerns about potential conflicts of interest were dismissed.[3] Strach declined to be interviewed by a reporter for *Indy Week*, which reported Dr. Striker's concerns, but in an email Strach said she had no role in the legislature's selection of Ogletree Deakins and that she did not believe her family made money from the case.[4]

Courts eventually struck down the voter ID portion of the new law, along with the reduction in early voting hours. The other changes remained, including both the elimination of straight-party voting and the standardization of the absentee-ballot request process. Standardized absentee-ballot request forms allowed GOTV programs to be implemented locally and also by well-heeled national organizations. GOTV with absentee-ballot requests began to replace or supplement hauling during early voting as a means of ensuring votes for third-party groups who needed to produce results. It was not necessary to have a reason to vote absentee-by-mail. "No excuses" absentee-by-mail voting, with standardized forms that could legally be downloaded and reproduced, became an important part of GOTV efforts.

CHAPTER 3

THE 2014 SENATE RACE

IN RETROSPECT, IT was crazy to bite off a huge statewide race for a first run at a political office. Mark's previous political activism had been during the 1980s. He had no idea how much had changed. "Retail politics," or "grassroots" politics as Mark had known it during his teenage years, was largely over. Consultants, fundraising, and data had replaced getting out and meeting people, according to some. A consultant actually described getting out among voters rather than simply sitting in an office making calls to raise money as "playing candidate."

Thom Tillis, speaker of the North Carolina House, was considered the front-runner for the GOP nomination to try to take out Democrat Senator Kay Hagan. Tillis represented the Republican establishment. As Speaker of the North Carolina House, Tillis was credited with engineering the supermajority and advancing the Republican agenda. As North Carolina's regulatory and tax climate became friendlier to business, the state began to attract companies. In addition to these successes, however, Tillis was also saddled with baggage over a deal with a private company to open toll lanes on Interstate 77 through Charlotte. North Carolinians were unfamiliar with tolls. We had a gas tax and a highway fund, which the formerly Democrat General Assembly had frequently raided, and there were loud voices demanding that the state fix the travel problem on I-77 without tolls. In addition, Speaker Tillis refused to step down from his position in the North Carolina General Assembly during the Senate campaign. This troubled some.

A Raleigh obstetrician with a fairly large online following as a Libertarian-leaning conservative, Greg Brannon, was the choice of the more conservative Tea Party wing of the party. We did not understand those dynamics at first and simply started trying to build support through connections we had across the state. A persistent rumor developed, completely false, that North Carolina-GOP chair Robin Hayes recruited Mark to run to foil Brannon's chances of defeating Thom Tillis. People don't step away from their paychecks, travel the state, keep a grueling schedule, and subject themselves to all the nastiness of a political campaign just to foil someone else's chances. People run because they want to win, and anyone who says otherwise has most likely never had the guts to step out and put his name on a ballot.

Because Robin Hayes was the only member of Republican leadership Mark knew, Mark did reach out to him for his support. Mark had invited Hayes to a groundbreaking ceremony for our church in Clemmons when Hayes was a Congressman, and Hayes attended. Whether Robin Hayes gave Mark his support sincerely, or to somehow secretly help Thom Tillis, only Hayes knows.

Mary Frances Forrester, the widow of Jim Forrester, also supported Mark. Dr. Jim Forrester had worked for a decade to get the marriage amendment out of committee and into the hands of voters when he served in the North Carolina General Assembly, but sadly he passed away before the amendment become part of the North Carolina Constitution after its approval in May 2012. Mary Frances liked Mark for his boldness and willingness to take stands. We were grateful for Mary Frances; she was as experienced as it gets as far as North Carolina politics.

Mark was not in a position to ply special interest groups for money, nor to seek out major Republican donors from all over the country. He simply went to work, and with the generosity and support of a network he built around the state, raised almost a million dollars for the 2014 campaign.

The campaign was hard, but it was also fun. I took everything and everyone at face value and enjoyed hearing from those who were well spoken enough to articulate the Republican agenda for North Carolina. The Senate candidates, without Tillis, participated in numerous county and GOP club debates and candidate forums. One of our first events was a small forum put on by the Gaston County GOP at a sandwich shop in Gastonia. We were crammed in the shop, and the atmosphere was relaxed, despite the fact that the candidates were debating on the issues.

During the 2014 Senate Campaign, I paid possibly my first visit ever to Bladen County, North Carolina. We had a friend, Cameron, who pastored there in a small town. He lived at White Lake, an interesting natural lake fed by springs. The spring water has a very low pH, so not much can grow in the lake. Consequently, its water was known for being crystal clear.

A member of Cameron's church graciously held a meet and greet for Mark at his home. It was at this meet and greet that I began to get educated on what was happening in rural North Carolina politics. There were quite a few Democrats in attendance at the meet and greet. They were conservative people who felt trapped.

The culture in small North Carolina communities in rural parts of the state dictated that to get anywhere with a political agenda, you had to be a Democrat. As long as the Democrat Party had a stranglehold on North Carolina politics, membership in the Democrat Party was expected for civil servants and law enforcement. These conservative Democrats now saw a light at the end of the tunnel. They were considering leaving the party, as they felt it had left their values behind. More than one person expressed that "Daddy would roll over in his grave" if his child registered Republican, but people were willing to move over to Unaffiliated. Unaffiliated voter rolls grew by 62% in rural Bladen County after the 2010 flip of the North Carolina General Assembly to Republican.[1]

Traveling the state in 2013 and 2014, we frequently saw fellow candidate Heather Grant and her husband Michael at grassroots Republican events. Heather was a former medical professional in the armed forces and a very likeable candidate. Like us, Heather and Michael slogged through rain, sleet, and snow to get to every event possible all over the state. I came away impressed with the dedication of the local grassroots GOP folks who put the forums and debates together and resolved to tell other Christians that they needed to attend such events, to meet candidates in person.

We had so many fundraisers in homes of incredibly lovely and gracious people that I lost count. These were not $10,000 per plate dinners of the kind that special interest and political party groups put together. Although these small meet and greet events did not usually generate large sums of money, they remain in my memory as the most enjoyable parts of the campaign. I was blown away by the effort hosts made to create the meet and greets. One woman had hand towels embroidered with "Mark Harris for Senate." Another had customized M&Ms as part of a fun candy station. I have hosted these events in my home, and it is quite a task to do ironed linens, fresh flowers, food and drinks, and all the other touches that make an event feel special. My heart was touched that people we often didn't know, but who perhaps attended the church of a pastor we did know, would open their homes to us. A relative of one of our staff did a meet and greet in the eastern part of the state, and snow was on the ground from a freak snowstorm. This too was a beautiful event made special by that rare eastern North Carolina snow.

As the Senate primary neared, it was exciting when four of the eight candidates were considered serious enough contenders to make the televised debates. Mark was joined by Thom Tillis, Greg Brannon, and Heather Grant for the first debate at Davidson College. One of Mark's answers at the first debate was brilliant and hilarious. When the candidates were asked which ACC basketball team they supported, as their final "lightweight" question, Mark replied that he had sent a child through UNC-Chapel Hill and had a child at Wake Forest, but based on the Biblical truth that "where your treasure is, there your heart is also," he would have to go with (the more expensive) Wake Forest. The auditorium at Davidson College rang with laughter. With that question, Mark had relaxed and the "real Mark" came through.

As the campaign began to wind down in spring 2014, Mark's father passed away. Everette Harris will always be a hero to Mark, who still speaks about his father's experiences as a prisoner of war. At the end of Everette's life, his mind was sharp, but his body had been in decline for some time. Everette cast an absentee-by-mail vote for his son Mark in early April and then died on April 17th.

When the election was held in May, Thom Tillis won the primary. Greg Brannon came in second. Mark came in third with 18% of the vote and Heather Grant came in fourth. After the election, we got a nasty surprise when a Democrat named Cynthia Burke successfully challenged Everette Harris's ballot. Everette's ballot was thrown out. I cannot describe what a slap in the face that felt like. Here is a man who fought for his country, suffered for his country, and lived the rest of his life as a contributing United States citizen, only to have his final vote thrown out. And that vote for his son—his fifth child—to boot.

The story behind the challenge was that some people in another part of North Carolina were angry because their deceased cousin's vote had been challenged and thrown out. They wanted the law to be changed and they wanted a high-profile case to draw attention to it. They had to recruit a Democrat from Everette's precinct, where ironically Everette had given his time for years as a Democrat precinct judge, to make the challenge. That's where Cynthia Burke came in. Their explanations were not soothing to me in the least.

The North Carolina House passed the Everette Harris Act in June 2014. The Act said a legal ballot cast early or by mail would have to count even if the voter died before Election Day. Unfortunately, the bill was never considered by the North Carolina Senate and thus did not become law.

Both Mark and Heather Grant proved they were team players and supported Tillis fully through the general election. As a result, both

Mark and Heather Grant were invited to play a role at the state GOP Convention that year, and we enjoyed attending. The keynote speaker at the big convention banquet was Mike Huckabee, who had been kind to us and generous with his time when Mark reached out to him about what to expect when running. Soon he and Janet would become good friends, and remained supportive of us throughout our two subsequent runs.

An article I read after the 2014 election troubled me, although I didn't fully understand all of its implications at first. The article praised Thom Tillis for running "a disciplined campaign." In my observation "disciplined" had meant being all over the country raising money while simultaneously avoiding any opportunity to appear before the citizens of the state to go on record with a position on any issue. I didn't yet understand "the money."

Within three months of the primary two of our three children married, so life moved on very rapidly, as life has a way of doing. Once again, my thoughts were at home. I chalked 2014 up as an anomalous experience on the heels of the 2012 Marriage Amendment, but I did resolve to get more directly involved with helping worthy candidates. Previously, any activism on my part was isolated to the pro-life movement.

We became more and more involved in local GOP clubs, and in our official county GOP organization. Mark was in demand as a speaker. He spoke about his burden for the direction of our country, and how pastors could play a role in shaping that direction. He continued to be dismayed at how few Christians even voted. Mark became a significant voice for the evangelical community. Candidates courted his support as 2014 turned into 2015.

On June 26, 2015 the Supreme Court ruled in *Obergefell V. Hodges* that, just like the High Court's ruling on abortion in 1973, state laws and even state constitutions were irrelevant, and that same-sex couples could marry based on the Due Process and Equal Protection Clauses of the 14th Amendment. The Marriage Amendment that so many, including Mark, had worked for in 2012 was thus null. That night, the White House was lit with rainbow lights, a display funded by gay-rights groups. That symbolic act felt like Obama thumbing his nose at conservative Democrats who had voted for him in 2008 and again in 2012, even while they also voted to define marriage as "the union of one man and one woman" in North Carolina. Obama would later say to a Gay Pride Reception that the rainbow lighting was "one of the most special moments of my Presidency." [3]

University of North Carolina law professor Maxine Eichner, an advocate for same-sex marriage, seemed to intuitively grasp that the public wasn't ready to embrace the radical LGBTQ agenda. Eichner was quoted in the *Charlotte Observer* in response to a 2014 North Carolina court ruling supporting gay marriage: "The speed of this is breathtaking. It makes the mind reel."[4] North Carolina would later grapple with conscience protections for magistrates after at least one magistrate refused to perform same sex weddings. It is difficult to quantify the effects of any one of these events on the electorate, but it is clear that the decline in the number of registered Democrats accelerated in rural North Carolina.

Closer to home, our children were establishing their lives as adults. They had completed their college educations, married, and in April, November, and December of 2015 we welcomed the first round of beautiful grandchildren. Careers also took them away from us, as one took a job with Sam's Club corporate in Arkansas, one moved to Washington, DC for a clerking position with a judge on the DC Court of Appeals, and one moved to St. Louis for her husband's job. I worked part-time at a museum but enjoyed being free to travel as needed to be with them, especially since all three families had infants.

While I continued to stay engaged in the Republican Party and tried to help advance Republican candidates I believed in, I did not expect Mark to run for office again, at least not anytime soon. A phone call on a spring day in early 2016 changed all of that.

March for Life 1990, Washington DC. The rally of over a half million pro-life citizens was my first trip to Washington.

June 14, 2014, Charlotte, NC. Our daughter married just after Mark's first campaign, the 2014 U. S. Senate primary. Photo credit: Allison Fowler Photography

September 22, 2017, Monroe NC. When Mark launched his 2018 campaign, we had five grandchildren.

CHAPTER 4

A FATEFUL PHONE CALL

I WAS ENJOYING a warm, sunny day at the beach in Pawley's Island, South Carolina in early March 2016. In fact, I was enjoying a nice life in general. Within the past year I had welcomed three grand-children, two girls and a boy. My husband was the senior pastor of a large church in downtown Charlotte, North Carolina. We had just crossed ten years at the church, and people were beginning to call him pastor and mean it, as the saying goes. Yes, I was living a nice, monogrammed, Sunday-brunch-at-the-club, Southern life.

Mark had his phone with him. He always had his phone with him, so much so that sometimes I rued the day he learned to use a smart phone. Generally he was quite an old soul and had been very slow coming into the information age. Mark picked up his phone and commented that he had to call this guy back, Dave. Dave had been trying to connect with him for several weeks. He had something to do with the American Renewal Project, Mark thought. The American Renewal Project was attempting to help train Christians to run for office, and Mark sometimes spoke at their events. "He probably just wants to schedule me for a conference," Mark said nonchalantly while he dialed Dave's number. While we sat in two white plastic pool chairs at Pawley's Island in March 2016, Mark talked to Dave, and life changed forever.

Dave talked to Mark about running for Congress in the Ninth

Congressional District. The districts had been completely shaken up by the courts, and Dave thought Mark had a strong chance to emerge victorious in a special election for the Republican primary, despite the fact that an incumbent was running again in the Ninth District.

North Carolina's primary elections were originally slated for March 15, 2016. The incumbent Congressman for the Ninth District, Robert Pittenger, had filed to run for re-election in December. In February, a federal court ruled that North Carolina's congressional district maps were racially gerrymandered and ordered the North Carolina General Assembly to redraw them.

With the March 15th date looming, the North Carolina legislature appealed to the US Supreme Court for an emergency stay to keep the old districts in place while it went to work redrawing the map of North Carolina's Congressional Districts. In mid-February 2016, the Supreme Court refused to grant a stay, and the legislature was forced to both approve new maps and postpone the state's congressional primaries, despite the fact that the March 15th election date was less than a month away. Ballots had already been printed, and absentee ballot voting was already underway.[1] Filing would re-open for North Carolina's congressional races in March 2016. New elections would be held June 7th.

Congressman Robert Pittenger didn't have stellar conservative ratings, although he did have a strong pro-life record. We already knew Pittenger was uber-wealthy from controversial land deals and had engaged in an extremely nasty Republican primary campaign in 2012. As Dave explained to Mark, Pittenger had previously represented only about a quarter of the newly drawn district. He wasn't a leader, his name ID would be low, and in essence, this was a new seat. This was almost an open election. The old North Carolina Ninth District no longer existed.

The old North Carolina Ninth District included all the affluent parts of Charlotte, along with both its northern and southern suburbs, including the western part of Union County, which was also in the Charlotte Metro region. Union County consistently voted Republican.

29

The newly drawn district now comprised only fifty precincts in South Charlotte. Charlotte's northern suburbs were stripped out of the district. The new Ninth District stretched approximately 150 miles east of Charlotte, encompassing all or parts of North Carolina's poorest rural counties. The district now included all of Republican-leaning Union County, not just the part of the county adjacent to Charlotte.

It also included counties full of farmers and blue-collar entrepreneurs who traditionally voted Democrat. Although the new Ninth District encompassed far more Democrats than it had previously, these were rural conservative Democrats. Not only had the rural counties in the newly created district supported traditional marriage in overwhelming numbers, Mark had over-performed in them during the 2014 Senate campaign. In Anson County, one of the counties placed in the Ninth District in 2016, Mark had actually placed first among all eight candidates for the GOP Senate nomination in 2014. Dave thought Mark's chances of winning the primary in the new Ninth District were high. Dave also strongly believed that the Republican primary on June 7, 2016 would in essence be the election.

I remember exactly what I said after hearing Mark's summary of his call with Dave. I don't know why I remember it so distinctly, but I do. Sitting in the warm sunshine, it was hard to be down on the possibility of another run. Trouble seemed far away and happiness close at hand. Usually I am quite risk averse, but on that day at the beach when Mark hung up the phone and recounted his conversation with Dave. I said, "That's a game-changer."

In the re-drawing of North Carolina's districts, another new district had been created north of Mecklenburg County: District 13. One of Mark's friends, a Gaston County Commissioner, had already been trying to convince Mark to throw his hat into the ring for that race. I thought that idea was silly.

There would be possibly ten or more in the primary for the new District 13 seat. We didn't even live in the district. In a large field of many candidates, the one with the most money typically wins. Ted Budd had already announced his intent to run in District 13. We knew the extended Budd family tangentially, through their company Budd Services, which provided janitorial services to First Baptist Church, Charlotte, where Mark was the pastor. They were a good family, and we had no desire to run against Ted, who was backed by Club for Growth, a conservative group, and who had personal resources.

The new Ninth District *was* a game-changer. The possibility of running against an incumbent hadn't really crossed our minds before, but the more we investigated his record, the less impressed we were with Robert Pittenger. *Conservative Review* gave him extremely low "Liberty Scores," mostly due to votes for massive spending bills. The only bill he had successfully shepherded through the legislative process into law was the first bill he introduced in 2013, the Kilah Davenport Child Protection Act of 2013. Mark also felt that he was a much better fit for the more rural Ninth District than Pittenger, who lived in an exclusive community on a golf course in Charlotte. Mark also had many connections with pastors throughout the district from his work on the Marriage Amendment in 2012.

Todd Johnson of Union County had also announced his intention to take on Pittenger in the special election. Because the circumstances were unique with the court-ordered special election, candidates were running for about nine weeks in essentially brand-new districts. The campaigns would be sprints, not marathons.

As we contemplated running, I was concerned that Mark should perhaps resign from First Baptist. By the nature of the special election and its circumstances, however, the campaign would be truncated. Its demands would be much less than the 2014 Senate campaign and the period of time for the campaign would be much, much shorter. We invited special friends in leadership at First Baptist out for dinner when we returned from vacation to share the phone call and get their thoughts. They were supportive and felt that it would not be necessary for Mark to resign unless he won the primary.

Later Mark called all the leadership together for a meeting. He offered to resign from First Baptist Church to run for the Ninth District seat. Since the campaign was only nine weeks long, the church's leaders generally felt that he should not do so, although that decision was not viewed as the right one by all parties at First Baptist.

Mark decided to hire Victory Enterprises of St. Louis, Missouri to run a campaign. One of Victory's principal consultants, Steve Michael, had also spoken at a few of the American Renewal events. There was little fanfare about Mark's run. He filed alone at the Raleigh Board of Elections on Good Friday, March 25, 2016, which was the final day for candidates to file to run in the June 7th special congressional election. My part-time job usually required me to work Thursday through Saturday, so I was unable to accompany Mark to file. Mark asked one of the workers there to snap a photo of him with his phone to record the event.

We were worried about Mark getting such a late start in the campaign. Pittenger had been running since December, and Johnson had announced by the February round of Lincoln Day GOP dinners, updated since the one we attended in the 1990s to now be called "Lincoln-Reagan Dinners."

The North Carolina State Board of Elections had also determined that everyone who had ordered an absentee ballot for the March primary would automatically receive one again for the special election, without having to personally request it. This was the first (but certainly not the last) instance in which the intersection of leftist lawsuits, court rulings, and State Elections Board decisions would change North Carolina's absentee ballot procedure. This gave Pittenger a great advantage, we thought. There was much to be done in a very short amount of time before those absentee voters began casting their ballots.

I found the campaign difficult. The novelty of 2014 had worn off. The district stretched from south Charlotte, where we live, following Highway 74 to part of Bladen County, which is just south of Fayetteville, North Carolina. The twelve Bladen County precincts added to the Ninth District in 2016 represented the least populated and most remote corner of the new district. It is a three-hour drive to get to the small communities in Bladen County from my house in

Charlotte. My Charlotte ZIP code (pop. 31,525) covering a 12 square mile area[2] has almost as many people living in it as the entire population of Bladen County's 874 square miles, (pop 33,190.)[3] During the short 2016 campaign, we didn't engage much with Bladen County voters.

While I was no stranger to a demanding schedule, the constant travel up and down dismal Highway 74 and the rural highways that intersected it became a grind. Some days we spent six- plus hours in the car in addition to events, GOP meetings, and going door-to-door meeting voters. Because we were both also working, we often left Charlotte between 2:00 and 5:00 p.m. and returned home after midnight. The gritty towns of Lumberton, Fayetteville, Laurinburg, and Wadesboro were dirty and economically depressed.

We did meet many wonderful people all over the district. These were the Trump voters. They had screamed about the destruction of manufacturing when Bill Clinton rammed NAFTA through in the 1990s, but no one listened. One strip of Highway 74 through the business district of Rockingham, North Carolina reminded me of photos I had seen of Europe after World War II. Former manufacturing plants, piles of partially collapsed brick, sat abandoned near the road. Apparently, there wasn't even enough money to tear the ruins down.

Behind the collapsing façades, however, stands an immaculate Veteran's Park, where annually the citizens of Rockingham raise money to put up a new monument. They honor their war dead on Memorial Day and eat hamburgers and hot dogs together afterward. For these citizens, even an Olive Garden is an hour's drive away and would be considered a luxury, as it would have been for me when I was growing up in small town North Carolina.

Now these voters had a champion in Trump, as it was apparent that he would be the 2016 Republican nominee. I cared about these citizens' concerns and often felt heartbroken when I visited their towns, but I was also worried about fall-out at First Baptist Charlotte. Trump was unpalatable to many evangelicals. If Mark were the nominee, he would have to support Trump. What would that mean? I wasn't sure.

People in wealthy Charlotte had the luxury of being ideological.

People in Lumberton, in North Carolina's largest and poorest county, Robeson County, didn't have that same luxury. Robeson County had also been added to the Ninth District in 2016. In Robeson County, citizens weren't worried about Trump's tone or tweets. They were worried about recruiting businesses when their school buildings were crumbling. I heard the angst in their voices at GOP meetings as they agonized over whether to approve a plan for new school construction that would be privately funded, with the county leasing the buildings from the company that built the schools. Schools would be larger, with children on buses longer, but schools would be newer.

Somehow government was failing these people, but how could we even unravel the failure? It existed on so many levels. I began to understand what candidate Trump meant when he talked about the swamp.

During the three-way primary that spring of 2016 between Mark, Todd Johnson, and Robert Pittenger, Pittenger relied heavily on endorsements. Getting endorsements was a kind of trademark for him. At a GOP event back in the winter, before the 2016 districts were redrawn and Mark decided to run, Pittenger approached Mark with an envelope already containing an endorsement that awaited Mark's signature. I can't recall whether Mark took the envelope or not, but he declined to endorse.

Pittenger's craving for endorsements blew up in his face the day before the June 7th primary. Teresa Rucho, wife of then State Senator Bob Rucho, recorded a robo call in which she cheerily announced "good news." Donald J. Trump had endorsed Robert Pittenger. Because we live in the Ninth District, we got the robo call.

Mark found it hard to believe that Donald Trump would be handing out endorsements in primaries as he faced a potentially rebellious Republican National Convention later that summer. In North Carolina's March 15th presidential primary, Trump defeated Ted Cruz, his last real opponent, by just 39,792 votes. In contrast, Hillary Clinton defeated Bernie Sanders by 155,897 votes. Among my evangelical friends, support had been divided between Mike Huckabee, Ben Carson, and Ted Cruz early. By March 2016 Carson and Huckabee were out, and evangelicals hoped to put Cruz over the top. When that didn't seem possible, there was serious talk among activist Republicans of attempting to deny Trump the nomination at the Republican National Convention.

A call to Mike Huckabee produced a Huckabee call to Corey Lewandowski, who confirmed that Trump had not endorsed Pittenger. Pittenger was caught red-handed in the lie about the Trump endorsement as well as a Huckabee endorsement up on his website. Mike Huckabee is a personal friend, and although he had endorsed Pittenger in the 2012 general election, Huckabee had specifically spoken to Pittenger and asked him not use that old endorsement in 2016 because of our friendship with him. The fiasco produced an article in the *Charlotte Observer* called "Robert Pittenger's No Good, Very Bad Endorsement Day." [4] The article was a lucky break for us on election morning, and Mark's persistence in getting to the bottom of the robo call had paid off.

I had no idea what to expect on election night. We had a small meeting room at a hotel in Charlotte booked for the party to watch the results and close out the campaign. We didn't have enough money left for a really nice party. I had bought a red dress on the spur of the moment just in case Mark won. I'm not really a huge fan of red, but you have to wear red if you are a Republican. I was happy to see that Mark led for a good bit of the evening, and I was touched when one of the part-time campaign staff came up to me at the party and thanked me for knowing his name. As the final precincts came in from Mecklenburg County, Mark's lead evaporated, and Mark ended the evening just below Pittenger, but close enough that a mandatory recount was required.

When all the dust settled, Mark lost the 2016 primary to Pittenger by 134 votes in a turnout that was heavier than predicted, with 26,606 votes cast. We actually achieved the target number of votes projected by Victory Enterprises as needed to win. All in all, the campaign was extremely successful, so it was discouraging to come up short, particularly in that Robert Pittenger won only Mecklenburg County, and actually came in third in most of the other seven counties of the new district. Mark won two counties, and Johnson won the rest, including Bladen County.

We noticed a high number of absentee-by-mail votes for Todd Johnson in Bladen County, but when we asked an attorney who was handling the recount about the absentee ballot number, he had not seemed too concerned. Johnson had come in third, and the Bladen County absentee-by-mail votes did not affect our race with Pittenger.

I was happy to leave town the morning after the 2016 primary election for the Southern Baptist Convention in St. Louis, where our daughter, her husband, and their baby girl had moved in March. While Mark was tied up in committee meetings, I visited and saw the sights of St. Louis with Laura and my baby granddaughter.

One week later, we flew straight from the Southern Baptist Convention to Guatemala, joining a group from First Baptist that was already there doing mission work. I loved Guatemala, and the people we partnered with there. I was excited to plant vegetable gardens alongside them, and to work with women each morning on everything from personal hygiene to Bible study. For me, the campaign happily receded into the background. I was glad that it was over and had no desire to ever do it again.

For Mark, it became the single greatest question mark in his life. Should he run again? He had come so close. One hundred thirty-four votes. He had achieved so much with so very little time to work on a campaign. What would it mean for First Baptist Church if he did run again? Over time, would he lose the desire to run, or would he always feel that he missed something he was supposed to do? What about the nagging burden he had felt ever since attending the Watchman on the Wall conference in 2012? If not him, then who?

It was impossible to live in North Carolina in 2016 and not feel a certain burden about the direction of our country. For North Carolina, 2016 was a watershed year. The hard-core left decided once and for all that North Carolina's red legislature had to be crushed into submission to the narrative that North Carolina was purple. In addition to the lawsuits that constantly kept our congressional districts in flux, 2016 brought the wrath of the LGBTQ movement on our heads, Black Lives Matter into our streets, and Hillary for America attorney Marc Elias and his law firm Perkins Coie into our state elections.

CHAPTER 5

WE WILL DESTROY YOU AND YOUR STATE

DURING FEBRUARY AND March 2016, while the North Carolina General Assembly was being forced to redraw congressional maps by the courts and Mark was deciding whether to run in the 2016 Republican primary in the redrawn Ninth District, a different battle raged in Charlotte.

Jennifer Roberts, a Democrat who lost a bid for the Ninth Congressional District seat in 2012 to Robert Pittenger, was elected Mayor of Charlotte in the fall of 2015. Immediately she proposed a new ordinance with two major components. The ordinance gave special legal protections to those who identified as homosexual, and more radically, the ordinance codified gender fluidity. This second component became known as the "bathroom bill." Individuals could use male or female bathroom and changing facilities based on their feelings at the moment they had to perform a bodily function, change clothes for PE, or wash their hands. On February 22, 2016 the Charlotte City Council was slated to vote the ordinance up or down. Citizens would be allowed to speak for exactly one minute before the vote. The Dems had the votes to pass the ordinance.

Tami Fitzgerald of North Carolina Values arranged a rally for the hours just prior to the vote. Mark would speak alongside other activists. After running around town doing errands on the unseasonably warm afternoon of the rally, I hit the sidewalk outside the Mecklenburg County Government Center in a short-sleeved shirt and light sweater. A cold rain set in as early winter darkness fell. As we all huddled together under umbrellas, I heard a member of our church comment that she had not voted in the mayor's race. Shivering, I thought how easily this day could have been avoided. Just one or two of Charlotte's largest churches could have assembled enough votes to defeat Roberts.

Roberts' Republican opponent in 2015 was Edwin Peacock, a moderate who held no interest for evangelicals. I took a shift making calls for Peacock one morning in October weeks before the November election, and I was literally the first person to have done so. Christians keep waiting on perfection, but we are getting insanity by not voting. Elections matter.

After the rally, as I thawed out at home, I watched the City Council meeting on television. Mark was at the meeting. I recall one woman who questioned the City Council during her one minute. Might the city one day require kitty litter boxes to be placed in every bathroom for those who felt like cats that day? She cited a man in another part of the world who believed he was born to be a parrot. This misguided soul had his eyelids tattooed and his ears cut off to look more like his pet birds. Where would it stop? The bill passed the Charlotte City Council on February 22, 2016 in a 7-4 vote.[1]

Many restaurants in urban Charlotte already had unisex single bathrooms with full closed-door privacy. One Methodist church downtown had male and female bathrooms plus one "transgender" fully private bathroom. Under the ordinance, the church's solution wasn't good enough. The Charlotte City ordinance gave no exemptions for churches or schools, organizations which might find extensive bathroom remodeling cost-prohibitive. With only weeks before the ordinance would take effect, churches that did not have single-occupancy gender-neutral bathrooms would have to figure out their response to the ordinance.

The ordinance was set to take effect in April. Immediately, confusion set in. Not long after the ordinance passed, I waited outside a restroom near my gynecologist's office in Novant Presbyterian Hospital's tower. I had on jeans, a cute top (at least I thought so) and a wool blazer. I'm tall and I have my dad's broad shoulders, but my hair was done, and I had on make-up. As I waited, a hospital employee approached with her cleaning cart. She looked me over, looked at the two doors marked "women" and "men," and then hesitantly asked me which I was about to use.

Other unintended consequences quickly became apparent. On a frigid Sunday night between the date of the bathroom bill's passage and the date it was to go into effect, Charlotte's First Baptist Church was, as always on Sunday nights during the winter, serving as an overflow shelter for the homeless. Women and children get space first, followed by men if there is room. Usually the overflow group is co-ed. There are strict requirements for bed space, etc. so that guests feel safe and have a small degree of privacy.

Part of the evening routine is offering a hot shower to guests in our gym facility, which has semi-open stalls separated by individual shower curtains for the women. There is a separate bathroom with showers for the men. On this particular evening, a person known as a male to the women in the shelter told the volunteers he was transgender and demanded to be allowed to shower with the women. The women became irate. These women, after all, were experiencing homelessness, carrying their belongings with them all day and bedding down each night in a different church or shelter.

The volunteers called one of the First Baptist staff and worked out a solution for the man to shower alone. I have no doubt he was treated with dignity and compassion, and I also have no doubt the women in the group were treated with dignity and compassion as well. Had this incident occurred a few weeks later, would the City of Charlotte have fined First Baptist if the male complained? Would he have the basis for a lawsuit? How long would it take for Charlotte's churches to eliminate such programs in order to shield themselves from heavy-handed government fines and potential lawsuits?

The North Carolina legislature responded to public pressure. Charlotte acted unconstitutionally when it created its own discrimination standards and demanded that both public and private facilities allow men into women's restrooms. The General Assembly passed House Bill 2, shutting down Charlotte's "bathroom bill." Myths abound about HB2. Chief among them is that HB2 enshrined discrimination.

Section 1 of the bill, the section that directly responded to Charlotte's ridiculous ordinance, was simple and direct. **Public** multiple-occupancy facilities in which individuals would be in a state of undress would be designated by biological sex. HB2 included a provision permitting single-occupancy facilities to be developed and used at the discretion of any school.[2] In other words, a large open girls' locker room would be for biological girls, but a school could provide single-occupancy changing and bathroom facilities that were gender neutral if it chose to do so. This common-sense solution put decisions about students back in the hands of the people who were best equipped to handle them: parents, teachers, and school administrators.

In 2012, the Left was embarrassed by North Carolina's 61% passage of the Marriage Amendment. In 2016 the Left became enraged. Governor Pat McCrory relates that a lobbyist for a powerful LGBTQ interest group threatened that they would destroy him and his state. Another representative of a powerful Progressive interest told McCrory they would make sure his legacy of economic growth and infrastructure improvements was destroyed and he would be remembered as the George Wallace of his generation.

PayPal pulled out of a planned operations center they were going to place in Charlotte, claiming it was due to HB2. I immediately called and canceled my PayPal account. The woman who helped me didn't argue or try to persuade me to stay. She sounded weary. I wondered how many other North Carolinians were taking the same action that evening.

Swiftly, the Left began a campaign of misinformation and retribution. The NCAA moved seven championship games out of the state. Musicians canceled performances. The ACC pulled out, as did the NBA All-Star game. All because someone dared to say that schoolgirls didn't have to let boys into their locker rooms and homeless women didn't have to let a man see them shower.

During and after Mark's nine-week campaign for the special congressional elections in 2016, North Carolina Republicans faced persecution by the rabid left over HB2. The corporate sheep who kowtow to the Left panicked under the unrelenting pressure. They in turn pressured North Carolina's legislators. For North Carolina's elected officials, 2016 was eye-opening. Those who still believed the myth that reasonable people on both sides of the political aisle would get fair treatment by the media had their illusions shattered.

I saw genuine hurt in the eyes of public officials who tried to do the best they could with what Charlotte's radical mayor forced down their throats. They had acted responsibly, not hatefully, yet the entire state faced brutal condemnation. In one of the most hypocritical acts of the ever-hypocritical left, New York City Mayor Bill di Blasio issued a "travel ban" on North Carolina in March 2016, then started a program whereby the city's homeless were transported to cities in North Carolina and their housing funded for one year to get them out of New York.[3]

North Carolina Speaker of the House Tim Moore dispatched an emissary to meet with Mark, literally in the dead of night. Judge Marion Warren, whom we met during the 2014 Senate campaign when he was also running for a judicial position, had told Speaker Moore that Mark would be reasonable and was an ally for Republicans. The North Carolina General Assembly needed to repeal HB2, because of the omnipotent "business interests" they always cite when they take the coward's way out of anything.

The emissary wanted Mark's thoughts, but mostly he wanted Mark's help to make sure Christians didn't rebel and stay home from the polls in November, in the 2016 general election. The nighttime meeting took place while we were staying at a relative's home near the site of the North Carolina GOP Convention, which we were attending. I was so upset I cried.

The evangelical community had staged a massive support rally for the North Carolina General Assembly members, with thousands on the mall at the Raleigh legislative complex. Evangelicals were organizing like never before to re-elect members of the General Assembly and particularly Lt. Governor Dan Forest, who never wavered on HB2.

As always, it was about the money. A friend who held elected office privately shared with Mark and me that short of 100,000 people on the mall, the money would speak more loudly than the voters. He proved to be correct. HB 2 was repealed, although not until after the 2016 elections. Only State Senator Dan Bishop of Charlotte spoke against the repeal in the General Assembly.

Charlotte faced more woes in the fall of 2016, when Keith Lamont Scott was shot and killed by a police officer. Scott was black, and the officer who shot him was also black. Jennifer Roberts' predecessor as mayor was black. Police Chief Kerr Putney was black.

The city erupted in riots. I was in shock. It was eerie to watch television news coverage of rioting in the streets and recognize the landmarks of my own city. An NBC News Op-Ed implied that clean, prosperous Charlotte had finally gotten what she deserved when parts of the city were damaged. Life in Charlotte wasn't so great after all, according to the Op-Ed.

The area of downtown Charlotte impacted by the riots spread nearly to First Baptist Church. The outer edge of looting and destruction stopped just one block away from the church, at Buffalo Wild Wings, a casual restaurant whose management was always kind and accommodating to the church. The restaurant's glass doors were shattered, but looters did not get inside. One person was fatally shot during the rioting.

The next day, I drove to the church and walked over to Buffalo Wild Wings and spoke to someone there. I wanted to do something. I wanted to pick up a broom and help. Most businesses said they had to wait for insurance adjusters before cleaning up.

Mark was out of town at a conference the night the riots began. By phone, we organized an informal prayer meeting in the church worship center for the next morning, which I attended while he traveled home.

Eventually, Pastor Leon Threatt, a good friend, and the Billy Graham Evangelistic Association first response chaplains organized a way for faith leaders to engage with protestors as throngs of people continued to gather in Uptown Charlotte each night. Pastor Threatt is black, a former marine, former police officer, and had run for Congress in another district, District 12. Pastor Threatt was one of few Republicans advocating for criminal justice reform before President Trump began to highlight the issue.

After a second disastrous night of rioting on September 21, 2016, Democrat Mayor Jennifer Roberts at last reached out to Republican Governor Pat McCrory, himself a former Mayor of Charlotte, and asked for help. The HB2 Controversy still raged, pitting Roberts and McCrory against each other in a way that never should have been, but for the radical left driving the narrative. Her slow response to the riots, coupled with her radical agenda, caused voters to oust Roberts in favor of the more moderate Vi Lyles in the Democrat primary the following year.

By Saturday night, the fourth night of protests, we found ourselves downtown with Pastor Threatt's group. Some we spoke with were hysterical with fear, not anger. Mark and Pastor Threatt tried to speak calmly and give people an outlet to express themselves. We spoke with and tried to encourage the National Guardsmen and law enforcement officers. It was clear that there were two distinct groups in downtown Charlotte that night: locals, who were scattered about, nervous and shaken, and the main block of more professional protesters, sponsored by Black Lives Matter. Some protestors admitted to us that they had come from out of town and that they would be leaving the next day because they would not be fed any longer. Just before 9 p.m., the main body of protestors passed us by in a sort of parade.

Many of the insignia and signs represented radical LGBTQ views. There were some shouts of very foul language. Mostly, someone just beat a drum, and everyone marched along. At the side of the group was one man I thought looked like a local. He looked both weary and resolute, and he had his arm on the shoulder of a boy who looked to be about ten years old and wore a Carolina basketball jersey over a t-shirt. The man and the boy carried the look of the middle-class South. I locked eyes with him briefly and smiled. I wondered what his life experiences had been like as a black man. I knew something made him determined that his son or perhaps grandson needed to be walking in solidarity with the protestors.

Just as the main body of protestors moved beyond us, my cell phone rang. Our daughter-in-law had gone into labor. We were needed to stay with their eighteen-month-old daughter. It was very hot and humid for late September. I was wearing an App State t-shirt and sweating through it. We didn't have time to go home, but immediately walked the several blocks back to our car and headed straight out of town.

Robert Pittenger was the Republican nominee for the Ninth District and a sitting Congressman during the Charlotte riots. Pittenger told BBC News Night September 22, 2016, "The grievance in their minds—the animus, the anger—they hate white people, because white people are successful and they're not." [4] Pittenger then tried to tweet that he was misquoted, was quoting someone else, and finally, that he was heartbroken over his city and regretted his comments.

The Democrat candidate for the Ninth District congressional seat that fall of 2016 was Christian Cano, a nice man, but one not likely to get much grassroots support around the conservative Ninth District, since he was a Latino Progressive who switched his support from Hillary Clinton to Bernie Sanders in the 2016 Democratic presidential primary. Nor did Cano seem to have the national connections that would later prove so valuable to Dan McCready, Mark's opponent in 2018. Despite Pittenger's baggage, it appeared that he would defeat Cano without much difficulty in the 2016 general election.

Throughout that fall of 2016, Mark worked hard to get President Trump elected. Trump's personal life made it difficult for some Christians to vote for him. Many of these same evangelicals had a hard time with Mitt Romney's Mormonism in 2012. The long view, which included Supreme Court appointments, often seemed lost on them. Mark took calls from all sides and tried to be a peacemaker. It was an exhausting fall for him.

I worked the polls for the Republican Party slate of candidates throughout early voting. I was a team player. Each day that I stood outside the South County Regional Library I shared the sidewalk with the same female Democrat. We were both tired of the vitriol, and we pleasantly chatted while offering our material to voters entering the library.

Election Day 2016 was a long day. That evening, Mark and I stopped by a party for some young people who had given a tremendous amount of time volunteering in Charlotte. As usual, Mark had helped a national organization make arrangements for the young people and had been highly involved with them, including a lot of behind-the-scenes grunt work with voter guides. Also as usual, local Republican candidates wanted to get in on the action by showing up to speak to the group at various times during their stay in Charlotte. Republican candidates make a good show of courting the evangelical community. Afterward we went to State Senator Dan Bishop's home with other GOP candidates and volunteers to watch the returns for a while. I think we left the party around 11:00 p.m. A local Republican lost a seat in the North Carolina General Assembly, which dampened the mood, but it appeared that Trump might win the presidency and that Pat McCrory would retain the governorship.

Governor McCrory was in a heated race with Democrat Attorney General Roy Cooper. When we arrived home, I was too exhausted to stay up and watch into the wee hours of the morning. I went to bed sometime just before midnight, believing that both President Trump and Governor Pat McCrory would be elected. Before Mark came to bed at around 2:30 a.m., it was clear that Donald Trump was going to be president. I woke up the next morning to the horrible news that Governor McCrory was down by a thin margin after a midnight-hour dump of 94,000 ballots from Durham County.[5]

By Wednesday afternoon Democrat Roy Cooper led by 10,257 votes, including his 122,137 votes in Durham County, which was 78.56% of the county's vote. The McCrory-Cooper race was the last race in the country to be settled, and the closest gubernatorial race in the nation in over a decade.[6] In the weeks following Election Day 2016, a simmering pot boiled over in North Carolina. The fire beneath it was stoked by the Left's anger over Donald Trump's election, election protests in the Cooper-McCrory governor's race, and the seemingly unstoppable exodus of rural Democrats from the party of their fathers. This exodus escalated in the Trump era and began to include elected officials who switched parties. We didn't know it, but many of the same forces at work in the aftermath of the 2016 general election would array themselves against us in 2018.

CHAPTER 6

THE POT BOILS OVER

WITH DONALD TRUMP'S election, the anger of the Left reached a crescendo not seen since the '60s. This anger had an eerie staged quality to it, like an advertising company generated it. First President Trump was "illegitimate" because he lost the popular vote and there were calls to dismantle the Electoral College system. Television commercials ran asking electors to "vote their consciences." Carefully groomed network personalities fumed about Trump's reality show persona, then artfully cut to commercial to promote their evening line-ups of backstabbing, survival-of-the-most-manipulative reality show fare.

Protests and violent rhetoric filled Washington. Celebrities like Madonna, Johnny Depp, and Kathy Griffin talked about blowing up the White House and killing the president. Griffin's photo of Trump's bloody, severed head in her hands may never be topped for sheer tastelessness.

In North Carolina, the weeks following the 2016 general election were filled with different kinds of protests: official ones. The North Carolina State Board of Elections fielded allegations of fraud in the Cooper-McCrory contest for North Carolina Governor. As November turned to December and the January swearing-in ceremonies for state offices loomed on the horizon, the protests had to be resolved. The McCrory team mounted multiple protests across several counties alleging that felons voted, illegal aliens voted, and political operatives fraudulently voted on behalf of others.

Media headlines portrayed McCrory as a sore loser who wouldn't let go. *Politico* described allegations of fraud as McCrory's "bid to hang on."[1] CNN opined, "governor refuses to accept vote count."[2] McCrory lost the election after a late hour dump of 94,000 ballots from Durham County added to Cooper's vote count. Was McCrory really just trying to hang on? Were the protests just political ploys?

There is absolutely no good reason to file a frivolous election protest. Protests come with expensive legal fees. Usually changes in vote totals are insignificant. Was there a reason to believe misconduct had occurred in the 2016 election, perhaps even enough misconduct to affect the election's outcome? Yes, but the mainstream media never reported it.

As early voting got underway in the Cooper-McCrory race in the fall of 2016, the North Carolina State Board of Elections closed an investigation into problems in Durham County during the March 15, 2016 primary. On October 12, 2016, local media outlets reported that the state elections board had referred Richard Rawlings, an elections official in Durham County, for criminal charges.[3] A tote containing at least 300 ballots went missing after the March 15, 2016 primary election. In April 2016, an audit discovered issues with the March election. In May 2016, over 1,000 voters in Durham County recast their ballots for the March primary at the direction of the North Carolina State Board of Elections. In addition to missing ballots, the State Elections Board reported:

> Other ballots that should not have counted may have been added to initial tallies, and some ballots appear to have been counted twice when the county first transmitted its results.[4]

Rawlings later pled guilty to the misdemeanor charge of failure to discharge his duty by mishandling ballots.[5]

Missing ballots, inflated vote totals, ballots counted twice. This information never made it into national news stories, even though these improprieties happened in the same election year in the same county as the 94,000 ballots dumped in at midnight in the November 8, 2016 general election.

Perkins-Coie, the law firm in which Marc Elias is a partner, represented the Democrat gubernatorial candidate Roy Cooper in the election's aftermath. Elias also served as counsel for Hillary for America 2016. This is the same Marc Elias who in April 2016 retained Fusion GPS to create opposition research on Donald Trump. That "research" eventually resulted in the discredited Christopher Steele dossier. [6] The Steele dossier was a major element in the Russian collusion narrative sold to FISA courts and the media in order to spy on and smear Donald Trump. An FBI agent eventually pled guilty and received probation for his role in creating a false narrative presented to the FISA court as factual evidence. Elias gave the Democrat Party line to the willing media:

> More North Carolinians voted for Roy Cooper than Pat McCrory, and did so by a close but significant margin. There is nothing Gov. McCrory or his legal team are going to be able to do to undo what is just basic math. [7]

Just basic math. North Carolina elections had always been about the math. In fact, North Carolina law specified that the State Board of Elections had up to one year post-election to investigate allegations of potential criminal conduct. If the election's outcome was not in question, precedent indicated that the election should be certified and then investigations could follow.

In the Durham County 2016 primary, in which it was determined that criminal misconduct had occurred when an elections official didn't count some ballots and had others run multiple times through the machine, three incumbent Durham county commissioners who lost requested that another election be held. The answer from the North Carolina State Board of Elections: No.

Why? The state elections board said that the number of votes in question *was too low to change the election's outcome.* [8] (Emphasis mine.)

More than one thousand mishandled ballots were not enough for the State Elections Board to order a new election in 2016. An official's mishandling of those ballots, resulting in criminal charges, was not enough for the State Elections Board to order a new election in 2016. Improperly counted ballots that inflated vote totals were not enough for the State Elections Board to order a new election in 2016. Three hundred ballots that disappeared were not enough for the State Elections Board to respond to officially filed candidate protests and give the candidates a new election.

Pat McCrory's campaign attempted to consolidate voter protests in various counties, not just in Durham. The McCrory campaign asked the State Elections Board to take jurisdiction over the county protests. On November 20, 2016 the appointed State Elections Board, which oversees the bureaucratic agency of the same name, held an emergency meeting by teleconference. Prior to the meeting, a letter was emailed from the offices of Perkins-Coie. The Perkins-Coie letter concluded that the McCrory protests were irrelevant.

> These protests-taken together-fail on their face because... North Carolina law is clear that a protest must be dismissed if "there is not substantial evidence of any violation, irregularity, or misconduct sufficient **to cast doubt on the results of the election.**" See North Carolina Gen Statute 163-182.10 (d) (2) c.[9] (Emphasis mine.)

The letter also mentions that County Boards of Elections were under tremendous time pressure to complete their official vote tallies (canvassing) by the legal deadline and must be left alone to work quickly.[10] The letter assures the Board that they will be taking on "substantial legal risk" and that "any voter whose vote was improperly discarded following a rushed hearing could sue in federal court" if the State

Board of Elections pursued protests and delayed Cooper's victory.[11]

According to the Official Meeting Minutes of the State Board of Elections for the November 20, 2016 emergency meeting, board members discussed the legal determinations "yet to be made" involved with assuming jurisdiction over county protests. After discussion, Democrat Board member Joshua Malcolm of Robeson County moved that the Board decline to take over the county protests. The motion passed unanimously. [12]

A lawsuit followed. Plaintiff Francis DeLuca, who at that time led an organization called Civitas Institute, requested a preliminary injunction and in essence demanded that the State Board deal with the situation in Durham. Immediately, the League of Women Voters and the NAACP came alongside the North Carolina State Board of Elections and filed a counter motion asking that DeLuca's case be dismissed. The counter motion claimed there was no evidence to question 3,000 provisional ballots from Durham County.

There was one glaring exception to the State Elections Board's decision not to hear protests concerning possible illegal activity in the 2016 general election. Again, Joshua Malcolm made the motion. Allegations "known and unknown" in Bladen County related to the election of November 8, 2016 needed to be heard by the State Board.[13] The state elections board assumed jurisdiction over two Bladen County protests.

Leslie McCrae Dowless, Jr. filed one of those protests, accusing the Bladen County Improvement Association (BCIA), a Democrat GOTV operation that included a PAC, of absentee ballot fraud. Kenneth Register, a BCIA-PAC contributor who lost a county commissioner contest to Republican Ashley Trivette, a Dowless client, filed the other. A hearing to take up the protests was set for December 3, 2016.

In 2016, dueling GOTV programs ran full force in Bladen County. McCrae Dowless worked for Republicans. The BCIA-PAC worked for Democrats. Dowless was a political operative who grasped both the exodus of conservative Democrats from the party and the phenomenon of Donald Trump. Dowless realized eastern North Carolina politics had reached a tipping point.

Although Dowless, like most people over fifty in rural eastern North Carolina, had been a Democrat all of his life, in the spring of 2016 he changed his party affiliation to Unaffiliated. Months later, he changed again to Republican. For the average individual, this would be a relatively insignificant act: a form filled out, a different answer given to a poll worker on Election Day. For Dowless, this change ended financial relationships and created bad blood with former associates.

In 2014, McCrae Dowless had joined with principal registered agent Jens Lutz to form a company called Politico Management Services, based in Lumberton, North Carolina, in Robeson County. That company was dissolved by the State of North Carolina in January 2016 after the company did not file its annual report for 2015. Lutz never followed up to try to reinstate the company.[14]

On July 14, 2014 another Dowless associate, Jeff Smith, appeared as the treasurer for a new PAC called Patriots for Progress.[15] Patriots for Progress was a low-budget operation, and appears to have helped only local Democrat candidates at first. Politico Management Services was one of a handful of donors to Patriots for Progress, and at the same time McCrae Dowless was paid a salary by Patriots for Progress in 2014.[16] Whatever else the relationship between Jeff Smith, Jens Lutz, and McCrae Dowless was, it was financially interdependent. All three men had also faced criminal charges in the past. Smith allegedly owned a lucrative gambling operation in a video poker parlor.

Until 2014 the Bladen County Improvement Association–PAC, or BCIA- PAC, which is the Democrat GOTV machine for black voters, ran the main game in town in Bladen County as far as aggressive absentee ballot GOTV. The PAC had been formed back in 1996 when a conservative PAC had also been formed in the county. The Bladen County Citizens for Conservative Government folded in 2000, while the BCIA grew unchallenged until 2014 and Patriots for Progress.

By early 2016, relationships among political operatives were ending in Bladen County. In a filing with the North Carolina State Board of Elections dated 1-22-2016, Patriots for Progress informed the state elections agency in a hand-written letter that McCrae Dowless was no longer a member.[17] McCrae Dowless voted as a Democrat for the last time in North Carolina's presidential primary on March 15.[18] He changed his registration to Unaffiliated before the June 2016 primary and changed it again to Republican after the November 2016 general election.[19] Dowless broke with Democrat operatives Jeff Smith and Jens Lutz and went solo by April 2016.

Although we did not know it until after the fact, Republican Todd Johnson hired Dowless and paid Dowless and his associates Tabitha Joyce and James Singletary a total of $9,756 over eight and a half weeks for GOTV in the special congressional election of 2016.[20] With Johnson, Dowless hooked a high-profile congressional race for his GOTV program. In the 2016 general election, Dowless worked for victorious Republican Ashley Trivette, among others.

Democrats in the rural county had to be discouraged by the results of their efforts. In 2016 Bladen County Democrats lost the presidential contest, the governor's race, North Carolina's Senate race, and the North Carolina lieutenant governor's race to Republicans. Republican Ray Britt, a fifteen-year veteran of the Bladen County Board of Elections, finished second behind BCIA powerhouse Michael Cogdell for Bladen County Commissioner at large. By contrast, in 2012 there had been only two Republicans on the ballot in local Bladen County elections. From national contests to local races, whether Dowless ran GOTV or not, Democrats lost ground in Bladen County in the 2016 election, even with huge absentee-by-mail numbers for Democrat candidates, produced by the BCIA's aggressive absentee ballot program. Dowless had read the tea leaves correctly.

The final slap in the face for the BCIA in 2016 had to be McCrae Dowless's victory in a race hardly anyone normally cares about. Dowless won the post of Soil and Water Conservation District Supervisor. He was the only person who filed to run. This little race, literally at the bottom of the ballot every time, became the battleground for BCIA vs. McCrae Dowless in 2016.

I can almost hear the meeting in a corner booth at Hardee's now: "We can't let Dowless get away with it. He switched parties. We've got to mount some resistance..." The BCIA pushed Franklin Graham as an alternative to Dowless. Because Graham had not filed, he would have to be a write-in candidate. The results of the Bladen County Soil and Water District Supervisor's race are quite interesting.

Dowless received 7,786 votes, which amounted to 67.47% of the vote. There are also six named write-in candidates against Dowless. Five of those write-ins got fewer than fifteen votes. Then there is Franklin Graham, the BCIA champion. Franklin Graham got 3,356 votes for 29% of the vote total.[21]

In a race in which only one candidate (McCrae Dowless) actually filed, a write-in candidate got almost one third of the votes cast. This result prompted my curiosity. Who got the most write-in votes in the history of the United States? That appears to be presidential candidate Ralph Nader in 1996, with an impressive 685,000 votes. [22] Nader's numbers aren't as impressive in context, however, as that represented only .71% of the 1996 vote total. That's less than one percent. Below one percent for the man who got the highest number of write-in votes ever.

1996 was the second year Ross Perot found his way onto the ballot with his Reform Party. Perot garnered 8% of the vote in 1996, after gaining 18.91% in 1992.[23] In some of the highest vote totals in American history for third-party and write-in candidates, no one came close to Franklin Graham's 29%.

How were these votes generated? That's what McCrae Dowless wanted to know. And that's where attorneys for Governor Pat McCrory saw an opportunity to get votes thrown out and narrow the gap between Cooper and McCrory. Dowless filed an official election protest against the BCIA. A law firm representing Governor Pat McCrory connected with Dowless and other voters who filed complaints in Bladen County.

The Dowless protest was covered fairly widely in North Carolina media outlets. I read about it, and I even saw a photograph of hand-writing samples that formed the substance of the protest. A hand-writing expert concluded that many of the write-in votes for Franklin Graham were done in the same handwriting.[24]

The witnesses on the absentee-by-mail ballots with the question-able write-in votes were known operatives for the BCIA- PAC. Brian Hehl, an appointed member of the Bladen County Board of Elections, wrote a letter to state elections agency chief investigator Joan Fleming outlining his concerns about the questionable absentee ballots he had examined. He mentions a small, but significant detail.

> I do not recall seeing any of them [the ballots] with written documentation that they [the witnesses who both signed the ballots and wrote in the write-in votes] actually assisted the voters, only that they witnessed the voters filling in the ballots.[25]

In other words, Hehl asserts that members of the BCIA- PAC fraudulently voted ballots instead of voters. Republicans also accused the BCIA of running an "absentee ballot mill" [26] to collect ballots. From the public's perspective based on media reports, problems with absentee ballots in Bladen County originated with a Democrat PAC.

Agency documents show that investigators interviewed voters and suspects between October 24 and November 28, 2016. This shows that state elections agency investigators knew of the problems with absentee ballots in Bladen County prior to the December 3, 2016 hearing on the McCrory protests. The State Board held meetings on November 19, 20, 22, 27, and 30 prior to the hearing into the Bladen County protests. Five meetings gave plenty of time for a briefing.

McCrory had not yet conceded. The 2016 final canvass had not yet been completed. All options were legally on the table as of December 3, 2016. The State Board could accept the candidate pro-tests. Ballots could be thrown out or recast, as had been done in Durham County in the 2016 primary. The State Board could have delayed certification of any race pending further investigation.

Raleigh attorney Roger Knight, who represented the Pat McCrory Campaign, appeared at the December 3 hearing of the North Carolina State Board of Elections regarding Dowless's protest. Knight requested that the allegedly fraudulent ballots be thrown out. For Dowless, the ballots were irrelevant, as he had won. For Republican Governor McCrory, the "approximately 400" ballots"[27] called into question by the protest could be meaningful. Throwing out specific ballots affected by fraud or mishandling represented the way North Carolina election law had always been understood. Removing affected ballots was a limited, logical remedy. Remember, it had always been about the math. Marc Elias said so. The board had recently allowed over 1,000 voters to recast ballots in the 2016 primary election. The board did not call for a new election over those 1,000 ballots. In fact, it denied the requests of three candidates who filed protests asking for a new election as their remedy.

The transcript of the December 3, 2016 North Carolina State Board of Elections "hearing" into the protests by McCrae Dowless and Kenneth Register runs 253 pages. Many who have looked at the transcript from this 2016 hearing believe 2018 was payback for the McCrory protests. Kim Strach, Executive Director of the state elections agency was present with counsel, as were five appointed board members: three Republicans and two Democrats. While McCrory was still governor, Republicans held the State Elections Board majority. That would flip if Cooper were declared the winner. One of the Democrats on the State Board was Joshua D. Malcolm, the same board member who suddenly made a motion to pull Mark's certification as winner of the Ninth District race in 2018.

Malcolm moved to dismiss the McCrae Dowless protest regarding Bladen County Improvement Association write-in votes, saying there was "not substantial evidence of a violation of election law or other irregularity...*sufficient to cast doubt on the results of the election.* [28] (Emphasis mine.) Malcolm didn't reluctantly vote to dismiss the protest; he made the motion to dismiss it because the outcome of the election was not in doubt, despite highly credible evidence from a handwriting expert that many write-in votes were done in the same handwriting. Malcolm did not seem the slightest bit interested in withholding any candidate's certification pending further investigation into activities in Bladen County.

The other protest heard on December 3, 2016 by the North Carolina State Board of Elections concerned the Ashley Trivette-Kenneth Register race in Bladen County. Losing candidate Kenneth Register (D) cited "absentee-ballot irregularities" among the reasons he filed a protest asking for a hand recount. Although Joshua Malcolm questioned Register sympathetically, Malcolm concluded, "You know, your belief that something happened doesn't get us, in my opinion, **over the [numeric] threshold** to order a recount." [29] Like McCrae Dowless, Mr. Register found himself rejected after a motion was made by Dr. Maja Kriker (D) to "dismiss the protest for lack of evidence of any irregularities, any difficulty, **that would change the outcome of the election.**"[30] (Emphasis mine.) The motion passed 5-0.

At the conclusion of the December 3, 2016 hearing into the two Bladen County protests from the general election, State Elections Board member Joshua Malcolm made a motion to immediately refer "all information in our possession, notes and otherwise, regarding the election that took place in Bladen County, North Carolina" to the United States attorney for the Eastern District of North Carolina. To the casual observer of the 2016 elections, the issues with the election in Bladen County, North Carolina revolved around fraudulent write-in votes by a Democrat group. No internal investigations from the state elections agency were made available to the public at the time.

On January 30, 2017 state elections agency Executive Director Kim Strach sent a one-page letter to Acting US Attorney for the Eastern District of North Carolina John Stuart Bruce. The letter stated: "our investigations team has conducted a lengthy investigation into various allegations of absentee ballot fraud in Bladen County." Strach tells Bruce that Joan Fleming will provide the contents of her case files and any other information. The letter from Strach is the only public document available regarding the elections agency's referral of the Bladen County cases to federal prosecutors.

Pat McCrory conceded in early December and Roy Cooper was sworn in as North Carolina's governor in early January, in a rare southern snowstorm that ruined his inauguration celebrations. Cooper, like other Democrat candidates, benefitted greatly from the BCIA absentee-by-mail ballot operations in Bladen County.

In the 2016 general election in Bladen County, Hillary Clinton got 627 absentee-by-mail votes. Roy Cooper received 629. Rising Democrat star Josh Stein, who won the North Carolina Attorney General post in 2016, got 627. Linda Coleman, who lost to Dan Forest for lieutenant governor, got 622 absentee-by-mail votes in Bladen County. [31] That's a mere five-vote difference between absentee-by-mail votes for President of the United States and Lieutenant Governor of North Carolina.

What's unusual about such a scant difference in votes between the office of President of the United States and Lieutenant Governor of North Carolina? Most voters tend to pay attention only to those races that will impact their concerns. A pro-life voter may vote for president, governor, and state attorney general because, in the voter's perception, those offices matter. A voter who is pumped beyond belief about Donald Trump may have no idea about any other races on the ballot. This produces a phenomenon known as "voter roll-off." Voter roll-off describes the tendency of voters to vote only in top races, skipping the lower-level state and local offices.

For Republican candidates in Bladen County in 2016, we see the expected pattern of voter roll-off in absentee-by-mail votes. Donald Trump received 389, Pat McCrory 385. Attorney general candidate Buck Newton got 335, and lieutenant governor candidate Dan Forest got 294. By the time you drop down to North Carolina insurance commissioner candidate Mike Causey, he got 261. That's a "roll-off" of 128 voters from president down to insurance commissioner.

Yet among Bladen County Democrats, not only did the top three council of state candidates receive almost exactly the same number of votes as presidential candidate Hillary Clinton, North Carolina Insurance Commissioner and Democrat activist Wayne Goodwin got 644 absentee-by-mail votes, more than Hillary Clinton.

For Cooper, the 629 absentee-by-mail votes were incredibly significant, as Pat McCrory won twelve of Bladen County's seventeen precincts on Election Day. McCrory even defeated Cooper in early voting in Bladen County by 748 votes, which is rare for a Republican due to Democrat hauling operations during early voting.

In 2016 the Democrat BCIA-PAC took in record contributions, including four contributions directly from candidate committees.[32] The Bladen County Improvement Association PAC shows forty-one disbursements for Get Out the Vote in 2016 that do not correspond to dates of early voting or Election Day. In other words, the Bladen County Improvement Association PAC was performing some type of GOTV activities unrelated to working at the polls or hauling voters to the polls during the time the polls were open.[33]

No one from the Bladen County Improvement Association has ever been criminally charged with the allegations that they collected ballots and even voted them as improper "assistants" in the 2016 election, despite Kim Strach's letter from January 2017 referring the elections agency's information to federal prosecutors.

Unknown to us, the state elections agency launched simultaneous investigations into the GOTV activities of both the Bladen County Improvement Association and McCrae Dowless right after the 2016 general election. These investigations never saw the light of day prior to the 2018 general election. Although I read about Pat McCrory's protests and generally developed the opinion that Democrats were cheating in Bladen County, I did not follow the cases closely. The protests had been dismissed. The investigations were not publicized.

Mark certainly did not follow the protests closely. He was gratified that his efforts had paid off and we were going to have President Donald J. Trump rather than President Hillary Clinton. He was also haunted by his 134-vote loss to Robert Pittenger in the 2016 Republican primary. He began to talk a lot about possibly running again. He would make statements like, "It's the people with the votes who really shape the direction of our country." Nothing I said persuaded him that he possessed a tremendous amount of influence on public affairs.

The stress of the spring congressional campaign, the fall presidential campaign, and a busy church and home life had taken a toll on us. Our discussions about whether Mark might run again kept escalating into arguments. Earlier in the fall we had decided we had to get away after Christmas. We took a trip to a beautiful resort where we rang in the New Year at a poolside party, rested a lot, had a couple of water adventures (our jet ski ran out of gas once) and generally talked and reconnected with each other. I fought back tears when I had to load the van to depart the warm, sunny island and come back home. The great question was still hanging over Mark's head. I was going to have to come to grips with the fact that he wanted to run again.

CHAPTER 7

2018: IT'S YOUR TIME NOW

NOT LONG AFTER the special primary election in 2016, Mark had a conversation with a friend, Judge Marion Warren. Warren told Mark that he wished he had known he was running in 2016. If he had known, Warren asserted, he would have introduced Mark to McCrae Dowless.

In the spring of 2017, Warren and Mark reconnected over the issue of sentencing reform. North Carolina Chief Justice Mark Martin wanted pastors to rally around sentencing reform. Justice Martin wanted Mark to line up some pastors for a press conference on the issue.

As Warren and Mark chatted, Dowless came up again. Warren assured Mark that McCrae Dowless was a hard worker who did everything above board and offered to make an introduction. With what limited experience we possessed in the political world, we had learned one thing: it is a world full of people who overpromise and underperform, and also full of laziness. There's a lot of talk. So if McCrae Dowless actually worked hard, Mark, who also possessed a strong work ethic, would be glad to meet him.

As the conversation continued, Mark realized that Dowless must have been the man responsible for the large number of votes Todd Johnson received in Bladen County during the 2016 primary.

Mark was making inquiries and considering whether to run in

2018. Congressman Robert Pittenger had agreed to limit himself to three terms. By that standard, the 2016 election should have been his last. But signals were clear that he was planning to run again in 2018. In late 2016/early 2017, as Mark contemplated running again, he knew he would need close to a year to defeat Robert Pittenger, and victory was far from certain.

Following up on their earlier conversation, Marion Warren, who was at that time Administrator for the North Carolina courts, helped connect Mark to leading Republicans in Bladen County. A meeting was arranged.

In April 2017, Mark had his first meeting with McCrae Dowless at a furniture store in Elizabethtown, North Carolina owned by Ray Britt. Britt was the chairman of the Bladen County Commissioners and was present at the meeting. A leading businessman named Pat Melvin was also there, along with Walter McDuffie, Bladen GOP Chair. We learned that Britt was a client of Dowless's, along with Sheriff of Bladen County Jim McVicker. Sheriff McVicker was supposed to have attended the meeting, but instead was attending a funeral. These men vouched for McCrae. They said that his opponents hated him because he simply outworked them. They claimed that he followed the law completely.

A few weeks later, I also met McCrae Dowless. Mark and I were going to be in Bladen County for a big annual fundraiser. This event is called "Bladen We Care" and it is brilliant. Someone came up with the idea that since the county was small, each non-profit shouldn't compete with other non-profits for limited donor dollars. Instead, every year they have a dance party with a really good oldies/beach music band and a fun theme with fun food to match the theme. The dollars from the Bladen We Care event are distributed among various charities. It was nothing like the stiff, boring, three-hour-long fundraising banquets we so often attended. Ray Britt and his wife Wanda are fantastic dancers, particularly when it comes to Carolina beach music dances like the shag. Ray and Wanda thought the event would be a great way for us to start meeting people from Bladen County. I was really looking forward to the evening, because I love to dance. As a middle-aged Baptist pastor's wife, weddings are about the only opportunities I ever get to cut a rug.

A friend of ours was planning to run for Charlotte City Council in a heavy Democrat district. Only two Republicans held seats on the eleven-member Charlotte City Council. I knew the Mecklenburg County GOP would not devote its resources to our friend, because that seat was not realistically winnable. But with God, all things are possible.

After hearing Mark explain McCrae Dowless's GOTV program with absentee-ballot request forms as a means to track supporters, we wanted our friend to hear Dowless's program and possibly hire him to help bring workers up to Mecklenburg County to work for Pete. We met again at Ray Britt's furniture store for Dowless to explain his program to our friend. That has now been almost four years ago, so I can't recall everything said in the meeting, but I do recall the program being explained and the phrase being used, "You never touch a ballot."

Eventually our friend had McCrae Dowless meet with Michael Dickerson, director of the Mecklenburg County Board of Elections, to explain the GOTV program to someone who knew election law. Dickerson signed off on Dowless's program as described. Dickerson never raised red flags.

Dowless asked Mark to make a contribution to Patriots for Progress as a good faith act that if Mark decided to run, he would hire him. Mark did so, writing two checks to Patriots for Progress. These checks were from Mark personally and were donations made prior to the Mark Harris for Congress Campaign's launch. The Mark Harris Campaign directly hired McCrae Dowless individually in July 2017. Back in early May 2017, we were still making decisions.

There was a lot to think about. We had decided that Mark would step down as pastor of First Baptist Church Charlotte if he ran again. I was working only part-time, and Mark did not want me to return to work full-time. He wanted me to be able to be with him on the campaign. We had financial decisions to make. Plans had to be laid so that we could live for a year and a half on basically no income.

We gave ourselves a deadline of June 30, 2017 to make a final decision on running against incumbent Robert Pittenger again in the 2018 midterm election. If we announced early enough, and could be taken seriously enough, perhaps no one else would get in the race. If we were running, we would open our campaign committee the first week of July.

As we were contemplating these things, our world was rocked. Our little two-year-old granddaughter Nora had an accident in the nursery at her church. Nora was diagnosed with moderate hearing loss at birth and wore hearing aids. In the nursery she pulled over a heavy wooden play refrigerator, which knocked her to the floor. After demonstrating symptoms of a concussion, she was sent to Levine's Children's Hospital in Charlotte for an MRI. Just getting the MRI accomplished with a two-year-old was a very trying experience for my son and his wife, as you might imagine.

Nora was recovering well when the results of her MRI came back. I was driving north on Providence Road toward downtown Charlotte, heading up to First Baptist Church to prepare for children's Wednesday activities. It was a brilliantly sunny day, and pleasantly warm.

Our son Matthew called. I was utterly unprepared for the words he spoke.

"They think Nora might have a brain tumor."

I started to cry but tried to hold myself together to get the facts straight. I kept repeating them back, trying to digest Matthew's words through a mind turned into mush by terror.

I hung up the phone and started to both cry and pray in a completely irrational manner. "Take me, not her," I pleaded with God. "Let me suffer, not her," I asked, as if God wasn't big enough to just heal her on His own, or as if I could move Him from His will through any type of transaction.

When I got to church, I went to find Mark. He had also gotten the news and we held each other for a moment and cried. I had to pull myself together by 3 p.m., when Brookstone School's afterschool program would begin. Along with several members of the church staff and volunteers, I helped provide a program that allowed the students from Brookstone, an academically rigorous school for low-income students that leases space in the First Baptist building, to do their homework, have a recreation time, eat dinner, and then stay for Wednesday- night church activities at First Baptist.

Our associate pastor at that time, Terry Long, helped talk me through my initial reaction to the news about Nora as we watched the Brookstone students play outside on the playground. I will always remember his wisdom and kindness, and I knew that he and his godly wife Joyce would be praying for us through it all.

That night Mark and I decided that we couldn't pursue the massive life change of leaving First Baptist and running for the Ninth District seat if Nora had a brain tumor. Matt and Mallory would need us too much, as their second daughter, born the day after we left the Charlotte riots, was just a baby. We wouldn't be in a good place to undergo the emotional rigors of a campaign. All plans were on hold until there were more answers on Nora's condition.

The North Carolina GOP Convention was held the first week of June. Mark has a lot of fans among the grassroots of the GOP, as he is viewed as a strong leader who doesn't cower in fear of economic interests when it comes to matters of principle. He was kind of a rock star as he walked around the convention. Many people approached him, and usually they asked him about a future run. His outgoing nature caused him to speak too freely about that possibility. Others, not so friendly, were apparently in earshot, and word began to travel that he was running, even though we had not made a final decision.

A few days later, Robert Pittenger made that decision for us.

By June 7, 2017 Robert Pittenger felt so threatened by Mark that he made the tactical blunder that would, alongside his vote for the massive omnibus spending bill in spring 2018, cost him his next election.

We received word that first full week of June that our little Nora did not have a brain tumor. We were euphoric. It was a hectic week, as we were preparing once again to depart for Guatemala that weekend. Our Guatemala trip would last just over a week. We would be planting gardens, checking on a simple water project that had been completed in February, and leading a Vacation Bible School for children in two villages.

I was also hosting a fundraiser in my home that week for our friend running for Charlotte City Council in the "doomed" heavily Democrat district. The week was interrupted when an email landed on the desk of the administrator of First Baptist Church, forwarded there by the headmaster of Brookstone School.

Robert Pittenger had sent a fundraising email. In it, Pittenger stated that Mark Harris would be resigning from First Baptist Church Charlotte in July in order to challenge him once again for the Ninth District congressional Seat. According to the email, although Mark was "just a pastor" without Pittenger's worldly experience, Mark did have a following, so Pittenger needed all of his supporters to ante up.

A Brookstone school board member who was on the Pittenger email list immediately forwarded the email to Brookstone's headmaster with the question, "Are all of our contracts firmed up at First Baptist?" A pastoral transition often means a change of direction for a church, and that could affect Brookstone. A new leader might not share Mark's staunch support of the school for low-income children.

Pittenger's email had both immediate and far-reaching implications. The immediate implications were bad for us, the long-term bad for Pittenger. We were now forced to either move full speed ahead with resigning from First Baptist and launching a campaign, or we had to make an unequivocal decision not to run and assure the church leadership of that decision.

Obviously, there was a great deal of hurt on all sides, because Mark had not had the opportunity to tell the staff and congregation before they heard the news second-hand from Robert Pittenger.

Mark canceled his flight to Guatemala and prepared an announcement he would read to the congregation during Sunday services. I would share the same announcement with the Guatemala team. Our dear friend and life group leader Chris Horne was kind enough to read Mark's prepared statement for me in Guatemala as the team sat around long tables with a view of a smoldering volcano in the distance.

Mark would be resigning as the pastor of First Baptist Church and opening his campaign committee July 1, 2017 to run for the Ninth District congressional seat in 2018. Another friend who was on the Guatemala trip had relatives in one of the Ninth District's rural counties, Scotland County, who were still holding on as Democrats. Our friend was angry about Pittenger's email, especially his implication that Mark wasn't worthy to run because he was "just a pastor."

"There will be some people changing their registrations," our friend declared emphatically.

Pittenger's presumption to speak for us infuriated me. I made up my mind that I didn't care how hard the campaign was or how much it got on my nerves, I would work as hard as I could to make sure Mark won the election. I would do the things I hated, like door-to-door canvassing, and I would do the things that I enjoyed, like behind the scenes clerical work. From that point on, I never spoke in terms like "maybe" or "hopefully" or "if it's God's will" when it came to our 2018 primary.

I spoke with certainty and clarity. "Mark will win. We will win." Others spoke that way too. "It's your time, now" was a common phrase we heard.

It is conventional political wisdom that you don't win your first race, but once you have built up enough name identification and enough grassroots support, you can win on a subsequent outing. GOP insiders seemed to believe that we would be successful this time around.

Legitimizing Mark as his major rival was a huge tactical mistake by Pittenger. As a challenger, Mark had proven formidable in the 134-vote loss in 2016. But rather than making Mark pay to get that message out, Pittenger had delivered it on Mark's behalf early enough to scare off any other serious challengers. The move got us media attention and made fundraising easier. Some folks who had seemed afraid of Pittenger in 2016 were less so, believing Mark could actually win. Pittenger had also sold his troubled Pittenger Land Investments Company to South Street Partners, cutting many Charlotteans' financial ties to him.

In the first full quarter of the campaign, we out-raised the three-term incumbent Congressman, raising over $250,000 from July 3, 2017 to September 30, 2017. The *Charlotte Observer* switched our numbers with Pittenger's in its headline for first-quarter campaign reports. I was quite frustrated by this. Many were watching for first-quarter reports to be sure Mark was up to snuff. Was the numbers switch accidental? Only the Harris-haters at McClatchy News really know the truth.

By September of 2017 we were ready with a full-scale launch of the campaign. We did stops around the district, concluding with a rally at a historic courthouse in Monroe, North Carolina, the county seat of the "red wall" of the district, Union County. By the time of the launch, all three of our children had returned to North Carolina. One of my favorite pictures of all time is of our two little toddler granddaughters holding hands as they look down at the Firefighters' Memorial at that rally.

Here in Piedmont, North Carolina, it can still be blazing hot in September and even into October. The day we launched the campaign was one of those hot days, yet the men who stood to speak for Mark at the rally gave their best, even dressing in suits. A kind member of First Baptist Church entertained two-year-old Nora by letting her play with her necklace. My daughter-in-law Mallory and my daughter Laura were juggling strollers and diaper bags for their second children, born in late 2016 and early 2017 respectively.

At the back of the crowd, we noticed Robert Pittenger's campaign manager with another staffer in tow. Pittenger sent his campaign staff to many of our public events. Larry Shaheen even showed up at First Baptist Church Charlotte on a Sunday morning. He came into the early service and snapped pictures of empty pews at the back of the enormous sanctuary. He attempted to hide behind a column of the church as he spied on the service. This was how it was going to be. I had to get used to it, but I found it pathetic that people would stoop to that.

October 28, 2017 found us in Bladen County for a weekend of events McCrae Dowless organized for the campaign during a local festival called Beast Fest. Dowless was in essence our field director for Robeson, Bladen, and Cumberland counties during the 2018 congressional campaign. The media has portrayed Dowless as a low-life crook. My experience with him on the campaign was quite different. In addition to his GOTV program with absentee-ballot request forms, McCrae lined up vendor spots and volunteers for the Harris campaign at local festivals and arranged our participation in parades. He coordinated distribution of our campaign signs, which is a much larger job than folks outside of a political campaign realize, and he lined up campaign workers across three counties at polls for early voting and Election Day voting, also a much larger job than most realize. In North Carolina, we have court-mandated early voting that lasts for twelve hours a day for two and a half weeks. We even have early voting for half a day on Sundays.

When Hurricane Florence was predicted to hit North Carolina, McCrae took up all the campaign signs he had placed, and then put them all out again once Florence's flooding subsided. McCrae connected Mark to locals who were coordinating relief efforts after the hurricane so that relief supplies donated in greater Charlotte could be distributed as quickly and efficiently as possible in Bladen and Robeson Counties, which were extremely hard hit. If McCrae Dowless was in charge, it was going to get done and it would be done right.

That last weekend of October 2017 was a good time to be in Bladen County. It had finally cooled off. The mosquitoes bred in the county's swamps had died down. McCrae Dowless and Ray Britt had put together a fish fry for Thursday night before the Beast Fest festival kicked off on Friday. It was a great casual event, held at a beautiful venue in a vineyard. The Sheriff of Bladen County, Jim McVicker, attended, along with his wife. The air was crisp as the sun set. We enjoyed the meal in a barn-like setting outfitted with quaint string lights and one open side from which we could see the colors of the twilight.

The next day, Mark and one of our staff made visits to key leaders around the eastern part of the district, while I stayed behind at the hotel and addressed invitations to another upcoming event. I always liked to hand-address things as much as possible. A great team of ladies often helped me with this enormous task. We enjoyed coffee around my kitchen table many afternoons while addressing thousands of invitations to events and pieces of campaign mail.

Saturday was the day Mark and I were slated to post up at Beast Fest to meet voters. McCrae had gotten the campaign a prime spot among the festival's vendors. He had obtained a tent and volunteers to man the tent during the two days of the Beast Fest festival. The outdoor festival was rural North Carolina at its best. There were beauty queens, vendors selling collard green sandwiches and muscadine grape slushies, and local talent showing off on an improvised stage in a parking lot.

That late-October day as I stood on a black top parking lot sandwiched between the old brick buildings of downtown Bladenboro waiting for the arrival of "The Beast," I learned the story of the Beast of Bladenboro. In 1953, something started killing livestock and pets around the edge of the swamp that skirts the town of Bladenboro. The killings were vampire-like. Some folks occasionally spotted a beast said to resemble a large cat. Others said the beast resembled a bear. People got scared and started hunting for the mysterious creature killing their animals.

Eventually the hunt for the beast became more dangerous than the creature's nighttime raids. Outsiders were swarming into the county to hunt the beast. Back in 1953, with growing numbers of armed parties shooting up the woods and swamps, local officials got concerned. Bladenboro leaders came up with a creative solution. They ran the skin of a big cat up a flagpole and declared the beast conquered.

Around 10 a.m., the Beast Fest mascot, which I can only describe as a cross between the North Carolina State Wolf and the Duke Blue Devil, rode into the festival on a vintage fire truck while AC/DC's

"Back in Black" blasted through the sound system. He threw confetti on the crowd, fake attacked a few public officials, and then posed for pictures with the festivalgoers.

When I think about Bladen County, North Carolina and the events surrounding the 2018 midterms, I think of that legend of the Beast of Bladenboro. There's something about the story of the hunt for the beast that reminds me of our experience in aftermath of the 2018 election.

For the Mark Harris Campaign, it was a long, hard road to the May 8, 2018 primary, with many short nights. We went everywhere and did everything we needed to do across eight counties to campaign. In parts of the district, crime was high, and going door-to-door canvassing voters on Saturdays took us to house after house with rickety porches but thousands of dollars of fencing and surveillance cameras. People's mistrust was palpable as we walked the formerly quaint small-town streets, particularly in Robeson County. One young man there told me in no uncertain terms to get out of his yard the minute I said that my husband was running for Congress. Going door-to-door could be unpleasant, but it was necessary. The odds of a voter actually casting a vote for a candidate go way up if the voter has interacted in person with the campaign.

This was, as explained to us, the heart of what McCrae Dowless provided with his GOTV program. He seemed to know everyone in Bladen County. His plan involved hiring individuals to canvass voters. There is nothing unusual about that. Campaigns and national third-party groups constantly hire people to go door-to-door campaigning. What McCrae provided was that people in the county trusted him. He also provided follow-up on the initial canvassing. McCrae or one of his workers would encourage voters to vote absentee-by-mail. He would keep copies of their request forms (not ballots) for follow-up to make sure they voted. This was completely legal under North Carolina law at that time.

An individual who lives in Bladen County told me that McCrae never asked for his ballot in all the many years that he had known

McCrae Dowless. He said that McCrae would frequently call and "bug" him, asking him if he had mailed his ballot yet.

The crime McCrae Dowless has been charged with is collecting thirteen voters' ballots across three election cycles and mailing them. In all, between McCrae and his workers, there are charges that twenty-nine ballots were improperly mailed to the Bladen County Board of Elections in 2016 and 2018. Taking a voter's absentee-by-mail ballot is illegal in North Carolina, even if that ballot is mailed to the Elections Board.

In the 2018 general election, which was the election overturned by the state elections board, Dowless is charged with improperly mailing two ballots. Others have been charged as well, for a grand total of ten ballots improperly mailed in the Harris-McCready congressional race per the criminal indictments issued by the state of North Carolina.

Dowless worked the eastern part of the Ninth District, which included Robeson County and parts of Bladen and Cumberland counties. This was the least populated area of the district. As the months of campaigning continued, Mark focused heavily on Union County, just southeast of Charlotte, with the attitude that he needed to run like he was running for county commissioner there. Union County was always the key to the Ninth Congressional District. Since the campaign was now his full-time job, Mark spent about two to three hours every single afternoon going door-to-door in Charlotte and Union County meeting voters and speaking with them.

I can't explain it, but the 2018 primary did feel like our time. I think we knew it, and I think Robert Pittenger knew it, too. While we watched the news and generally kept up with current events, we had little idea of the ongoing battle that continued to rage in North Carolina between the forces of the Left and the North Carolina General Assembly. It was clear that the Left had found an ally in Democrat Governor Roy Cooper and Attorney General Josh Stein.

CHAPTER 8

UNCHARTED TERRITORY

THROUGHOUT 2017 AND early 2018, while we were preparing to run for the Ninth District seat once again, North Carolina's Republican legislature and Democrat Governor Roy Cooper were engaged in a court battle over the politically appointed board called the North Carolina State Board of Elections. The North Carolina State Board of Elections has oversight over the elections agency of the same name. The North Carolina legislature, which is constitutionally empowered to oversee elections, had combined the appointed State Elections Board with another board to create the North Carolina Board of Elections and Ethics Enforcement. The legislature had restructured the appointment process so that they, and not the governor, selected the members of this new Board of Elections and Ethics Enforcement.

Legislators also continued to try to advance no-nonsense reforms, such as voter ID. After a federal court struck down North Carolina's 2013 Voter ID law, the North Carolina legislature began preparing a Voter ID requirement that could survive a court challenge for 2018. Ultimately, the legislature created a constitutional amendment to put before the voters in the general election of 2018. If passed, voter ID would be part of the North Carolina Constitution.

During these court challenges to the North Carolina legislature's right to execute its constitutional duties, the appointed State Board of Elections stopped meeting for almost a year, from April 26, 2017 to March 21, 2018. From the time Mark's congressional campaign launched in July 2017 until one month before early voting started for the May 8, 2018 primary, the State Elections Board never met to deal with elections issues. The agency that actually ran North Carolina's elections was left on its own. Finally a meeting of the politically appointed board was called for March 27, 2018, with new members.

At this March 27, 2018 meeting, the new appointed board, now called the North Carolina State Board of Elections and Ethics Enforcement, approved a list of County Board of Elections members, with the instruction that new members should be sworn in by April 2, 2018,[1] just five weeks before the May 8, 2018 primary election. In the same way that the state elections agency has a politically appointed board to oversee it, each county of North Carolina also has a politically appointed board to oversee county elections employees.

Despite the fact that appointed board members are not to engage in "electioneering," one of the names approved March 27, 2018 was Jens Larson Lutz of Bladen County. This is the same Jens Lutz who had formed Politico Management with McCrae Dowless in 2014 when both were Democrats. In other words, Lutz came straight out of running a political consulting business into a position as an appointed elections official in Bladen County. Lutz later told media he formed the company to keep tabs on Dowless and "solidify any suspicions of wrongdoing."[2]

That statement strikes me as odd. Why do you plunk down the $125 filing fee to create an LLC in North Carolina just to spy on someone in a small town where everyone knows everyone else's business? Why do you pay that person to do GOTV for said company? If Dowless broke the law while doing GOTV for Democrats, Lutz was complicit in it. Lutz never complained about Dowless until Dowless switched political parties. Perhaps, on the other hand, Lutz was expressing the wishful thinking of someone with a hero complex when he told the *New York Times* he was keeping tabs on Dowless. Lutz at one time was a firefighter, and he was criminally convicted for impersonating a police officer.

Once Lutz was sworn in as a member of the Bladen County Board of Elections in April 2018, he began boasting to associates. Local sources indicate that Lutz said he would "finally be able to take McCrae Dowless down," and that he was "working undercover" for state elections agency investigators.

The elections agency had officially handed over material from its 2016 investigation to federal authorities in early 2017. Authorities apparently had little interest in following up on the investigation. In early 2018, elections agency Executive Director Kim Strach corresponded with Bladen County District Attorney Jon David. Strach warned that if action wasn't taken to stop the aggressive GOTV programs in Bladen County, she feared the election could be compromised. David responded that he had turned everything over to Wake County District Attorney Lorrin Freeman. No charges were filed against anyone in Bladen County over the 2016 election. Jens Lutz stepped into the void created by the lack of follow-up on the 2016 election.

Lutz had phone calls with appointed North Carolina Board of Elections and Ethics Enforcement member Joshua Malcolm. Neither Lutz nor Malcolm has been forthcoming about their conversations. Had it not been for lawsuits filed by WBTV in Charlotte, Malcolm's communications as a member of a public board that is supposedly transparent would be forever hidden.

Lutz had a meeting with elections agency chief investigator Joan Fleming, and FBI and SBI investigators. McCrae Dowless's former business partner spewed speculation. Lutz claimed that Dowless had worked for Mark Harris in 2016, and that he had worked for a local candidate, David Edge. Both of these statements are false. David Edge has publicly asserted that he has never met Dowless or ever engaged him to do any work on his campaign. Publicly available campaign finance reports clearly show that Dowless worked for candidate Todd Johnson in 2016.

Lutz also told investigators in spring 2018 that the office of the Bladen County Board of Elections was not secure, and that individuals had access to voting results and other sensitive materials. The chairman of the Bladen County Board of Elections, Bobby Ludlum, later filed an affidavit repudiating Lutz's assertion that voting materials were not secured. Bobby Ludlum is a retired Air Force Command Chief Master Sergeant. At that time, Ludlum had served on the Bladen County Board of Elections six years, since 2012. In his affidavit, Ludlum declared flatly, "Mr. Lutz's affidavit contains false information."[3]

Astonishingly, state elections agency Executive Director Kim Strach apparently never came to Bladen County to see the office for herself before the 2018 general election in November. Strach repeated Lutz's allegation regarding unsecured office space during the hearing into the Ninth Congressional District election as evidence that the election was tainted. Did elections agency investigator Joan Fleming communicate Lutz's allegation to Strach in April 2018? I would like to know the answer to that question.

Once Lutz was in place on the Bladen County Board of Elections, someone warned the Democrat GOTV group Bladen County Improvement Association that an active investigation was underway in Bladen County. Horace Munn, Bladen County Improvement Association president during the midterm elections, told WBTV he got a warning from an individual he refuses to name. Munn was told that his Democrat group should back off in 2018 to avoid getting into trouble.

Munn stated specifically that he was warned about the investigation before the 2018 primary election was held on May 8. Munn told WBTV that he even called the state elections agency's chief investigator Joan Fleming and spoke to her about it. Munn claims he told Fleming that his group would not do GOTV with absentee ballots in 2018 in order to keep itself clean.[4] Munn obviously felt comfortable contacting Fleming to get information on investigations at the agency—investigations that were not publicly released until after the 2018 midterms.

The warning had an effect on the Bladen County Improvement Association's GOTV activities. Only four disbursements appear for

GOTV work occurring outside of early voting days or Election Day in 2018.[5] That number stands in stark contrast to forty-one disbursements of GOTV payments occurring outside of voting days in 2016. Contributions to the PAC in 2018 were half of what they were in 2016.[6] Testimony during the 2019 "evidentiary hearing" held by the State Board of Elections indicated that certain BCIA operatives worked independently in 2018, rather than as part of the BCIA-PAC. The logs produced as evidence from the Bladen Board of Elections for the 2019 hearing into irregularities in Congressional District 9 support that statement. BCIA Democrat operative Lola Wooten logged in hundreds of absentee-ballot request forms, which is perfectly legal, as did McCrae Dowless, who was working for Mark Harris for Congress.

In Bladen County as early voting got underway in the 2018 primary, the North Carolina State Bureau of Investigation (SBI) and the FBI placed Dowless under surveillance. They observed Dowless going to an ATM and meeting some people at a convenience store on May 3rd.[7] Surveillance was revealed when search warrants for Dowless were made public. Dowless's activities would make sense to me as him connecting with campaign workers for early voting and paying them a day's wage in cash, which is perfectly legal. This was pretty standard practice across the eastern part of the district.

I visited at least one early voting site in every county in the Ninth District during the 2018 election. In Cumberland, Bladen, Robeson, Scotland, and Richmond counties, paid campaign workers set up tents and worked all day passing out campaign material to voters. In fact, in Scotland County, where the Harris campaign had no paid workers, locals told us that it would be proper to tip workers who were advocating for another local Republican candidate but also mentioning Mark Harris.

On May 3, 2018 while Dowless was under surveillance at early voting, the appointed North Carolina State Board of Elections and Ethics Enforcement held a hearing. This hearing reveals how board members felt about delaying election certification and also shows that they were well aware of their limited role in election certification.

As CNN anchor Chris Cuomo so deftly read from his teleprompter while President Trump's team was protesting allegations of voter fraud, there are duties that are called "ministerial." The sign-off by Congress on each state's electoral college certificate is considered "ministerial," a legal term for "without prejudice." Cuomo was making the point that it wasn't Congress's job to analyze criminal activity or investigate voter fraud. It was Congress's job to simply say that the letter in the envelope from each state with the state's vote count was a true representation from that state. In other words, the outcome of the election has already been certified. Get on with it.

In North Carolina, the members of the appointed State Elections Board sign off on county election certificates in multi-county races. This is also a "ministerial" action. The State Board members are political appointees, as opposed to county elections board employees who have counted the vote tallies and certified them. County officials handle allegations and protests. Counties could withhold certification of a race if a protest were ongoing in that race. The county would not transmit the name of an official winner of the race in question to the appointed State Elections Board if the Board agreed to hear a protest, as it did in the governor's race in 2016.

Final election certification is the ministerial duty of the appointed State Board of Elections. Investigation is not the job of the partisan board appointees. North Carolina's elections agency has up to a year to investigate allegations of misconduct in an election, even after that election is certified. As Cuomo's producer, no doubt in communication with lawyers for the Democrat Party, placed in his news report, a "ministerial" duty is one done without passing judgment.

The May 3, 2018 hearing of the politically appointed State Board revolved around a candidate who had requested a delay of certification in advance for his upcoming 2018 primary race. Legal complications involved with a challenge to his candidacy were going to make certain deadlines tight for him, and the candidate wanted ten days of wiggle room for legal maneuvering. In other words, the candidate wanted the State Board to pre-approve a ten-day delay in certifying the results of his race.

Democrat elections board member Stella Anderson asked, "Doesn't canvass represent certification for this race?" [8] In other words, Anderson is acknowledging that the county's vote count equals certification. The act of the canvass, or county counts, once completed, is synonymous with certification. The State Board **approves** the canvass in multi-county races thus giving final certification, but the canvass represents **the outcome.** Anderson is acknowledging that the appointed State Board simply says that the county tallies are correct, just as Chris Cuomo asserted that Congress was simply there to say that each state's certificate of election was correct in the Trump-Biden presidential race. Anderson is expressing hesitancy about the State Board voting to delay certification in a race that should be confined to one county.

During this May 3, 2018 hearing, counsel for the state elections agency Joshua Lawson made the statement "...we are in uncharted territory." The turmoil of the court fight over the very structure of the agency and delays in getting county boards certified had created confusion for candidates, the state elections agency, and the appointed State Elections Board.

Lawson clarifies for the State Board that if the candidate in question had brought an **official protest**, the candidate would be entitled to a ten-day stay of certification. (Emphasis mine.) Without a candidate protest, there was no legal precedent for the appointed State Elections Board to withhold certification in a race. That's what Lawson is saying. "We are in uncharted territory." No protest, no clarity.

As we will see, when it came to Mark Harris's victory in the 2018 midterms, the state elections agency director vouched for the county results literally moments before appointed Democrat State Elections Board Member Joshua Malcolm made a motion to pull Republican candidate Mark Harris out of the list of official county-certified winners. The state board then cited an obscure court case as the basis for taking jurisdiction over the Ninth District race.

Democrat congressional candidate Dan McCready never filed a

candidate protest. McCready had already conceded the election to Mark. Yet such was the agency's desire to get Dowless, such was the success with which appointed State Elections Board member Joshua Malcolm played his hand, that the election agency's director Kim Strach bent over backward to rob Mark Harris of a victory he rightfully won. This was truly "uncharted territory."

CHAPTER 9

HARRIS STUNS PITTENGER

BACK IN CHARLOTTE, we were oblivious to State Elections Board hearings and surveillance on McCrae Dowless. It was spring 2018. The campaign was in full swing, with events practically every night, and door-to-door voter canvassing practically every day. It was a beautiful spring in Charlotte, with plenty of warm days and pleasantly chilly evenings.

On March 23, 2018 President Trump did something uncharacteristic. He signed a bill he opposed. The bill was officially titled the Consolidated Appropriations Act of 2018. That's government jargon for a massive spending bill with everything but the kitchen sink thrown in. The bill ran over 2,200 pages. Members of Congress had only about three days to attempt to read it before they voted on it. President Trump called the bill "ridiculous" and apologized to his supporters for signing it to ensure necessary military spending. The bill called for 1.3 trillion dollars of government spending. The president vowed he would never sign another such bill.

Bills like this infuriated Mark. These omnibus spending bills represented everything that was wrong with the swamp. As I said, Mark embodies old-school American values like hard work and thrift. As we had educated ourselves on Congress, we were both dismayed by the charts we read showing less time in committee meetings, less time in debate, and no reasonable effort to come up with a proper budget.

Four days after President Trump signed the massive spending bill, the most important candidate forum of the 2018 Republican primary was held in Union County. Mark would debate Robert Pittenger, and a third candidate from the Fayetteville area who had filed back in February, Clarence Goins. The debate would take place in a historic courthouse in downtown Monroe. The morning of the debate, I got a phone call. The campaign was going to do something bold at the debate. I needed to go purchase enough reams of paper to equal 2,200 pages. Fortunately, I was able to obtain the paper easily. I called back. "Got it."

Late that afternoon we rode to the debate with our campaign manager Jason Williams. Two ladies who were incredible campaign volunteers and became my good friends through the campaign, Mary Chapman and Leigh Ann Patton, met me at the historic Old Courthouse in downtown Monroe. I knew both were sincere when they said they were praying for Mark to excel in the debate. Both were very active in the Mecklenburg County GOP and went out on a limb to support Mark in the primary.

It was a dramatic moment in the debate when one of our campaign staff hauled the 2,200 pages of paper to the podium where Mark was speaking and plunked it down.

Robert Pittenger could only counter that sometimes you had to make compromises to govern. He pulled out Ronald Reagan's "take half a loaf" analogy.

Mark destroyed this argument in the debate, pointing out that Republicans did not control the House of Representatives when Ronald Reagan took office. Reagan's Speaker of the House was the Massachusetts liberal Tip O'Neill. At the time of the 2018 Republican primary, Republicans controlled all three branches of government. There was no excuse for Republicans to create massive spending bills without reading them.

We had many supporters at the debate, so it wasn't so much about persuading them, but Mark's performance solidified their support for him. Among our most ardent supporters, it ramped up enthusiasm. After that debate, we felt the momentum definitely going our way. Polls nonetheless showed Pittenger with a huge lead. Our internal data gave different results, so we never really trusted the polls.

Finally, early voting began. Early voting in North Carolina is a two-and-a-half-week grind. We kicked off the first day of early voting on April 19, 2018 with a rally at the Hal Marshall annex in downtown Charlotte, the only site open for the first couple of days. Reporter Joe Bruno of WSOC TV in Charlotte was assigned to cover us during the campaign. He brought a little crew out to film the rally. I was over the top, telling them Mark Harris was going to win for sure and generally whooping it up. We kept laughing with the TV crew. It is so much fun to be an outsider candidate.

There I had one of the more unforgettable experiences of the campaign, when a redheaded white girl yelled at me from afar that I looked like "the perfect example of white privilege." I can only presume it was because I had on a blazer and nice slacks. I vocally took issue with that comment, as she knew nothing about me, nor my ancestors, who toiled first on farms and later in textile mills, and eventually I asked a sheriff's deputy to come over and speak to her, as she was taunting others. The deputy removed her from the property.

A few days into early voting, I got a call just as I was climbing into bed one night. My daughter-in-law had gone into labor. I got up, got dressed, and drove to Raleigh to stay with my two-year-old grandson. I kept tabs on the campaign from afar for the first full week of early voting. That same week, our campaign manager's wife gave birth to their sixth child, on Mark's birthday! Jason sent us a picture of the baby swaddled up with a "Mark Harris for Congress" sticker on his little blanket.

When I returned home, I took my usual turn working the polls at the South County library. It was intense working at the polls in a contentious primary. In a general election, everyone knows where everyone else stands. You can be nice. But in the primary, it was dog eat dog. Once while I was at South County, an elderly female volunteer for Mark drifted past the sign posting the boundary for electioneering. One of Robert Pittenger's young congressional staff, who took vacation to come campaign for Pittenger because he had almost no volunteers, immediately pulled out her phone and started filming our volunteer. I had to go over and point out to the volunteer that she was a couple of feet over the line. She was gracious and nice. This incident is a sign of the times we live in. No one wants to resolve issues by talking. No one assumes the "other side" is decent. It's phones and cameras, secret recordings, and media leaks. Solving problems is not on the agenda.

By the last day of early voting, a Saturday, our team was worn out. State Representative Bill Brawley treated a bunch of poll volunteers to lunch at a restaurant in Mint Hill. Mark had been campaigning at his usual spot at the Union County Board of Elections in downtown Monroe, forty-five minutes away, so he couldn't make it to lunch. Several of our young staff, key volunteers, and I enjoyed the lunch so much. We had the giddiness that often arises from a combination of exhaustion and camaraderie. Each of us joked about what our chapter would be in the "tell all" about the campaign and we came up with silly titles that were inside jokes to us. My favorite was "There's Always the Hardees in Laurel Hill," referencing one of the few places to go to the bathroom *and* get coffee on a particularly rural stretch of the 9th District's main artery, Highway 74.

On Election Day I worked from 6:15 a.m. to 7:24 p.m. at Olde Providence Elementary School, passing out campaign material to anyone who would take it. I ran home and threw on cotton pants and a flowing black top without even being able to take a shower. This campaign had been "all hands on deck." It wasn't about the red dress this go-around.

We pulled up the results from early voting on my laptop before we ran out the door to our election night watch party. Early vote results were usually posted immediately after the polls officially closed at 7:30 p.m. Mark was in the lead by around 1,000 votes.

Our party that night at The Bridge restaurant in Hemby Bridge was one of the best nights of my life. The restaurant was packed with supporters. It was hot and crowded. Two of our little granddaughters ran to us and jumped up in our arms as we walked in the door. The election results were projected onto a wall of the restaurant. Our staff didn't go to a private room, but just sat in a booth with everyone else around and watched results from specific precincts on their laptops. The mood was fun, friendly, and completely unpretentious.

I kept asking if the results had come in from Mecklenburg Precinct 233, but by late in the evening the room was so packed I couldn't get over to the booth where our guys had their laptops out. I kept calling out to my friend Mary Chapman, who was nearer the guys with the laptops than I was, "What about Matthews 233?" Precinct 233 in Matthews typically voted the most Republicans of any of the precincts in the Ninth District in Mecklenburg County. Mark won that precinct in 2016.

Mary couldn't even hear me with all the goings-on. She would put her hand up to her ear and then we would both start laughing. A rumor began to circulate that an accident had delayed the transport of ballots to the Board of Elections in Robeson County from one of the precincts. I kept trying to stay close to Mark so that I would be with him if anything happened. At the peak of craziness, Jason Williams, our campaign manager, bulldozed his way through the crowd toward Mark and me with his phone in his hand. "Pittenger's on the phone," he said with a smile. Jason grabbed Mark and took him outside for the concession call.

The next morning the *Charlotte Observer* carried the headline "Harris Stuns Pittenger in Primary Upset." We had beaten the odds through hard work and the unseen something that happens as momentum shifts. Pittenger's vote for the unread 2,200-page omnibus spending bill no doubt contributed to the momentum shift. From a poll that showed us down by 30 points, a poll we never really believed, as it did not match our data, we rebounded and won. We took Union, Anson, Scotland, and Bladen counties, while Pittenger took Mecklenburg, Richmond, Robeson, and Cumberland counties. District-wide we won the votes on Election Day, in early voting, and in absentee-by-mail. Our margin of 828 votes exceeded our absentee votes in Bladen County, which were 437 votes. Pittenger won four of Bladen's precincts, we won seven, and one tied. Pittenger won the other two counties where Dowless worked his GOTV program. Our total votes in Bladen County were 1,427. In Union County, where we had campaigned so heavily, we took 7,509 votes to Pittenger's 5,894, a difference of 1,615 votes. Our lead over Pittenger in Union County was more than our total votes in Bladen County.

Starting very early that next morning, Mark began to field calls from Republicans in congressional leadership. Everyone was friend-ly and helpful. The Ninth District was a targeted district by the Democrats, and we would have to raise a lot of money and work even harder, if that was possible. I had mentioned Dan McCready, the wealthy Democrat challenger in the Ninth District, a few times during the primary season. Mark usually pushed past any discussion that did not involve the primary, preferring to focus on one thing at a time. Now he would have to think about Dan McCready.

I didn't even think about the formal certification of Mark's 2018 primary. I'm not even sure I understood the slightest thing about the process. I vaguely knew it would be a few weeks before the results would be official, but the possibility of a disruption in that process never occurred to me.

Search warrants ordered unsealed after Dowless was indicted reveal that McCrae Dowless was the subject of investigations by the SBI and the FBI **before** the May 8, 2018 primary election. Jens Lutz had asserted to law enforcement that Dowless worked for Mark Harris in 2016, which although false, would cause me to suppose the State Board of Elections as well as the SBI and the FBI understood that Mark Harris for Congress hired Dowless in 2018. Dowless rode around town with two large Harris for Congress magnetic signs on the doors of his vehicle. Surely these would be noted if he were under surveillance. It is clear that the state elections agency, particularly chief investigator Joan Fleming, had formed the belief that Dowless was worth investigating as early as 2016. Mark Harris received over 400 votes by mail in Bladen County in the May 8, 2018 election. Did this escape notice?

These facts raise the question: Why was Mark's primary victory certified?

If Joshua Malcolm or other appointed state elections board members were so concerned about fraudulent activities in Bladen County, wouldn't they want to act immediately to investigate the 2018 primary election? The elections agency's chief investigator Joan Fleming had written a report on activities in the 2016 election. Agency Executive Director Kim Strach referred Fleming's findings to federal prosecutors by January 2017. The agency obviously believed it had already gathered enough material for prosecutors to consider criminal charges against Dowless.

Why not delay certification of Mark's primary win? Why not conduct additional voter and suspect interviews at that time?

If investigators had already established that Mark Harris was not conspiring with Dowless, why not give him what has come to be known as a "defensive briefing?" Mark Harris lacked access to any of the materials from the agency's investigation of Dowless in 2016. Attorneys later told us that had we even known to ask, we probably would have been denied access to the investigation, since it was an ongoing criminal investigation.

Certification of an election was understood in May 2018 to be final. During the May 3, 2018 hearing into a candidate's request for a delay in the certification of his race, attorney Brad Hill made this point. Arguing for the candidate desiring the delay, Hill stated, "An election, ***once it has been certified, cannot be reversed, even by an appellate court.*** Certification would be final."[1] (Emphasis mine.)

No one on the Board of Elections disputed this point when Hill raised it. Yet no one, not Democrat appointed State Board member Joshua Malcolm, not elections agency executive director Kim Strach, nor any other board member or agency member made a peep about the 2018 primary. Mark was given his certificate, which he still has to this day in his office. By 2019, however, not only were 282,000 votes thrown out and a new general election ordered, the North Carolina legislature also ordered a new primary election for the Ninth Congressional District.

CHAPTER 10

TAKING DOWN GOLIATH: THE 2018 GENERAL ELECTION

ACCORDING TO DAN McCready, it was President Trump's election that propelled his decision to run for office as a Democrat in the Ninth District race in 2018. In an interview with McClatchy reporter Katie Glueck "over chips and guacamole at a trendy tacos and tequila joint in a prosperous Charlotte neighborhood,"[1] McCready evaded Glueck's question about when he decided to run for office. She reported that she had to ask him five times about the specific moment he decided to run. Glueck stated that McCready "referenced his time in the Marines" and spoke in other generalities about broken Washington before he finally, on Glueck's fifth try to get a straight answer, claimed that it was in late 2016 after a conversation with his oldest daughter about the "leadership we have in Washington." Glueck followed McCready on the campaign trail and reported that he told a group at a meet and greet one day after he evaded her questions that he decided to run the day after Trump's election.

McCready later commented on HB2 to Glueck "…The problem we had in North Carolina—HB2 was one of the worst laws in the modern history of the state. We have no problems with bathrooms in North Carolina, but that law cost us thousands of jobs, cost us part of our reputation built up over decades."[2] In reality, according the US Bureau of Labor Statistics, North Carolina saw a net creation of 84,700 jobs between October 2015 and October 2016.[3] Evasion, refusing to take positions, and covering up well-laid plans for his political ambitions would be a McCready pattern throughout 2018 and the 2019 special election. By May 2017, McCready had secured two different domain names. One domain name, danmcready.com, was registered in 2012, a full four years before Donald Trump was elected president.

McCready was a Democrat who was in the process of getting filthy rich from a company he founded based on investments in solar farms.[4] In the summer of 2018, Dan McCready fit the profile of the handpicked Democratic Congressional Campaign Committee candidate for the 2018 midterms. A young veteran who also had elite educational credentials and wealth, McCready was a dream candidate in the mold of Conor Lamb. McCready's business partner Rye Barcott is the CEO of "With Honor," a group that recruits veterans to run for office. While at Harvard, McCready became friends with Seth Moulton, D-Massachusetts, whose Serve America PAC endorsed multiple candidates in Dem primaries while touting a plan to overthrow Nancy Pelosi as Speaker of the House.

McCready had no trouble raising money, with the majority of his early money coming from donors within his father's law firm, Robinson Bradshaw of Charlotte. Later the Democrat Party's giving vehicle Act Blue kicked in, and money poured in from the West Coast and the Northeast.

The McCready campaign targeted Republican women early, with letters full of nice-sounding sayings like "country over party" and "a new level of service." Around July 2017, nearly a year before the primary, I started receiving mail from the McCready campaign. McCready and the campaign's supporters had success getting op-eds into the McClatchy-owned *Charlotte Observer* and even national newspapers.

The McCready campaign was fond of listing its Republican supporters in its mailings and Dan McCready was initially viewed as "Republican lite" by many, an appealing description to urban and suburban Republicans in Charlotte who disliked President Trump and wanted a safe blue alternative for a punitive vote against Trump.

North Carolina's conservative political blog *The Daily Haymaker* quickly placed McCready on its list of candidates derisively described as having "made a trip to the candidate store." McCready did not vote in a primary from 2004-2016, according to his voter history on the state board of elections website.[5] His first vote cast in a federal primary was presumably for himself in the May 8, 2018 primary. Publicly, McCready touted only his Marine service and his solar company, actually an investment-in-solar company called Double Time Capital. He sold off oil and gas stocks to shore up his clean energy credentials, although he did not remove the CEO of Duke Energy from Double Time's board.

McCready's Democrat primary opponent in 2018, Christian Cano, who had been the Democrat nominee for the 9th District in 2016, openly expressed his dislike and distrust of McCready. Cano and Mark had always been cordial, despite their opposing political views, and I found Cano to be a very nice person. In my subjective impression, Cano appreciated those who clearly expressed where they stood on the issues.

The relationship between Cano and McCready became strained when Cano used social media to criticize McCready for not making a sharper attack on President Trump's remarks after the Charlottesville, Virginia incident. Later, during the Black Political Caucus Forum in Charlotte, McCready appeared to call Cano an asshole as he shook his hand at the end of the debate, according to video posted on the *Charlotte Observer's* website. McCready handily dispatched Cano, however, in the May 8, 2018 primary, winning 82% of the vote.

As May 8, 2018 approached, Dan McCready didn't even seem to know who Mark Harris was. According to a friend who attended a church service at which McCready spoke about defeating Robert

Pittenger, McCready was asked, "What if Harris wins? There is a competitive primary going on among Republicans." Dan McCready stared blankly and asked, "Who?" It was rumored that the McCready campaign had $200,000 worth of television commercials already in the can for an assault on Pittenger to begin immediately after the primary, likely based at least in part upon those remarks Pittenger made to the BBC during the riots in Charlotte months before.

McCready wasn't much of a campaigner. He seemed awkward around people at the events he attended. He appeared to love the camera more than the public. At the Hood-Hargett group, an ad-hoc group of business people that hosted separate private forums with each candidate and invited the media, McCready was so evasive regarding his political positions that even the Harris-hating *Charlotte Observer* called him out on it. At the Mallard Creek BBQ, an event that has become mandatory for office-seekers in Charlotte, McCready stayed only briefly, and was surrounded by handlers while he was there.

Furthermore, what McCready didn't say in all of those nice-sounding summer letters to Republican women was that he was endorsed and supported by the AFL-CIO, the Feminist Majority PAC, and ultimately House Majority PAC, a super PAC with close ties to Nancy Pelosi. Mark Harris was third highest in the country in money spent against him by House Majority PAC. As the summer wore on, political reality began to sink in for many Republican voters in the Ninth District.

If Republicans lost their majority in the House, control of not only the Speaker's chair but also the committee chairs would flip to the Democrats. The specter of Maxine Waters as chair of the Financial Services Committee was sobering to many in Charlotte, the number two financial center in the nation behind New York. Waters had already let slip her belief that the energy sector should be nationalized, in a grilling of oil executives posted online. In other words, she held socialist beliefs, even if she didn't use that word to describe them. Not long before the general election, Fox News carried a speech she made in which she vowed punitive action against Republicans for what they had done to Dodd-Frank banking regulations. She promised that she indeed would be the Chair of Financial Services, and that she would "give back to them what they did to us."

McCready's high fundraising numbers put Mark between a rock and a hard place. Whose money could he afford to reject? This is the very tough position principled candidates find themselves in when they run in competitive districts. Do you take money from PACs and special interest groups, or do you lose? Do you try to play nice with everyone at the risk of losing some of your hard-core grassroots supporters, or do you alienate sources of contributions and lose the election, in which case your supporters certainly will not be represented? Mark had pledged during the primary to join the Freedom Caucus, and he was not going to go back on that promise.

State GOP Chair Robin Hayes called Mark and told him that if he would promise not to join the Freedom Caucus, Robin would help him raise funds. Mark told Robin he had already pledged to join and could not go back on it. We really didn't hear from Robin again until we saw him at the end of the summer, in what turned out to be a very embarrassing moment for him.

Nancy Schultz, one of the organizers of the Women for Trump bus tour, called me and told me that she was praying in her chair at home and God told her to help Mark Harris. She was thinking about forming a PAC so she could do bus tours for candidates. As she moved forward with forming her PAC, I could not coordinate with her, so I didn't know the details, but an attorney gave approval that I could join the bus tour she was creating called "Women for Harris" if the campaign paid my expenses, and I was simply given an itinerary of when to show up and speak. God kept providing these new avenues of support for Mark when establishment Republicans backed off. Nancy hired some local people to help with the tour, and it was phenomenal.

We hired a second local fundraising expert with a wider circle of national connections than our finance director, who was from

Charlotte and had mostly worked for local and state candidates. The mantra this gentleman kept before us was Trump, Trump, Trump. If President Trump will come for you, it's over. You've won.

By August, we got the news we had hoped for. President Trump would come and do a joint fundraiser for Mark and Congressman Ted Budd. Many, many details had to be pulled together for Trump's visit, which was scheduled for August 31, 2018. Personally, I didn't have to do a lot with the legal, fundraising, and technical sides of the Trump visit. I was primarily concerned with what I was going to wear. I would be escorted out with Mark to stand beside the President of the United States on a stage set up for the event at Carmel Country Club in Charlotte.

It was going to be hot, but I wanted something long-sleeved. I thought that would look better in photos. I wore my black campaign skirt that I wore everywhere with a black top, and a full-length pale-blue jacket I found for the occasion. I had so many products on my hair that I was afraid it was going to go flat in the hours of waiting before President Trump's arrival. Few times in my life have my feet been killing me as much as they were that day! I don't think I sat down for six or seven hours straight.

President Trump was due to arrive between 4:00 and 5:00 p.m. We had to arrive at Carmel Country Club around 11:00 a.m. We had to check in through security just like everyone else. People had to show that they had tickets, and they had to show ID, of course. Then we were given identification credentials for the event. Our daughter and her husband, who had moved back from St. Louis to a Charlotte suburb, met us at the country club. They both looked gorgeous. It was exciting.

While we were standing around outside the club in the credentials area, North Carolina GOP Chair Robin Hayes approached us. We chatted for a time as we waited to get our credentials, as Robin Hayes had a small part in the program. Suddenly, the Trump people nixed that. They did not want Robin to appear at the event with the president. Robin kind of smiled, shrugged it off, and left. Later we learned that Robin was under investigation by the FBI as part of a big operation initiated by North Carolina's new Republican Insurance Commissioner Mike Causey. Robin later pled guilty to one count of lying to the FBI. As we think about this in hindsight, it gives us pause. There was a reason Trump didn't want to be seen with Hayes. Yet he had no qualms about being seen with us. At that time Dowless had been under investigation by the FBI for approximately four months.

While waiting at the country club, we were told we would get a few moments with the president. Those moments came in a darkened hallway as President Trump was heading in to take photos with people who had paid a great deal of money for that privilege. It was my first meeting with Donald Trump. He was completely professional. He chatted with us for a couple of minutes about how the campaign was going. We were also able to take a photograph with him. In the photo, my clothes look great. My hair looks perfect. My expression looks like…well, if a deer in headlights could look overwhelmed, that would be me. Every time we see that picture, Mark and I laugh. It was a long day, but a great day. We went home to gear up for the following week, which began with the Labor Day holiday.

On the day after Labor Day, we had Janet Huckabee speaking at a women's event. This was "my" event. I had gotten a group of friends together to plan it. We called it Pearls of Power. Janet is the wife of Governor Mike Huckabee and mother of Sarah Huckabee Sanders, but she is also an incredible woman in her own right. She is a cancer survivor and was the Republican candidate for Secretary of State in Arkansas in 2002. My friends helped with everything, even down to decorating, because I was so busy. Their work was amazing. Our finance director took care of the fundraising aspects.

I was spurred to do a women's event by Dan McCready's attacks on Mark for preaching the biblical model of family. Naturally, the mainstream media hopped on the bandwagon. ABC News did a story on one of Mark's sermons. The hypocrisy of anyone at the network that introduced *The Bachelor* claiming Mark Harris didn't respect women because he honored the roles of wife and mother boggled my mind. Which gives a woman more dignity—her children "rising to call her blessed" because of her work ethic, intelligence, strength, and devotion to her family (Proverbs 31) or competing for the affections of a hunk along with a couple dozen other young women while the voyeurs of the American public tune in?

We had events that same week in two counties outside of Charlotte and then a reception at the end of the week with Senator Tim Scott of South Carolina back in Charlotte. Absentee-by- mail voting was about to launch statewide for the November election. In Bladen County, both McCrae Dowless and Lola Wooten, who frequently worked for the BCIA, were turning in hundreds of absentee-ballot request forms as part of legal GOTV done over the summer.

While we were campaigning in North Carolina that first week in September 2018, in Washington the Senate Judiciary Committee was holding its first hearing for Brett Kavanaugh's Supreme Court nomination. After the first Senate Judiciary Committee hearing on the Kavanaugh nomination, all hell broke loose. The Kavanaugh debacle ended Dan McCready's ability to survive as "Republican lite" on happy slogans. On a smaller scale, all hell broke loose at the state elections board that same week, when the board met in response to a Justice Department investigation into illegal aliens voting in the 2016 election.

CHAPTER 11

WE WILL NOT CONSENT

AS I WAS worrying about my hair and wishing I had worn flats while I waited for President Trump's arrival the last day of August 2018, fax machines (yes, that's right, fax machines) were humming in forty-four County Boards of Elections offices around Eastern North Carolina and at the state elections agency headquarters in Raleigh.

In January 2017 the executive director of the elections agency, Kim Strach, had written to the acting US Attorney for the Eastern District of North Carolina, telling him about the agency's investigation into possible criminal activity during the 2016 general election.

On August 31, 2018, the agency's headquarters in Raleigh received a subpoena by fax. The subpoena indicated that ICE (US Immigration and Customs Enforcement) was getting involved in investigations into election activity in North Carolina and a grand jury had been convened. The subpoena was issued by the United States Justice Department and was signed by an assistant US Attorney. The forty-four counties under the jurisdiction of the federal court for eastern North Carolina also received similar subpoenas. In the infamous Cooper-McCrory governor's race, voters filed protests stating that illegal aliens had voted. Apparently, the Justice Department was taking a look into these allegations. The elections agency was given until September 25 to produce the subpoenaed material.

The agency's reaction was not what one would expect given that

Director Kim Strach had written a letter asking the US Attorney to take a look at activities from 2016. The elections agency's chief counsel Josh Lawson reached out to the US Attorney's office with the complaint that the agency could not possibly fulfill the August 31 subpoena by the required date of September 25.

On September 6, 2018 Lawson got a reply. In it, the United States Attorney's office indicated that the agency could have until January to prepare the subpoenaed documents. That's a four-month extension. The assistant US Attorney also indicated that the purpose of the subpoena was to prevent destruction of materials from previous elections based on standard agency document retention policy.[1] With a grand jury convened, the Justice Department wanted to be sure potential evidence was not destroyed.

The subpoena federal prosecutors issued to the state elections agency requested materials related to voter registration, absentee ballots, and write-in votes.[2] Agency Executive Director Kim Strach would later refer to this subpoena as "exceedingly vague."[3] Absentee ballots and write-in votes were two of the issues the agency itself had investigated and referred to federal law enforcement.

A board meeting of the State Board overseeing the elections agency was called for Friday September 7, 2018. Democrat Board Chair Andy Penry went ballistic over the subpoena. Penry fumed, "We have not been given a reason as to why ICE wants that information and candidly I can't think of any reason for it."[4] Penry continued ranting that the subpoena came "out of the blue" and insisted, "had a call been made in advance, we would have worked to resolve this. But that didn't happen, unfortunately."[5]

During the meeting, Penry complained about the four-month time frame given to produce the documents. He also complained about the state elections agency having to produce subpoenas while the 2018 general election was occurring. The "job of this Board is to administer elections," Penry continued. Referring to the September 6 letter, Penry says, "Once they realized there was an election in November and we had a role in it, they decided it wasn't that urgent."[6]

You can practically see Penry rolling his eyes as you listen to the recording of the September 7 meeting. Then, true to form, the elections board went into closed session. What they discussed regarding the US Attorney's investigation into illegal aliens voting in North Carolina is not publicly available.

The outcome of the closed-door session was a vote by the board to demand that North Carolina Democrat Attorney General Josh Stein "quash" the subpoenas for the state elections agency and also for the forty-four counties of eastern North Carolina. The motion to refuse compliance with the subpoena was made by Democrat Board Member Joshua D. Malcolm. Malcolm's motion ends with a declaration:

> But, this Board will... not stand idly by and consent to any agency attempting to obtain records and documents that violate the principles of overreach by the federal government, as in this circumstance."[7]

Malcolm's motion makes the Board's position crystal clear: We will not consent. Malcolm, who later had to drudge up an obscure case from a remote mountain county to justify his motion that Mark Harris should not be certified as the winner of the 2018 midterm election, announces he must take a stand against federal overreach.

After the board's vote to approve Malcolm's motion, the board issued one of its omnipotent "orders" via Executive Director Kim Strach. North Carolina Attorney General Josh Stein was ordered to quash the subpoena both for the elections agency and for the forty-four individual county election agencies. The "quasi-judicial" state elections board ordered the chief prosecutor of North Carolina to defy the constitutionally superior United States Justice Department on its behalf. A bureaucratic agency that exists wholly to secure elections refused to cooperate with a grand jury composed of American citizens that was convened to examine voting by illegal aliens.

Ironically, the exact time period granted as an extension to the elections agency by the US Attorney's office in its September 6th letter is the same time frame two different attorneys gave as necessary to produce the documents the same agency demanded from Mark Harris for Congress: four months. Initially, the Mark Harris campaign was given eleven days to fulfill a subpoena for which over 100,000 documents corresponded to queries for the subpoena terms. One attorney, whom we ultimately were unable to hire, explicitly stated that he thought the purpose of the vague and broad subpoena issued to the Mark Harris campaign was to get past the January 3, 2019 swearing-in date for the new Congress. He actually laughed when he saw the subpoena on my smart phone. This same attorney estimated that it would cost one million dollars to get through the state elections board's "evidentiary hearing."

This is perhaps the most troubling aspect of replacing constitutionally elected officials with supposedly non-partisan government boards and agencies. Government agencies give you the rules *you* have to play by, but they are exempt from any rules. They are autonomous, without any accountability. Agencies can declare, like the State Board of Elections did, "We will not consent." That's the bottom line of Joshua Malcolm's passionate motion. The State Board of Elections told the U. S. Attorney for the Eastern District of North Carolina they would not comply with a Justice Department subpoena.

Who tells a "quasi-judicial" agency, as the State Board of Elections was defined at that time, what it can and cannot do? Not the voters. The agency's staff members are not elected officials. The board that oversees the agency is not elected, but appointed by the governor.

Can the governor reign in the agency? The agency is not in the executive branch, although the governor appoints its members. The agency is statutorily defined as independent. What about the legislature? Unless the legislature goes to the trouble to actually pass laws pertinent to agency specifics, the legislature has no control over the independent agency. How about the courts? If a citizen is willing to go to the expense of filing a lawsuit, that citizen will quickly discover agencies are protected by the doctrine of "sovereign immunity."

A quasi-judicial, independent agency of "experts" to oversee elections sounds so good on the surface. Yet as we have seen over and over in the past five years, the best-intentioned bureaucrats can be led by the worst partisans appointed to oversee them. The worst intentioned bureaucrats can destroy citizens' finances and reputations with selective investigations. Those investigated by bureaucratic agencies don't have the same rights as the criminally charged. Investigations become show trials, without discovery or due process. Meanwhile, agencies that do the investigating simply shrug their shoulders and declare that they do not have to consent to be controlled by any part of the constitutional government.

Elected legislative bodies have today been reduced to being nannies for unelected agencies, attempting to oversee them without even really being able to understand their scope. Due to regulations created by government bureaucracy, I have to keep hand sanitizer in a locked cabinet in my classroom away from teenagers who are taking driver's education and hitting Interstate 485 at 70 MPH when school is over. This is one of my pet peeves of all time. When a kid sneezes, I have to stop my lesson, go to my desk and get a key, walk to the back of my classroom and unlock a cabinet to retrieve the hand sanitizer for him. The reason? Hand Sanitizer is marked "Keep Out of Reach of Children" and "children" are defined as less than eighteen years of age in the layers on layers of safety regulations schools must obey.

There are people who actually check on this, and I will get scolded if the potent and dangerous gel is sitting on my desk. This is insanity, but only mildly annoying insanity. Terrifying insanity comes when bureaucrats and partisan board appointees use their powers selectively based on political agendas. As North Carolina conservative blogger Brant Clifton put it after what he dubbed The Mark Harris Show Trial, "...our leaders are chosen by far-off interest groups and deep-pocketed 'investors.' If they don't like what we do on Election Day, they'll simply call out the lawyers and 'fix' our 'mistakes.'" [8]

CHAPTER 12

SPRINT TO THE FINISH

WE WERE IN the throes of the most intense part of the 2018 general election campaign when the state elections board issued its refusal to cooperate with the Eastern District of North Carolina's grand jury examination of illegal aliens voting. I never knew it happened. I only knew that we were in a neck and neck race with a candidate who was funded at twice what we were, despite Mark's having raised an incredible $2 million for his campaign, the vast majority of it from within North Carolina. Then fate lent us a hand.

Just after the first confirmation hearing for Supreme Court nominee Brett Kavanaugh wrapped up, a bomb dropped. An accuser took center stage in a surreal show trial for Kavanaugh when a second public hearing was held. There were many, many questions, particularly about the timing of the revelation by California Senator Dianne Feinstein, who had been contacted by Kavanaugh's accuser in July.

Suddenly a tepid, divided Republican base had a rallying cry. Kavanaugh!

People I had never seen before started showing up at the campaign headquarters looking for signs. In fact, we ran out of signs and had to print more. Our volunteer slots filled. Our internal polling showed Republicans solidifying behind the Republican candidate at around 92%, while Democrats were at 88% behind their candidate. Two polls done by the *New York Times* gave Mark the lead, although in the one done just prior to Election Day his lead was slim indeed. Mark was going door to door every afternoon, meeting voters. Each Saturday the campaign had "days of action" with Mark and volunteers going door-to-door in a different county of the district.

The McCready campaign's decision to attack Mark's teaching from the Bible on the family, a decision personally approved by Dan McCready, further energized Mark's evangelical base, as well as the hard left base. Some Charlotteans, particularly soft Republican women, began to feel paralyzed. Wealthy Charlotte Republicans who shared McCready's elite 28207 ZIP code began to fear that giving Dems control of the House might be a bridge too far.

Despite their dislike of Trump and the doubts about Mark that McCready had successfully raised with millions of dollars of television ads, Charlotte's Republican women weren't fully settled on McCready. One Charlotte Republican woman told *Politico* she might not vote in the 2018 midterm election at all, as she did not want to vote for Harris. The woman said that she probably would not make up her mind about voting until the morning of Election Day.[1]

In a district characterized as R+7 in its voting patterns, despite huge swaths of Democrats in parts of the district, McCready had to have Republican votes to win. Nice-sounding sayings were no longer cutting it, although McCready clung to them, and clung to his campaign strategy of refusing to take a position on anything. In the second and final televised debate, when asked directly by moderator Tim Boyum of Spectrum News whether he would vote for Pelosi, abstain, or vote for the Republican nominee for Speaker on his first day in Congress should Dems flip the majority, McCready still wouldn't give a straight answer.

More big news for us came in October. President Trump would do a rally in Bojangles Arena in Charlotte on October 26 to help both Mark and incumbent Congressman Ted Budd.

On October 26 it rained a cold, cold rain all day. Various groups were set up in a parking lot outside the rally arena, including FRC-Action, who brought the Values Voter Bus and worked all day in that freezing cold. I sat and listened in as Mark did interviews under tents. A friend with a radio show had a heated trailer. I must confess I took a break in there during one of Mark's interviews.

I once again had agonized over what to wear. We were going to be able to meet Air Force One, and I knew that was going to be a huge photo-op. Still, it was so cold, and I wouldn't be onstage at the rally with Mark this time. I opted for black boots, black skirt, black turtleneck sweater, and a gray and yellow plaid belted blazer. That was a good choice, as I was outside for a portion of the day.

After the preliminaries wrapped up in the parking lot, we left with our driver to head out to the airport where Air Force One would land. When we arrived, we were ushered into a room where Congressman Ted Budd and his wife Amy Kate joined us. We were coached on the protocol for greeting the president as he came down the stairs from the airplane. Aides took our overcoats so we would be ready for our pictures.

As Mark and I stood there on the tarmac at the foot of Air Force One, one of us, I can't remember which, made the statement that his parents wouldn't believe this if they saw us waiting to shake the hand of the President of the United States. Mark is very emotional, especially about family. He tells his sister he loves her in their every conversation. I saw him getting tears in his eyes.

I said, "We're going to think about that later, 'cause it's going to make us cry, and we don't want to look ugly when we meet the president!"

President Trump descended the steps and made his way down the row of those of us waiting to meet him. Then he said, "Come on, guys."

We had been told this *might* happen, but it was a maybe. Now it was happening. The president invited the candidates and spouses to ride to the rally with him in the presidential limo, "The Beast." As we all crammed in the limo, I was a little nervous about what the conversation might be on the thirty-minute ride to the arena. I love President Trump, but I felt a little like I imagine people felt at the court of King

Henry VIII. One false move, and it's over.

I didn't say anything for a long time. Tariffs were discussed. At some point I made some comment, I believe. President Trump told us all about the features of the limo.

We arrived at the arena and pulled under a tented area to unload the car so that the president wasn't exposed. We entered by a back door, and I was surprised and touched to see a host of first responders who had been allowed to line up at the back door and meet their president. Phones were flashing as the first responders snapped pictures. We were not allowed to approach the first responders. Only the president did that.

I thought it was the greatest thing that someone thought of honoring these heroes by allowing them to get up close and personal with the president. I was also touched when a family whom I did not know was backstage for photos. This family had a child with them. I never learned the reason they had been selected to meet President Trump that evening, but I know it was a good one. Many elected officials were there as well.

Amy Kate and I were escorted to our seats while our husbands went to the stage area with President Trump. I kept waving to our volunteers and supporters when I spotted them.

Mark was on the program to speak at the rally, and he knocked it out of the park. So many people told me later that Mark had sounded presidential himself. It is an intimidating thing to speak to thousands of people in an open arena like that. It takes a degree of charisma to "hold the stage" in that kind of setting. Mark did it incredibly well.

President Trump had to depart immediately after his remarks. In fact, an aide was holding out the president's coat for him as he walked offstage with Mark and Congressman Budd. Mark told me later that as the president quickly slid his arms into his waiting coat, he turned to Mark and Ted Budd and said, "If you guys can't win in this state, you don't deserve to be in Congress." I love that story. That is classic President Donald Trump.

We worked the polls at Early Voting again beginning in October, the requisite two and a half weeks before Election Day. I enjoyed hanging out with some of the same people I had met during the primary, both Democrats and Republicans.

We were blessed with so many volunteers who were so well organized by Lee Ann Patton, who is now the GOP Chair for North Carolina's 12th Congressional District, which covers the parts of Charlotte not included in the 9th District.

At last, it was actually Election Day. On Election Day I finally came up close and personal with Dan McCready . . . almost. It was a weirdly warm, rainy morning on November 6, 2018, with a forecast of strong storms ushering in cooler weather. I was once again at one of the Ninth District's busiest polling sites, Olde Providence Elementary School, lined up next to the sidewalk voters used to get into the poll. We jokingly dubbed the line "spouse row." Olde Providence isn't the largest precinct in the Ninth District, but it comes close. Three other wives and a husband were with me. Some were Democrats and some Republicans. We amiably chatted about the demands of a campaign and asked voters to take our respective campaign materials as they made their way to the poll.

Around mid-morning a cameraman showed up, gaunt, scruffy, and looking like he had been dropped straight out of Manhattan into Charlotte, North Carolina. Other media outlets had been in and out during the morning, but this cameraman was different. He didn't approach any voters but hovered at a distance, taking photos.

I began to suspect that he might work for the McCready campaign. I had heard rumors that Dan McCready never went anywhere without multiple handlers and a camera crew. Concerned about getting caught in a lose-lose proposition of looking rude on camera or looking like I was too friendly with McCready, I consulted with two Republican candidates for judge who were also meeting voters with us at Olde Providence. We decided my best option was simply to return to my car and wait McCready out, should he arrive. One of the judicial candidates pointed out that McCready seldom stayed past the photo opp.

Almost immediately after the impromptu sidewalk consultation, I saw Dan McCready walking across the parking lot. He stopped at a median where his cameraman was set up, instead of approaching the voters. I decided it was time to get to my vehicle. I had to walk directly past the photo shoot to get to my car, and from about ten feet away I heard Dan McCready talking to the camera. "So let's go back and see how we got here today..." was all I heard as I hurried past.

Once in my car, I called Mark. Since it was Election Day, he felt that it didn't matter what the McCready campaign did or did not do regarding photographs. Busy working at the busiest poll in Mecklenburg County, he didn't have time for angst.

I returned to my post, successfully avoiding any interaction with McCready, who was now posted at the head of the line, where he stayed for maybe thirty minutes or so, taking selfies with folks before crossing back to his cameraman, his back to the voters. I found that so amazing that I climbed up on a bench and snapped a picture, which I posted on my Facebook page with the caption "alone with his cameraman." Shortly thereafter, McCready departed.

That night, November 6, 2018, I stood in the wings of a make-shift stage created for our Election Night Watch Party at Rolling Hills County Club in Monroe, North Carolina. This election was Donald Trump's midterm. Mainstream media pundits desperately hoped Trump would be repudiated by the results. Democrats had spent an obscene amount of money trying to flip the Ninth District and gain a seat in the House. But we were in Monroe, and Monroe was in Union County. Union County was Mark Harris country: deep, solid red.

It was going on midnight and it was a weekday. As I peeked around the curtain, I could see that many of our supporters had left. Earlier, the room had been packed to capacity. Many had also stayed. Some had driven more than two hours to attend from other parts of the district. The Mark Harris supporter represented the best of America. They were mostly middle-class people who worked hard, volunteered for their churches and communities, stood for the national anthem, and had strong opinions on how the government was out of control. The majority of people in the room that night were not regular political donors. For some, their involvement with the Mark Harris campaign represented their first foray into political activity. Those in the room with us had given of their time, money, and talents to get us here. Tonight was the culmination of a year and half of hard work. The race was close, but I wasn't nervous. I was too tired to be nervous after working at a polling place all day. The district leaned Republican overall. Final polls showed Mark leading by one point.

I fidgeted backstage. I never felt adequately dolled up for these election night events. At our primary victory in May, I hadn't even had time to take a shower before the party because I greeted voters at a Charlotte polling location until about five minutes before the polls closed at 7:30. On that warm May night I threw on pink ankle pants and a black crepe top with ruffled long sleeves. Tonight, I wore the same black crepe top for luck, but with a skirt and a red necklace. You must wear red if you are a Republican.

Our campaign staff was backstage with us. They had stuck with us through a bitter primary and here we were. Earlier in the evening, while I greeted our supporters in the ballroom, Mark and the staff had been huddled in a room watching the returns. Mark fielded encouraging calls from other Republican Congressmen and friends. As local and national media descended on Monroe, the numbers rolled in for each county in the Ninth District. When I thought there was someone Mark needed to talk to, or when close friends and supporters departed, I would butt in and tell him he was needed. It was quiet and tense in the room as staff watched their laptops. Our campaign manager, Jason Williams, was in communication with our opponent's team throughout the night.

Our daughter Laura, our oldest child, was backstage with us. She would introduce Mark to the crowd. She had two speeches: one if Mark won and one if he lost. Her husband was out of town on a business trip and her toddlers were asleep in a double stroller backstage with us. Our son Matthew and his wife Mallory were also backstage, along with our son John. Mark's siblings Sheila and Steve had worked the polls all day for Mark and were out front with the rest of the crowd. As Mark's lead extended to 1,800 votes, we waited for the concession call that never came from Dan McCready. Finally, at 11:43 p.m., Jason reached out to McCready's deputy campaign manager Aaron Simpson by text to ask if Aaron thought we would hear anything from Dan McCready.

"Hey man, doesn't look like it," came Simpson's reply.

Based on the results that were in, we decided to declare victory and celebrate with all the folks who had stayed with us for a long night. Jason went to the podium onstage and introduced a congratulatory video from our friend Mike Huckabee. Jason had arranged the video as a nice surprise for Mark. Laura introduced Mark to the raucous crowd. Mark and I went onstage. Mark stepped up to the podium microphone and said words that would haunt him in a few short weeks. "Thank God for Union and Bladen Counties." Of the eight counties in the district, Mark won just Union and Bladen, although in Election Day voting Mark held his own in blue and densely populated Charlotte, coming in just 144 votes behind Dan McCready. We happily posed for pictures and took a group photo with our staff.

A little later, walking across the parking lot of Rolling Hills Country Club, I was cold. I had been in a hurry and didn't think about bringing a heavy coat. Election Day had been quite warm, but a cold front had come through. By midnight, the skies were clear and the air chilled. We said good night to our campaign staff and to the supporters who stuck around to the bitter end. Mark's sister Sheila and I got into Mark's car. Sheila was staying overnight with us, along with our son John.

I was happy but cautious. We all felt a little on edge about the fact that Dan McCready had not conceded. Election night is not the end of an election. Absentee ballots postmarked by Election Day still have to be counted. Provisional ballots still have to be counted. Provisional ballots come from voters operating outside of standard procedure, such as voting out of their precincts. County officials have to examine the provisional ballots and decide which to accept. How much would these additional ballots change the vote totals? That question makes everyone in a campaign nervous. Conventional wisdom said that McCready was not going to close a gap of 1,800 votes with last-minute absentee-by-mail votes and provisional ballots. Still, I wouldn't rest easy until McCready conceded.

On the car ride home, I started answering texts. A journey of more than a year had ended, and now a new chapter in our lives would begin. First, we would sleep. The following Monday we were scheduled to attend our first week of orientation for freshmen Congressmen and spouses, along with Jason Williams, who would now take a role in the district. All three of us had risked everything for this. Mark had left his job as senior pastor of First Baptist Church Charlotte and I had remained in my part-time job at a small museum rather than try to return to teaching full time. I was needed for the campaign, and I had plunged in with both feet. We sold investments and tightened our belts. Jason left a business partnership with his sister to work for the campaign full time.

The next day I was at my daughter's house around 3:30 p.m., waiting for her to return from work. I had picked up my toddler grandchildren from preschool, as I did several days a week. They had just awakened from naps and it was play time. My phone rang. It was one of our campaign staff, frantic. Mark wasn't answering his phone, and Dan McCready was trying to get in touch.

I called our landline and said as loudly as I could into the answering machine, "Mark, if you can hear this message call me right now!" He picked up. His phone had died after a full day of constant calls and was charging. I relayed the message.

At around 4:00 p.m., Mark and Dan McCready had a brief conversation in which McCready conceded the election. Mark called me and gave me the play-by-play. McCready and his family then spoke to his supporters just in time for the 5:00 p.m. newscasts. I breathed a sigh of relief and jumped up and down in my daughter's house. I'm sure my grandchildren thought I was crazy. My daughter arrived home and we jumped up and down together.

It was over. We were going to Washington. We were going to single-handedly clean up the swamp, join the Freedom Caucus yet stay friends with everyone, and make sure Christians were not bullied and silenced by the government. In short, we were incredibly naïve.

The deadline for a candidate to file an official election protest came and went. Dan McCready went to Disney World, where one of our key campaign volunteers ran into him as she was taking a much-needed vacation.

The day for official canvassing of vote totals by each county came and went. Each of the eight counties in the Ninth Congressional District certified its tally of votes, the action State Elections Board member Stella Anderson had indicated equaled certification for single county races.

When the official county-by-county tally was complete, Mark won the election by 905 votes. Each county in the Ninth District declared Mark Harris the official winner of the 2018 midterm election. 282,717 votes were cast in the 2018 Ninth Congressional District race. Over a quarter of a million people made their choices known in absentee-by-mail voting, early voting, and Election Day voting. Just a few days more and it would really be over. Mark would get his certificate declaring him the winner of the election when the North Carolina State Board of Elections and Ethics Enforcement signed off the following week.

Finally, November 27th arrived, exactly three weeks after Election Day. We were in Washington for our second week of orientation for new Representatives and their spouses. The nine-member appointed board of elections was to hold a meeting in Raleigh to certify the election results that morning.

The appointed board gathered in Raleigh that day was a lame duck board, as a three-judge panel had ordered it to be dissolved. After 2016, the North Carolina General Assembly had combined two existing boards into one and created a new nine-member entity called the North Carolina State Board of Elections and Ethics Enforcement, appointed by the legislature rather than the governor. A constitutional amendment placed on the November 6, 2018 ballot to make the change permanent failed after fierce opposition by Common Cause and other progressive groups. The seemingly endless court battles over who would control North Carolina elections continued to elude resolution. A stay of the order to dissolve the Board had been granted to allow the existing nine members to oversee the 2018 midterms.

The certification of county election results should have been one of the now-defunct board's final acts. The list of races to be certified on November 27th by the North Carolina Board of Elections and Ethics Enforcement included the Ninth District congressional race. The Ninth District was not omitted like other races in which protests were ongoing. Mark Harris's name was printed on the list of county-certified winners sent to board members as part of their meeting agenda. Every indication was that Mark Harris won the election and would be certified as the Congressman-elect November 27, 2018.

Enter Joshua Malcolm, appointed Democrat member of the State Elections Board. On November 27, 2018, Malcolm knew things the Mark Harris campaign had no way of knowing. Former FBI agent and chief elections agency investigator Joan Fleming had launched an investigation into Patriots for Progress and McCrae Dowless in October 2016. The investigation was kept totally out of public view, but Malcolm knew all about it. He had known all about it since at least December 2016.

Malcolm had also been in communication with Bladen County Board of Elections member Jens Lutz, who was spying on Dowless and hanging out at the Bladen County Board of Elections office during both the 2018 primary and general elections. It took the threat of legal action from WBTV in Charlotte to finally make the State Elections Board hand over records revealing thirteen communications between Malcolm and Lutz, the final ones occurring on Election Day, November 6, 2018. The elections agency initially denied that any communication had occurred between Malcolm and Lutz. It is unknown to what, if any, extent Malcolm was directing Lutz in the "undercover work" Lutz boasted about to associates.

Furthermore, Malcolm had been in communication with Democrat candidate Dan McCready, which violated the State Elections Board's ethical standards, which by North Carolina Statute prohibit even the appearance of conflicts of interest. Malcolm and McCready texted just forty-eight hours before the November 27, 2018 board meeting, according to a report issued by the WBTV investigative team.[2] It has taken more than a year and a lawsuit by WBTV to obtain that information. Malcolm never disclosed these communications when the conflict-of-interest statement was issued at the beginning of the November 27th meeting. Further legal action is ongoing as WBTV attempts to gain access to Malcolm's full communications.

At the November 27, 2018 meeting of the appointed State Elections Board, North Carolina elections agency Executive Director Kim Strach presented the certified county results, which included Mark Harris as the winner in Congressional District 09. Strach even made a speech to the State Board as she was about to present the certified county list that day. Strach said, "I always like to tell the Board what we've done to ensure that the results you are getting are accurate." She then detailed audits of both ballots and equipment, even bragging that the Department of Homeland Security was present on Election Night.

Strach specifically stated that the agency looked carefully at close contests to make sure there were no irregularities around the outcome.[3] Despite two election protests with concerns over absentee ballots and equipment in Bladen County in 2016, Strach mysteriously does not seem to have been down to Bladen County to supervise the election during early voting or on Election Day.

Democrat State Elections Board member Joshua Malcolm suddenly made a motion that Mark Harris not be certified. Republican board member John Lewis later said he had no idea that Malcolm's motion was coming. Lewis thought he was there to sign off on the election results as the State Elections Board always did. No new material from new investigations had been shared with board members prior to the meeting. John Lewis had no clue that Malcolm would make such a motion.[4]

Democrat Malcolm wanted Mark Harris pulled from the official county-certified list of *unchallenged and unprotested* election winners. The State Elections Board then entered a closed session and emerged with a 9-0 vote not to certify Mark Harris.

The agency, which is subject to open records laws, has denied my request for the summary of this closed meeting. The agency does not keep detailed minutes of its closed sessions. It has taken a lawsuit by WBTV to obtain the data showing Joshua Malcolm's communications with Jens Lutz and Mark's opponent, Dan McCready. Malcolm's phone seems to have disappeared.

Much later, Josh Lawson, the chief attorney for the agency, told a crowd at Davidson College that the state elections agency did not know Dowless was working for Mark Harris until someone saw a Facebook post on November 20, 2018. I don't know what Lawson did or did not know, but is it possible that an FBI agent, an SBI agent, and the "undercover" Jens Lutz missed the giant Mark Harris for Congress car magnets displayed on Dowless's vehicle while he was under surveillance during early voting in the spring of 2018? Did someone miss Dowless standing under the tent with us at most of the festivals we attended in Bladen County? Did someone miss the fact that Mark Harris got 437 absentee-by mail-votes in the primary?

After its 9-0 vote to delay certification of Mark's victory, the State Elections Board agreed to meet again on November 30th to make a final decision about the Ninth District race. They would either certify Mark or determine that one of their "evidentiary hearings" was necessary.

The State Elections Board never contacted Mark or anyone on our campaign about its refusal to certify Mark's victory, or the reasons behind it. Instead, the elections agency issued a press release through its communications officer. The press release included Joshua Malcolm's motion to pull Mark Harris from the list of certified winners, which vaguely referenced "unfortunate activities" happening in his part of the state.

At 4:30 p.m., Mark was entering an interview for a potential congressional staff member when he got a text from our son John with a link to a news article. Our campaign manager Jason Williams had gotten a text from a friend at 4:09 p.m. also containing a link to a news report. Our campaign consultant Andy Yates heard the news on his car radio while traveling on I-95 in North Carolina. I had spent a pleasant day at events for congressional spouses on November 27, 2018. I believe I was on a bus returning to our hotel when a text popped up from my ever-prescient friend Mary Chapman: "They're going to try to steal the election," she texted. She included a link to a news article about Malcolm's motion and the Board's vote. And thus the nightmare began.

October 28, 2017, Bladenboro, NC.
"Beastfest" capitalizes on the legend of the Beast of Bladenboro.

August 31, 2018, Charlotte, NC.
President Trump did a fundraiser for Mark and Congressman Ted Budd. The same day, the United States Justice Department issued a subpoena to the state elections board, which it refused to fulfill.

November 2, 2018 Matthews, NC.
Our daughter was one of many "Women for Mark Harris" who campaigned at early voting sites across the district.

October 26, 2018 Bojangles Arena, Charlotte, NC. Mark spoke at a rally for President Trump and we were invited to ride in the presidential limousine. Many people told me that Mark looked presidential that evening himself.

CHAPTER 13

FREEZE THE TARGET

EVERY MOMENT OF that November week of congressional orientation was completely crammed with appointments and scheduled meetings. It was both exhilarating and stressful. We were planning the January 3, 2019 swearing in celebrations in Washington and a December 8 local thank-you barbeque we were throwing for campaign volunteers.

When the State Board withheld certification, I dropped my plans to look at apartments in Washington and I found myself talking to lawyers at the National Republican Congressional Committee (NRCC) headquarters along with our campaign manager Jason, who was there in DC with us. Mark carried on with staff interviews for his congressional office. We didn't take the situation seriously enough at the beginning.

The attorneys at the NRCC were incredulous. One of them kept saying over and over, "He won the damn election."

Another attorney was wary. She remembered 2016, and the extreme vindictiveness of the Democrats and progressive groups in North Carolina over the governor's race. Democrats had attempted to prevent her from ever practicing in North Carolina again after she assisted Republican incumbent governor Pat McCrory with election protests.

A third attorney expressed his incredulity in a more cerebral manner. "They [the state appointed board] are performing a ministerial duty. How can they say the numbers aren't what they are when each county already certified them? Their job is just to sign off on the county numbers."

I had no idea what was going on. None. The chatter was generally that Malcolm was throwing his weight around and showing off. No one from the state elections agency or the appointed State Board of Elections ever informed us of any issues with the campaign. We were always a step behind because we had to learn everything from the media, except for the subpoena issued to our campaign a few days later.

Most of what the North Carolina State Elections Board discussed on both November 27, 2018 and November 30, 2018 was done in "closed session" and kept totally out of the public's view. My request for the summaries of those meetings, made one and a half years later and one year after McCrae Dowless was indicted, has been denied. I have no idea of the veracity of any evidence presented to the State Board, except that whatever was presented clearly did not affect the outcome of the election. In the State Elections Board's own "Order of Proceedings" issued once a hearing was called, the language indicates that the election results were not in question in the Ninth Congressional District.

By Friday, November 30, 2018 Republicans on the State Board were less willing to deny certification to the rightful winner of the election, my husband Mark Harris. Standard operating procedure had always been to certify the winner if the numbers weren't in doubt, and then investigate and prosecute any individuals involved in impropriety.

Nonetheless, on November 30, the appointed State Elections Board emerged from another closed session with a 7-2 vote not to certify Mark. Only two of the four Republicans on the Board voted against denying Mark's certification. Late that same Friday night we arrived home in Charlotte after our second full week of congressional orientation.

We had believed we would get a brief respite from campaigning and that Mark would be serving the people of the Ninth District's eight counties. Instead, we came home to investigations, threats, false rumors spread by Republican vultures, and reporters on the lawn. In hindsight, we should have known that this is how the game is played these days. Sue till it's blue. Investigation-paralyzation. Media hit pieces. But I wasn't prepared for it. And unlike Dan McCready, Mark's Democrat opponent, we didn't have the money and national connections to insulate ourselves from it.

November 27, 2018 marked the beginning of a brutal three-month struggle for the Ninth Congressional District seat in the House of Representatives. At the center of the struggle is an enigma. What exactly did a man named Leslie McCrae Dowless do, or not do, in the 2018 midterm election? Dowless has been charged with illegally mailing thirteen absentee ballots to the Board of Elections over three election cycles. He is charged with mailing two ballots in the Harris-McCready race. Dowless has pled not guilty.

We were caught totally off guard when Malcolm fired the opening salvo in this struggle. But the Democrats weren't. Someone had planned for the moment created by Joshua Malcolm.

1960s radical Saul Alinsky is credited with developing a concept called "Freeze the Target." If you Google "freeze the target" you will get results that include Alinsky's book *Rules for Radicals*, some medical examples of using freezing to block nerves, and Ice Spells from several video games and the Harry Potter series.

I immediately think of the Disney movie *Frozen*. To say that two of my little granddaughters are obsessed with *Frozen* is an understatement. They have *Frozen* costumes, *Frozen* nightgowns, *Frozen* sleeping bags, and my favorite, the *Frozen* sing-a-long microphones I gave them for Christmas. The five-year-old is a triple threat. She sings and runs around the room dancing and acting out the part of Elsa while she sings. The three-year-old stands perfectly still in the middle of the room and sings her tiny little heart out straight into the microphone. They also love to "freeze" people. Sometimes when they get together with their cousins the game gets crazy.

"I froze you."

"I unfroze you with my powers."

"You don't have powers. I'm Elsa."

"I'm a boy and I have soup-pa pow-was."

Alinsky's version of a frozen target is something altogether different. In Alinsky's version, one person becomes the face of an issue. One person must be blamed and scapegoated. Propaganda relentlessly places blame on the target until the target is paralyzed.

When a left-wing lobbyist told Pat McCrory in 2016 that he would turn McCrory into George Wallace, he was talking about making McCrory the target. Pat McCrory would be the face of HB2. Propaganda would make HB2 seem hateful, and by extension Pat McCrory hater-in-chief. It didn't have to be true.

Mark Harris was now the target. The real issue for high-level Democrats was getting Dan McCready a new election. The real issue for Bladen County Democrats was getting McCrae Dowless out of the way. From the moment Joshua Malcolm made his motion to pull the Ninth District out of the list of certified races on November 27th, the Democrat machine grabbed the narrative and never let go. McCrae Dowless, and by extension Mark Harris, became the implied source of every irregularity in the 2018 midterms in North Carolina, real or imagined.

On October 29, almost exactly one month before Malcolm's motion to pull Mark Harris out of the list of certified election victors, Democrats started collecting affidavits. Two women, Emma Lee Shipman and Datesha Dwana Montgomery, signed affidavits alleging that a female came to their residences and took their unsealed ballots. Shipman's affidavit was witnessed by familiar Bladen County Improvement Association figure Michael Cogdell, who had been interviewed as a suspect in the 2016 furor over alleged Democrat ballot harvesting.[1]

Both women had already voted before the date they executed their affidavits. Shipman voted October 17 and Montgomery voted

October 18 at early voting-in-person. The two women's absentee-by-mail ballots were not the votes they cast in the 2018 midterm election. The women's affidavits were not filed as official election complaints at the Bladen County Board of Elections as in 2016. Instead, the affidavits were given to the Democrat Party of North Carolina. Later, Shipman changed her affidavit.

Once the appointed State Elections Board voted to approve Malcolm's motion to withhold Mark Harris's certificate of victory on November 27th and meet again on November 30th, the Democrat Party of North Carolina went into blitzkrieg mode.

Lucy Young signed a document on November 28, 2018 stating that she voted early, but afterward an absentee ballot she did not order arrived at her residence. Ms. Young didn't even live in the Ninth Congressional District. Bladen County was split between the 9th and 7th Congressional Districts in 2018. The five heavily minority precincts of Bladen County, one of which was Lucy Young's precinct, were in the Seventh District. Whoever ordered Ms. Young's absentee ballot did not do so on behalf of the Mark Harris campaign, yet it was part of the Democrat Party's "evidence" submitted in a press conference targeting Mark Harris.

Failed Democrat candidate Matthew Dixon of Bladen County executed another affidavit during the two-day blitzkrieg. On November 29 Dixon called Agnes Willis. Willis, who worked at the Bladen County Board of Elections during the 2018 midterms, had also worked with the Bladen County Improvement Association a time or two. Willis later testified at the "evidentiary hearing" held by the State Elections Board that a young man called her late one morning and asked if he could come to her house and collect an affidavit from her. She told him that she was retired, wasn't dressed, and would come to his office later. He told her that wasn't fast enough; he needed to be at her home within the hour.

Soon the man arrived and identified himself as Matthew Dixon, a local attorney. He assured Willis he was a Democrat. Dixon had an affidavit already written up. He reviewed it with Willis while placing several calls from her dining room table to someone she couldn't identify. The man spoke to his coaches on the phone about what he was supposed to do. Willis signed the affidavit and the man departed.[2] Matthew Dixon witnessed the affidavit and a female notarized it.

Willis testified that Matthew Dixon completed the hand-written portion of the affidavit while in her home. She indicated that the typed portion containing her name and personal contact information was already completed when Dixon arrived. The affidavit shows two distinct handwritings- one is Willis's signature and the other in the body of the affidavit is different.

The affidavit states that poll workers viewed the early voting "tape" and thus saw election results before they were supposed to be released. In the February 2019 "evidentiary hearing" the chief judge at the polling place denied under oath that this occurred. Willis testified at the same hearing that the tape was viewed, but that the incident involved a couple of official poll workers accidentally noticing the results of the Bladen County sheriff's race and commenting on them, nothing more.

Again, this incident had absolutely nothing to do with the Ninth District congressional race. Nothing. No one testified that results were given to McCrae Dowless or that Dowless had access to any early-voting results. Willis's affidavit does not mention McCrae Dowless. Yet like the affidavit of Lucy Young who lived in a different district, Willis's affidavit was presented as "evidence" that Mark Harris should not be certified and should be investigated.

Also on November 29, Dwight Sheppard completed an affidavit based on nothing but hearsay. Sheppard's affidavit claims that he overheard two conversations. In one conversation, Sheppard said that he overheard a statement that Dowless would get a $40,000 win bonus from the Harris campaign. This is completely false and was repudiated at the "evidentiary hearing."

Sheppard also claimed to have heard a voter say that a ballot came in the mail for him that he didn't order. A quick check of the voter database shows that the voter named by Sheppard voted in person and that no absentee-by-mail ballots were ordered in his name.

Sheppard is the husband of Bladen County Board of Elections member Patsy Sheppard, a Democrat who has been the subject of three formal complaints for incompetency, "slanderous and disrespectful remarks," and bearing false witness. In a recent complaint Sheppard was accused of saying that the Pledge of Allegiance was for white supremacists.[3] Sheppard and fellow board member Louella Thompson were behind a move to ban the Pledge of Allegiance from Bladen County Board of Elections Meetings.

The Democrat Party of North Carolina submitted these five affidavits, none of which had any bearing on the outcome of the Harris-McCready race, with a letter from Democrat Party attorney John Wallace to the State Elections Board on November 29, 2018. No wonder Matthew Dixon couldn't give Agnes Willis time to take a shower and get dressed and come to his office. He needed her signature before a press conference that afternoon. The Dems rolled the letter and affidavits out with a public flourish "presenting" them to the State Elections Board and doing what Democrats do best, demanding an investigation.[4] The letter links the affidavits directly to Mark's certification and demands that Harris remain uncertified while an investigation is done, "just as it was in 2016."[5]

I didn't catch it at the time, but even in this first propaganda move, the Democrats reveal how their hand will be played. This will be about proving the election is "tainted." John Wallace directly says that in his letter.[6] The Democrats will be playing a sleight-of-hand game in which they will release information that sounds really bad, but in fact does not usually directly connect to evidence concerning McCrae Dowless, the man at the center of the Ninth District investigation.

In this first release of Democrat propaganda, the facts are that two of the affiants voted in early voting. One lived outside of the Ninth District. Another's information had nothing to do with the congressional race. The final affidavit contains an assertion that anyone with a laptop could prove false in less than one minute.

The haste and carelessness with which these supposedly legal affidavits were collected is shocking. Haste, carelessness, even lies, would not be surprising if these were just rash statements made by political party operatives. These affidavits, however, were submitted as if they were some kind of evidence. An attorney demanding an investigation on behalf of the Democrat Party of North Carolina submitted them.

The Left banks on something I call the myth of reasonableness. People who have been taught to trust in our institutions simply would not consider that an attorney, whether his name is John Wallace or Marc Elias, would be partisan, careless, or even nefarious in his dealings. When the media reported on these five affidavits, the average North Carolinian accepted them as true and relevant to the Mark Harris race.

I know Democrats who differ from me in many of our political views. In my heart I know with certainty that these Democrat acquaintances would be horrified by this wanton carelessness. Careful, decent people don't throw around irrelevant, unproven, or false allegations publicly. Yet the Democrat Party of North Carolina, the DCCC and Dan McCready himself did so time and time again in the weeks following the November 2018 midterm elections.

We should have left Washington immediately when Malcolm made his move on November 27, but we didn't. In hindsight, Mark sees this as one of several failures in his leadership during the crisis. We were told this would blow over. We shouldn't have believed it would be that simple. The days of reasonable behavior are gone. Things don't blow over. Mark should have been out front, and I should have been home researching and discrediting the Democrat propaganda instead of picking out paint and furnishings for the congressional office.

We flew home late in the evening Friday night November 30, still having spoken to no one directly at the State Elections Board or the elections agency after the Board's second vote not to certify. It would be January before that would happen. An appointment was made to speak with two lawyers who handled such issues. They were coming from Raleigh on December 5, the following Wednesday.

Four days: December 1, 2, 3, and 4. December 1 and 2 were weekend days: Saturday and Sunday. That doesn't sound very long, yet these were the crucial days in which we didn't start fighting the Democrat narrative. These were the crucial days in which we listened to cautious attorneys who said, "Don't talk to anyone." Newscasters knocked on the door, cameras running. Reporters gave their stories from our cul-de-sac saying, "We can see Harris in his house, but he won't come out." CNN sent two young producers around to ask our neighbors about us. I'm told they gave us a good report.

Crazy stories were all over the media. Some stories, we knew, had no truth to them. It was not possible that someone saw McCrae Dowless on the street carrying 800 ballots. It seemed highly improbable that folks going door-to-door in Robeson County wearing "election staff" lanyards were McCrae's workers. That sounded a lot more other third-party groups who have been called on the carpet previously for wearing official-looking badges.

Third party groups played a heavy role in the 2018 midterms in North Carolina. Among them was a shadowy Clinton-associated group called The Center for Voter Participation (among its numerous aliases) that was fined $100,000 in North Carolina for suppressing black female votes in the 2008 Democrat primary to help Hillary Clinton against Barack Obama. The group recruited absentee by mail votes for McCready from single women and minority voters by sending them unsolicited absentee ballot request forms with pre-filled information and a stamped return envelope pre-addressed to their county elections board. In the Ninth District, this group sent thousands of unsolicited absentee ballot requests.

Many reporters seemed to have no grasp of the difference between absentee-ballot request forms and absentee ballots. Things that were not illegal, like witnessing absentee ballots, got reported as if they were spectacular and shocking.

We had no idea what was going on in Bladen County, which the media quickly determined was the center of controversy after the

Democrat Party's news conference.

December 1, the first day we were home from Washington, I called McCrae Dowless. I wanted to know what was going on. I had talked to McCrae frequently during the final weeks of the campaign, as he was not computer savvy and wanted to know the numbers from the state election board's daily 5AM posting of absentee and early voting. Since I downloaded that list each day to take over to our Union County office to address campaign mail, I would call and update him.

That December Saturday I asked the only question I could ask from my frame of reference after 2016. "Is there any chance some of the girls who worked for you also worked for the Bladen County Improvement Association, just for the money?" I thought perhaps they had collected ballots at the behest of the Democrat group.

He said no. He denied collecting ballots. He said that Jens Lutz had set him up. I asked if he had proof that he trained his workers "never to touch a ballot" as he had phrased it to us. He replied that he did not. I told him that he had better tell the truth, and I hung up.

I had to speak at lunchtime at the Christmas tea for Union County's Republican Women. I was going to talk about the beautiful White House Christmas decorations. I did that, but I also told them the one scrap of information I had time to look up, that Emma Shipman and Datesha Montgomery had voted in early voting. They had not been denied their right to vote. They had voted exactly as they wanted to. I didn't think fast enough to check their Congressional Districts. I didn't even consider that they might live in one of the five Bladen County precincts outside of the Ninth District, as affiant Lucy Young did. I too fell victim to the myth of reasonableness and failed to research all the possibilities.

We went about a host of "Congressman-elect" activities acting like Mark was going to become the Congressman. Between December 1 and December 5 when we met our attorneys for the first time, we had nine events stretching from Mecklenburg east across the eight counties of the district, including a swearing-in ceremony for another McCrae Dowless client, Republican Sheriff Jim McVicker of Bladen

County. McVicker's race had been certified without protest. In that same span of five days, we also received an email from our son John breaking off communication with us until the situation was resolved. John had just started a job as an assistant US Attorney. He could not be put in a position of discussing anything about the campaign with us, and he believed it was necessary to be able to prove that he had upheld that standard. No communication at all was the cleanest way to achieve that goal. I woke up on my birthday to John's email on my smart phone, sent late the night before.

We didn't realize it until it was too late, but the Democrats were playing an entirely different game from our team. We began researching the numbers, trying to prove that Mark won the election without his Bladen County absentee-by-mail ballots and trying to determine just how many people who ordered absentee-by-mail ballots had not *voted,* as opposed to the number that **had not returned absentee ballots**. These are two different numbers, as Emma Shipman and Datesha Montgomery illustrate. Deciphering the numbers is more complicated than it sounds.

The Democrats were focusing on a different section of North Carolina law. Another standard for overturning an election is "taint that casts doubt on the election's fairness."[7] In hindsight, I can see the focus on "taint" early in the propaganda war against Mark. In real time, I didn't. I only understood when we got to the hearing and Marc Elias kept using the phrase over and over again.

The Democrats, possibly via Joshua Malcolm, who would have understood the significance of the county canvass better than we did, realized that Mark had won the election. Period. Indisputable. The election had never hinged on Bladen or Robeson Counties, which are much less densely populated than Charlotte and its suburbs. In Mecklenburg County, where urban Charlotte is located, McCready's percentages of absentee-by-mail and early voting ballots were almost exactly the same as those of Harris in Bladen County, but the raw vote totals were much, much higher.

On Election Day Mark soundly defeated McCready in Bladen

County, but split Mecklenburg County's Election Day vote almost 50-50 with him in their combined vote totals.[8] The two candidates' raw vote totals in Mecklenburg County on Election Day were separated by a mere 144 votes: 19,779 for McCready to 19,635 for Harris. In Bladen County, Harris got just upwards of 5,000 total raw votes. The Mecklenburg County numbers dwarf those of rural Bladen County. By holding his own in the densely populated Charlotte metro area, Harris was positioned to win the election when the votes of Union County, the "red wall" between blue Mecklenburg County and the rest of the district, were tallied.

Union County contains both Charlotte suburbs and rural areas. It is the second-most populous county in the Ninth District after Mecklenburg. The Harris campaign concentrated its efforts there and was blessed with tremendous grassroots volunteers who lived in the county. Harris got 59.12% of Union County's votes, which nearly rivaled those of Charlotte's Mecklenburg County in raw numbers.

The Union County turnout was extremely significant. If turnout in every county were equal, a candidate could conceivably win the election based on Mecklenburg County alone, just as Robert Pittenger did in the 2016 Republican primary, when Mecklenburg County was the only county in the district he carried. In 2018, Union County's overall turnout was just over 55%. In the four easternmost rural precincts of the county Harris took 70%, 76%, 75%, and 85% of the votes with a very high voter turnout in those precincts.[9]

The Democrat Party and Dan McCready himself also had to know that getting a new election was an uphill battle. No one had filed a protest. Not candidate McCready, nor any other voter in the Ninth District. Each and every county had certified its official tally of votes. Deadlines had passed. When Joshua Malcolm moved to withhold certification, it was a Hail Mary at the midnight hour. This was truly the uncharted territory the attorney for the state elections agency referenced when an unusual request for delayed certification had come before the board in May 2018.

To throw out the votes of 282,717 citizens across eight counties based on unproven accusations was almost inconceivable. The State Elections Board needed to embrace the ambiguous legal standard of "taint that casts doubt on the election's fairness" as a legitimate reason to overturn an election. The public had to be convinced that the election was tainted, whether Mark Harris had any direct involvement or not. The taint simply had to be tied to Harris. The tie did not have to be based on facts, just perception.

I believe the Democrats had a strategically planned roll-out of weekly messages to freeze the target. They even paid for television ads. The first week, the message was ballot harvesting. Next came emphasis on the word fraud, linked with Mark Harris. Then came the more dramatic phrase "stolen election." Last was "Mark Harris should be in jail," as a confident Dan McCready proclaimed to media outlets just days before the State Board's "evidentiary hearing."

The deceptions continued in the Democrat Party's move to freeze the target and isolate Mark from support. When the Agnes Willis affidavit claiming that early-voting results were viewed didn't gain enough steam on November 29, the Democrat Party of North Carolina rolled it out again at a December 11, 2018 news conference and left the public to assume that "leaks" of early voting information had gone to Dowless. It would be months later before sworn testimony by Willis herself proved this to be a baseless accusation.

After the December 11 news conference by Wayne Goodwin, Chairman of the North Carolina Democrat Party, Mark Harris lost the support of the state GOP. No one bothered to actually read the Willis affidavit. Everyone blindly accepted the Democrat Party of North Carolina's spin on it.

Both North Carolina Republican Party Chairman Robin Hayes and Executive Director Dallas Woodhouse went public with statements that if early-voting results had been viewed, a new election was required. Dallas Woodhouse even appeared on MSNBC. Harris's political enemies and vultures on the fence salivating for the seat were having a field day.

Three days after the Democrat Party's December 11 news

conference I was entering a GOP event in another county outside of the Ninth District. I saw Dan Barry, former Ninth District candidate, in front of the venue with one hand in his pocket posing for the cameras as he gave an interview. Dan Barry knew nothing. He would not even return my call to him to speak to me directly about the situation.

Charlotte political consultant Larry Shaheen was on the phone "24/7" with the media, according to a local source. Someone kept posing as an insider on our campaign. Shaheen allegedly played so fast and loose with the truth that another Republican consultant, Paul Shumaker of Raleigh, called him and told him to cool it. Both Shumaker and Shaheen had worked for Robert Pittenger, who lost to Mark in the primary.

I was shocked one evening as I was about to get out of the car to attend a Republican women's Christmas party. Amy Gardner of the *Washington Post* texted me. She had been told by a source claiming to be close to our campaign that I was "heavily involved" in absentee ballots. Perhaps the source supplied her with my cell number, or perhaps she obtained it elsewhere. I do not know.

I closed the car door and responded to her text. When I informed her that all I had done was download the 5:00 a.m. posting of absentee and early voters from the elections agency website to print and take over to our Union County Headquarters, she texted back, "So you weren't chasing down ballots in Bladen County?"

"No," I responded. Gardner and Nick Ochsner of WBTV were the only reporters in America who had the decency to check out the tales handed to them. A relative in another part of the state told me a story was indeed printed by a different news outlet stating that I had been very hands-on with Dowless's program, which is an absolute lie.

The Democrat propaganda piled up. Someone leaked 159 absentee ballot container envelopes from the Bladen County Board of Elections to Joe Bruno of WSOC-TV in Charlotte. These were the outer envelopes voters used to mail their absentee-by-mail ballots. These outer envelopes required either the signature of a notary or two witnesses to show that the ballot inside was properly executed and sealed in the envelope prior to mailing to the county elections board. Workers associated with McCrae Dowless had witnessed many of the ballot containers, which is legal. Bruno reported, tweeted, and otherwise disseminated information gleaned from the leaked ballots at a frantic pace, as if he had just uncovered Watergate. In reality, anyone can be a witness to a ballot envelope, as long as only the voter mails it or takes the ballot to the county board of elections in person.

A voter whose ballot container envelope was leaked to Bruno spoke to me on condition of anonymity. This voter said that state elections agency investigators never interviewed him. The agency claimed it interviewed over 100 voters and attempted over 400 voter interviews concerning the 2018 midterms. This voter also said that he had known Dowless for many years, and that Dowless had never asked him to hand over his absentee ballot. He said that Dowless did frequently call him just to make sure he mailed his absentee ballot to the Bladen County Board of Elections. This voter indicated that many of the 159 voters whose ballot containers were leaked had switched their party affiliations from Democrat to Republican as part of the mass exodus of Democrat voters in rural North Carolina.

Two of the leaked ballot envelopes in the batch of 159 belonged to Republican Mayor of Bladenboro Rufus Duckworth and his wife. Democrat "protesters" showed up in Mayor Duckworth's driveway to harass he and his wife after the leak.

When an investigator for the state elections agency showed up at Duckworth's house, Mayor Duckworth threw the agent off his property. Duckworth was fed up, and he told the investigator not to come back with a few threats thrown in for good measure. Chief Investigator for the state elections agency Joan Fleming immediately called her man in Bladen, Jens Lutz, to see if Duckworth was dangerous.

Duckworth later called Fleming and apologized in a phone call he recorded and provided to the Voter Integrity Project. Nothing about the Duckworth family's ballots was irregular. One of Dowless's workers, Woody Hester, had witnessed both ballots. Duckworth witnessed his wife's ballot, and vice-versa, as the required second witness signature.

Mayor Duckworth personally delivered the absentee ballots for himself and his wife, who was undergoing medical treatments and did not want to vote in person, to the Bladen County Board of Elections. They were not improperly mailed (harvested.) This information is clear because North Carolina law provides for logs to be kept when absentee ballots are returned in person to a county elections board. Democrats are currently attempting to undo these provisions in state law by creating federal law that allows for ballot boxes where ballots can be dropped off without any record keeping.

The State Elections Board began to realize that the leaker had selectively chosen ballot envelopes for his enemies without rhyme or reason. After the leak of the ballot container envelopes, Dowless's former business partner Jens Lutz resigned from the Bladen County Board of Elections. Some media outlets reported that Director Kim Strach and investigator Joan Fleming of the state elections agency paid Lutz a visit just before his resignation, leading most to speculate that Lutz was the source of the leaks. Shortly thereafter Lutz took off to Arizona.

On December 17, a town hall was held at First Baptist Church on Martin Luther King Drive in Bladenboro. Travis Fain of WRAL news in Raleigh attended. Fain opened his news story with a familiar media refrain. Fain wrote,

> Frustrated by decades of racial unfairness and seeing its all-too-familiar signs in the current controversy over the 9th Congressional District results, more than 200 people packed the First Baptist Church on Martin Luther King, Jr. Drive in Bladenboro.[10]

Fain reported that "organizers railed about stolen votes" and that the NAACP President "bashed Raleigh Republicans as bigots." At least Fain did tell the whole story before he closed his article. After two hours, there was "sparse evidence" offered of a stolen election,

Fain reported. A show of hands from people who believed their votes had been mishandled brought "only a few" from the standing room only crowd.[11]

The propaganda at the meeting focused on unreturned ballots from high-minority precincts. What no one said was that the five high-minority precincts in Bladen County were not in the Ninth Congressional District. Lucy Young, who received an absentee ballot she didn't request, did not live in the Ninth District. Precious Hall, who did actually live in the Ninth Congressional District, later testified at the "evidentiary hearing" that she received an unsolicited absentee-ballot request, and that women from the Democrat Bladen County Improvement Association showed up a few days later to collect that unsolicited ballot from her.[12]

George Michael Cogdell, a Bladen County Commissioner who was investigated in 2016 for his role in irregularities committed by the Bladen County Improvement Association, grabbed the media spotlight. "The Lord turned that thing way around," according to Cogdell. Representatives from the Southern Coalition for Social Justice and the NAACP were on hand gathering names and contact information from attendees.

After months of this propaganda, I would imagine that if you had asked the average North Carolinian about Dowless's alleged activities, you would not get the answer "Improperly mailing two ballots to the Bladen County Board of Elections in the Harris-McCready race," as is charged in his indictment. Instead, you would hear accusations planted by Democrats via a willing media. "He stole thousands of ballots and destroyed them." Maybe you would hear "He cheated and cost Dan McCready the election." Maybe you would hear "voter fraud." Since criminal charges have been issued, the media is choosing its words more carefully. "Irregularities," "improprieties," and "mishandling" are now the words of choice since neither the State Elections Board nor the grand jury indictment accused Dowless of destroying ballots or fraudulently changing votes to either give them to Mark Harris or take votes from Dan McCready.

CHAPTER 14

MALCOLM TAKES CHARGE

AS THE DEMOCRAT propaganda machine ramped up, as usual there was chaos at the state elections board. On Saturday December 1, 2018 Board Chair Andy Penry resigned under pressure over his tweets in reply to @realDonaldTrump. State Board members are supposed to refrain from any partisan activity. It is illegal for them to "electioneer," or campaign for or against particular parties or candidates.

Penry's resignation led Democrat Governor Roy Cooper to elevate Joshua Malcolm, who had been vice chair, to board chair at the State Elections Board. Now Malcolm, who was in communication with Democrat candidate Dan McCready, would be in total control of the process regarding the Harris-McCready race.

Within a few days of ascending to the chairman's seat on the elections board, Malcolm made a decision. A "portal" was opened on the election agency's website for documents that were supposed to be relevant to the Ninth District Investigation. Among the first things to go up on the portal were the 159 ballot container envelopes leaked to reporter Joe Bruno. No personal information was redacted. Names, addresses, even voter signatures were available to the general public for 159 voters who believed they had cast confidential absentee-by-mail ballots. It is ironic that the same man who made a motion to quash United States Justice Department subpoenas to supposedly protect voter confidentiality had no qualms about exposing voters' personal information in a highly charged death match for a congressional seat.

On December 19, 2018 the report from the 2016 investigation conducted by the state elections agency was publicly released for the first time on the portal.[1] Documents damaging to McCrae Dowless, after sitting around for two years, were released during the peak of the Democrat Party's manufactured scandal concerning the Harris-McCready election. This nearly 300-page report, while I didn't read it carefully at the time, was a gut punch. Dowless certainly looked guilty of ballot harvesting. When I did take time to read the report, I was astounded at its conclusions.

In the weeks before and after the 2016 general election, out of public view, the North Carolina State Board of Elections started probing into both Patriots for Progress, the PAC formed with Jeff Smith as it treasurer in 2014, and the Bladen County Improvement Association PAC, or BCIA-PAC. Both organizations started as Democrat GOTV groups. Former FBI agent Joan Fleming created two separate cases, one for each organization. Although Patriots for Progress had submitted a letter to the state elections agency dated January 22, 2016 indicating Dowless was no longer affiliated with the PAC, [2] the investigation primarily focused on Dowless.

Both groups were investigated for "possible absentee ballot fraud."[3] Just over one year later, Fleming summarized her investigations in a 278-page document that was ultimately posted on the Ninth District document portal December 19, 2018, after Mark's certification was withheld. Fleming's summary is dated January 23, 2018, well before the 2018 primary. I looked at every single board meeting agenda post-January 23, 2018 through November 2018. No agenda item was ever posted regarding follow up to the 2016 elections protests and investigation by the agency. During the summer of 2018 the board entered closed session numerous times. Was the investigation discussed then? It is impossible for anyone in the general public to know that. It was impossible for Mark Harris to know anything about Joan Fleming's investigation until December

19, 2018, *after* the 2018 midterm election.

It seems obvious from investigation documents that almost everyone in Bladen County understood that the Democrat BCIA ran a program that involved absentee ballots. When Dowless began to work his GOTV program for Republicans in 2016, confusion set in among voters. They were used to the BCIA being the only game in town.

In October 2016 Brenda M. Register filed a complaint at the Bladen County Board of Elections. It turns out that Mrs. Register is the mother of Kenneth Register, a Democrat candidate for County Commissioner.[4] Kenneth Register donated to the BCIA-PAC and yet complained about absentee-ballot irregularities when he lost his election. Brenda Register was highly offended when a "young, Caucasian lady" came to her house and allegedly said that she was with the Bladen County Board of Elections.

The young lady wanted Mrs. Register to vote absentee and asked her to complete an absentee-ballot request form. Register declined to fill out an absentee-ballot request, asserting that she always voted at the polls. The young lady left.

Brenda Register immediately picked up the phone and called Cynthia Shaw, Director of the Bladen County Board of Elections. When Register explained what had happened, Shaw responded, "It may have been the Bladen Improvement Committee." Mrs. Shaw went on to say that "this was done every year." When Register demanded that something be done about it, Mrs. Shaw said, "No."[5]

Now, I'm not a trained investigator, but I can gather a couple of things from this telephone exchange. First, the Director of the Bladen County Board of Elections knew that the Bladen County Improvement Association did a door-to-door absentee ballot GOTV campaign and had been doing it for years. When Brenda Register's complaint was filed, Patriots for Progress had been in existence just over two years. Patriots for Progress could at most have been involved in the 2014 general election and the 2015 Municipal Elections. The BCIA had been in existence since 1996.[6] Second, the Director of the Bladen County Board of Elections had no hope of the group being stopped and no plans to try to stop them.

Dowless had started as a Democrat operative. In fact, Patriots for Progress was a Democrat GOTV organization. Dowless was paid individually for work for federal Republican campaigns in 2016 and 2018. Dowless eventually asserted to us that part of the reason he disassociated from Jeff Smith, who was listed as treasurer for Patriots for Progress in 2014, was that Smith collected ballots. Is that the truth? Possibly not, but Dowless came on the scene long after the BCIA's program was well established.

The investigation also followed up on a complaint to the Bladen County Board of Elections filed by retired school principal Linda F. Johnson-Baldwin. Ms. Johnson-Baldwin wrote a letter to the Bladen County Board of Elections dated October 4, 2016. Mrs. Johnson-Baldwin was so kind-hearted that she used a pseudonym for the former student at her school whom she accused of taking her ballot. Mrs. Johnson-Baldwin wasn't so much interested in complaining as making sure she could still vote. She did not want the young man who she says took her ballot to get in trouble.

When she contacted the Bladen County Board of Elections, Mrs. Johnson-Baldwin said that a young man called "Josh" told her he would be paid if she signed up to vote with an absentee-ballot request. He would take her request form, turn it in, and come back for her ballots when she had time to vote them.

This part of the transaction did not alarm Mrs. Johnson-Baldwin. She wanted "Josh" to get paid. She did, however, insist that he bring the ballots back to her so that she could personally mail them. She also insisted that she would vote exactly how she wished, and that might not be for "Josh's" preferred candidate.

Mrs. Johnson-Baldwin began to be alarmed when Josh did not return with her ballots on the appointed day. She was annoyed, too, as she arranged her schedule to be home at the appointed hour. Mrs. Johnson-Baldwin wrote a letter to the Bladen County Board of Elections asking them to disregard any ballots turned in for her and her sons, so that they could vote in person.[7] Her ballots were eventually returned to her with a letter of apology from "Josh."[8] The elusive "Josh" turned out to be alleged Dowless employee Matthew Mathis, who, along with Caitlyn Croom, was the focus of the 2016 investigation.

When investigators interviewed BCIA operative Michael Cogdell about his own issues with the law and ballots, he initiated a conversation about Mrs. Johnson-Baldwin's ballot. Immediately after telling investigators Joan Fleming and Marshall Tutor that the BCIA was "hands off" with ballots after serving as witnesses,[9] Cogdell said he was home one evening when a lady named Dorothy Johnson called him. Dorothy Johnson wanted Cogdell to know about a situation in which someone had collected a ballot (Mrs. Johnson-Baldwin's) and not returned it.[10]

My question is this: How did people know that Michael Cogdell was the one to contact when you had ballot problems? Why not call the Bladen County Board of Elections? Why didn't Joan Fleming ask Cogdell that question?

Once Cogdell learned from Mrs. Johnson-Baldwin that "Josh" was campaigning for Republican Ray Britt, Cogdell's opponent in his own election for county commissioner-at-large, Cogdell insisted on helping Baldwin file a formal complaint with the Bladen County Board of Elections.[11]

There were many red flags regarding the BCIA's activities. Candidates and campaign committees formed the bulk of the BCIA-PAC's donors.[12] Two of the six voters interviewed by investigators denied that the BCIA members who had signed as witnesses on their ballots were ever present with them when they voted.[13]

Seven additional ballots from the BCIA investigation show illegal activity involving someone signing as the voter on either the absentee ballots or absentee-ballot request forms. In other words, signatures don't match on both the request form and the ballot. In attempting to locate five additional residences for voters whose ballots may have been compromised, investigators indicated they were "unable to locate" the residence for three of them.[14] So three out of five potentially compromised ballots could have been fictional. Residences could not be located by professional investigators, one of whom is a former FBI agent.

Obvious questions were left unasked by elections agency investigators. In fact, when investigators learned that the BCIA had hired well-known civil rights attorney Irving Joyner, they stopped interviewing suspects altogether.[15] Only three members of the BCIA were ever interviewed as suspects in the 2016 write-in vote scheme, when a write-in candidate got 29% of the vote: Michael Cogdell and wife Barbara, and Deborah Monroe. Only six voters were ever interviewed regarding the BCIA, when virtually every Democrat candidate in Bladen County received over 600 absentee-by-mail votes and there were over 3,000 write-in votes for Franklin Graham.

Although elections agency Director Kim Strach referred both the BCIA case and the Patriots for Progress cases to federal prosecutors in the Eastern District of North Carolina, the investigative reports authored by Chief Investigator Joan Fleming for the two groups differed dramatically in their language.

Fleming described her interview with **BCIA operatives who admitted writing in Franklin Graham's name on voters' ballots** in her investigation summary:

> None of the witnesses who were interviewed appeared to have an understanding that by writing the write-in candidate's name on the voter's ballot, they were "assisting" the voter in marking their ballot, and therefore were required to sign the assistance certification on the ballot container-return envelope.[16]

In the next paragraph:

> Some of the voters [only six were interviewed] interviewed stated they knew the witnesses and trusted them to "help" them vote their candidate choices by making suggestions.[17]

In her report on Patriots for Progress, Fleming describes the suggestions of certain candidates to voters by Caitlyn Croom and Matthew Mathis like this: "Dowless allegedly instructed his workers to "push" votes for certain candidates while meeting with voters."[18] Thus, in her summary, Fleming describes fraudulently writing in the name of a Democrat who did not even file for the election as "helping," but she describes basic campaigning as "pushing" voters when it was done on behalf of Republicans.

Two voters interviewed by investigators claimed they never laid eyes on the BCIA members who "witnessed" the absentee ballots voted in their names. Fleming dismisses both voters' damning statements against the BCIA by saying the voters have "questionable credibility."[19] Investigators do not provide transcripts of such interviews. Usually they are not even recorded. Investigators create their own summaries, which a friend in law enforcement warned me are subjective. How did Fleming determine the credibility of suspects and victims? She concluded that BCIA suspects were trustworthy helpers who were seemingly unaware that they had to fill out a pesky little line on a form. Witnesses with damning evidence about the Democrat group voting ballots in their names without their knowledge or permission were dismissed as not credible.

Fleming's interview of Michael Cogdell, Bladen County Commissioner who is both a donor to and payee from the BCIA, provides another example of how easily the Democrat group's behavior was excused.

Cogdell was informed that it is a violation of North Carolina election law for a candidate to assist a voter by signing as a witness to their absentee ballot. Cogdell stated he was not aware of the law pertaining to candidates assisting with absentee ballots and he advised that if that was the case he had made an error that did not stem from malice or intent to harm anyone. [Cogdell was a past president of the BCIA-PAC and an elected official.] He advised that he would comply with the law in the future.[20]

A quick comparison is in order here. McCrae Dowless: criminally charged with ballot harvesting. Michael Cogdell: headed a PAC that ran extensive GOTV operations, and personally illegally witnessed absentee ballots but claimed he didn't know election law, not charged. Dowless and Cogdell held elected office for the full terms of their positions.

Mark Harris: did not harvest, witness or otherwise engage with ballots, and was deceived by Dowless if allegations against Dowless prove true. The elections agency has indicated in various forms at various times that the outcome of the Harris-McCready race was not in doubt. Yet Mark Harris was dragged through a media circus and a "hearing" with no due process. It was Mark Harris who lost the seat he and others had worked so hard to win. This is—and I will use a ladylike word instead of the word I am thinking—ludicrous.

2016 general election investigation reports when candidate protests were dismissed by the State Board of Elections and election winners were certified	2018 general election criminal charges against Dowless and his workers after a new election was ordered for the 9th Congressional District
167 write-in votes on the ballots completed by seven different BCIA operatives who did not identify themselves as "assistants." [21]	Ballots improperly witnessed on the **outside ballot container envelope.**
2 voters denied the right to vote due to ballot fraud committed by Caitlyn Croom and Matthew Mathis.	SBI and FBI interviews with suspects indicate **sealed** ballots were taken and shown to Dowless.
7 issues with signatures that appear to have been forged by members of BCIA on either absentee-ballot request forms or ballots.	10 sealed ballots possessed and mailed to the Bladen County BOE by Dowless or workers paid by him. Dowless mailed two ballots improperly.
1 entire ballot completed and signature forged by Croom and Mathis. (They filled this ballot out while the voter was on the phone with them.)	No charges for fraudulently voting ballots instead of voters.
Candidates file protests alleging fraud, appeal to the State Board of Elections, and seek relief through the courts.	No candidate protest filed by Dan McCready.

While the BCIA's alleged ballot harvesting doesn't negate alleged illegal actions by McCrae Dowless, that's not the issue. Mark Harris knew nothing about Dowless's activities and did not participate in them. Mark Harris has never even been interviewed by any member of law enforcement, and the district attorney handling the case took the rare step of publicly stating that Mark Harris was not going to be criminally charged and her investigation was over as far as Mark Harris was concerned.

Why was one election singled out and overturned in an action initiated by one board member, Joshua Malcolm, and supported by elections agency director Kim Strach? Many candidates paid Dowless for GOTV over nearly a decade. In 2016, there were more irregularities actually affecting ballots—voter intent—in Bladen County and in Durham County, and they were documented before the final vote canvass of the 2016 general election. Three legitimate candidate requests for new elections from Durham County were denied in 2016. Pat McCrory's protests were dismissed. Dowless himself won an election in 2016 and was certified on December 3 after the investigation into his activities was completed. So what was the difference?

In 2016, the main election in question was that of Democrat gubernatorial challenger Roy Cooper, backed by Marc Elias and the mighty law firm Perkins-Coie. In 2018, the election in question was that of a Baptist preacher who had somehow managed to defeat the Democrat Golden Boy Dan McCready.

That would be the same Dan McCready whom Alaina Malcolm must have campaigned for, since she was paid for her work on behalf of Democrats out of the federal account of the Democrat Party of North Carolina, and the Harris-McCready race was only federal race on the ballot in Robeson County, Joshua Malcolm's home.[22] That would also be the same Dan McCready with whom Joshua Malcolm spoke multiple times in the weeks between Election Day and the day Malcolm made his motion to withdraw Mark Harris's name from the list of certified election winners.

In 2016, the numbers mattered. The election was about just the math. The votes. In fact, Perkins-Coie threatened that if voter intent was not honored, civil rights lawsuits would result. In 2018, the desire to get a new election for the rich and well-connected Dan McCready mattered more, at least to Joshua Malcolm.

Elections agency Executive Director Kim Strach made it known that Malcolm was running the show in her communication to the Harris campaign legal team via counsel for the agency Joshua Lawson. When concern was expressed about the confidentiality of the hundreds of thousands of texts and emails that fell under the vague terms of the State Board's subpoena to the campaign, Lawson responded by sending an email to John Branch, a Raleigh attorney working for the Harris Campaign. Lawson quoted Strach:

"...staff is unable to bind a Board regarding the use of the documents...the Board chair directed disclosure under processes distinct from ordinary practice."

Strach's statement needs to be unpacked. She is shrugging her shoulders and saying she can't promise that anything submitted by the Harris team will not be fodder for the propaganda machine ahead of the hearing. More importantly, Strach indicates that she is not the person in control of those decisions.

Strach points out that it was Democrat Joshua Malcolm, acting as board chair for the lame duck board the courts had declared unconstitutional, who ordered "disclosure," meaning the public portal for Ninth District documents, such as the 159 leaked ballot containers. Strach also points out that Malcolm's decision, like the decision to pull Mark Harris from the county-approved list of election winners, was unprecedented. Malcolm acted in a way that was "distinct from ordinary practice."

The hearing was originally scheduled for December 11, 2018. That gave the Harris campaign just six days from our initial meetings with attorneys to produce documents. The search terms were so comprehensive, including words like "stamp" and names of towns across the district, that there was no way the subpoena could be fulfilled. The hearing was postponed until late December.

By late December, however, Malcolm lost his grip on the process when the courts stepped in once again. Courts rejected a request for another stay of the State Board's dissolution. The board would dissolve at the end of the last full week of December, on Friday December 28, 2018. Our attorneys wrote a letter requesting that the board certify

Mark in their final meeting the morning of December 28. The 116th Congress was to be sworn in on January 3, 2019. The Board ignored the request. Malcolm was gone as of noon December 28, 2018.

Now the Board had to revert to its old structure, and Governor Roy Cooper would have to appoint new board members. Cooper announced he would not take any action before January 31, 2019.

After all our hard work, I had imagined myself in the gallery watching Mark be sworn in on the floor of the United States House of Representatives. Debbie Meadows became my "big sister" in the Congressional Spouses Club. Elaine Norman of South Carolina had given me all the low-down on how to get our constituents into the White House when they visited Washington with their kids. As a history teacher, I was excited to think I could actually tour our families around the Capitol rather than dumping that off on interns.

It was all going up in flames. The uncertainty and waiting were unbearable. Governor Cooper's refusal to appoint a state elections board before the new Congress convened January 3, 2019 caused us to personally spend a ridiculous amount of money to have our attorney file a motion in court. We asked that the judge order the state elections agency to certify Mark's victory without the board's final sign-off. Each county in the Ninth District had already certified Mark as the election winner. It was our understanding that this had happened once before in the absence of a state board. Then, on January 12, Mark started experiencing a headache and chills. In less than a week, my perspective was going to radically change. Instead of fighting for a seat in Congress, Mark would soon be fighting for his very life.

CHAPTER 15

A VERY BAD PROGNOSIS

ON JANUARY 12, 2019 Mark had a breakfast meeting with Joe Bruno of WSOC-TV. Bruno had been assigned to follow our campaign during the 2018 season. When he hopped on the Democrat propaganda bandwagon in the first few days after Mark's certification was withheld, we were furious with his coverage. The meeting was to clear the air off the record. That afternoon, Mark was sitting in his recliner and told me he wasn't feeling well. He commented that he thought he might be getting the flu.

On Sunday, we got up and went to church despite Mark not feeling well. He kept saying he had a headache. After church, I offered that we could go home without making our usual stop for an early lunch, but he insisted on going out for our usual Sunday lunch. I interpreted this to mean he didn't feel completely terrible, so I didn't worry about him too much.

Later that afternoon, he continued to talk about having a headache and was starting to get chills. We turned on the gas logs in the fireplace, and he rested in the recliner all afternoon. By Monday, we thought a visit to the doctor was in order. I drove him to the doctor's office and went back to the exam room with him. Mark told our family doctor he thought he had the flu, so the doctor ordered a rapid flu test, which was negative. The doctor listened to Mark's chest and thought he heard some congestion, so he prescribed an antibiotic for bronchitis. That night, I experienced something I would experience the next three nights, something mystifying and scary to me. When Mark got in bed, his body began to shudder. He kept saying that he had the chills, but to me it didn't seem like chills. Every time I took his temperature, it hovered around 99.5 to 100.5—not normal, but not high enough to cause such extreme chills. His whole body just shook. I compared it to the shakes that often occur after childbirth as the effects of an epidural are wearing off. I tried to get close to him and put my arms around him, but that didn't make the shudders stop or make him more comfortable.

In the middle of the night Monday night, he got up to go to the bathroom. I told him to wait a second while I turned on the light since he was sick, but he stubbornly ignored me. Then he tripped over his jeans, which he had left on the floor next to the bed, fell, and hit his head on an easel where we keep my wedding portrait in the corner of the room next to his nightstand. By the time I turned on the lamp, he was on his hands and knees next to the bed. I helped him up and looked at this forehead, where it was clear he was going to have a bump and a bruise, but it didn't look severe. He got back in bed.

Tuesday January 15, the North Carolina-GOP was holding a belated press conference/Mark Harris rally. After both Chairman Robin Hayes and Executive Director Dallas Woodhouse made media appearances calling for a new election, Harris supporters had bombarded the North Carolina-GOP with complaints. Woodhouse thought we orchestrated a campaign against he and Hayes, which we had not done. People were just disgusted by their lack of support for Mark. When at last the North Carolina-GOP scheduled a support rally, Woodhouse told Mark to "call off the dogs." The North Carolina-GOP had developed a flier called "Joshua Malcolm: His Problematic Past," but it would take WBTV's unrelenting year-long effort, including legal action, to uncover the full extent of Malcolm's partisan activities while he sat on the North Carolina State Board of Elections and Ethics Enforcement. Hayes was to present the GOP's information on Malcolm at the rally.

Tuesday Mark seemed sicker, not better. His sister Sheila had come down for a visit. Sheila and I went to the rally, but Mark stayed home. I was starting to get worried, but figured a nasty virus compounded by bronchitis was getting the best of Mark. We were under incredible stress as the North Carolina State Board of Elections and Ethics Enforcement's "evidentiary hearing" was approaching. We did not yet even know the composition of the new board that would be installed sometime after Governor Cooper appointed its members January 31, 2019. We were one week away from the court date for our motion asking a judge to order the executive director of the North Carolina State Board of Elections agency to certify Mark's victory in the absence of an appointed board. Judge Paul Ridgeway would hear our case January 22, 2019. We were optimistic, since Ridgeway had calendared the hearing so quickly.

By Wednesday, Mark was no better. One of us called the doctor's office back and they called in a stronger antibiotic and prescription cough medicine. I had concerns that the nurse had not really listened to what we were saying about Mark's symptoms, but I picked up the prescriptions anyway. Again that night I tried to fall asleep, but Mark's shuddering body worried me. He was up and down during the night, and I was getting no sleep. I needed to sleep, because the next day, Thursday, I would have to drive to Raleigh, meet up with our attorney, and be interviewed by the North Carolina State Board of Elections agency director Kim Strach and chief investigator Joan Fleming.

A couple of friends with law enforcement experience had already spoken to me to express concerns about the interview. One told me in no uncertain terms that I did not need to attend. He stated that former FBI agent Fleming would just write a summary of the interview and she could create the summary to suit her purposes. He begged me to at least record the interview if I consented to it. A recording would preserve the interview verbatim. None of our attorneys, however, were remotely open to the possibility that I would not be interviewed or that I would insult Fleming by demanding to be allowed to record the interview on my phone.

From November 27 to the opening day of the hearing, every attorney involved with our campaign or us said that we had to cooperate. In the gray netherworld where a state agency is allowed powers constitutionally reserved for the courts, confusion reigned. Did we have to be interviewed just because they asked? What would happen if we said no? What would happen if we just didn't go to the hearing? Can an agency hold a person in contempt like a court? I asked some of those questions, but there were not clear answers. This wasn't the judicial system. Clarity was impossible.

I do not fault any of our attorneys for that, but in hindsight both Mark and I wish we had stood up to the North Carolina State Board of Elections. Mark had done nothing wrong, as the agency's own witnesses would attest at its "hearing." He had hired Dowless, but there were plenty of people serving in elected positions who had campaign workers that had violated the law without their knowledge or participation. In fact, Dowless clients in races involving only one county had been sworn into their elected offices in December and January. Those races had not required State Board approval. Those names were printed on the same ballots with Mark Harris's name. Only Mark Harris was blocked from taking office.

Furthermore, it hadn't even been proven that McCrae Dowless had actually violated any laws. The McCready smear campaign was running full steam, but other than that, neither the state of North Carolina nor federal authorities had yet presented hard evidence against Dowless. We should have told the Board that we would not expose ourselves to what amounted to a one-sided trial. We could not possibly be adequately prepared for the evidentiary hearing, because we didn't know the evidence or witnesses the agency would present. We would not be protected by standard legal procedure. But everyone, including Mark, kept foolishly clinging to the belief that since he was innocent of wrongdoing, things would work out.

I knew Mark wanted to be with me as I traveled to Raleigh. When he didn't fight me on staying home, I knew he was terribly sick. In fact, he seemed no better despite having started on a stronger antibiotic the previous day. I called our daughter and asked her to come by the house to check on Mark and try to get him to eat. I drove to Raleigh and agency director Kim Strach and chief investigator Joan Fleming interviewed me. Parts of the interview seemed strange to me. They seemed fixated on the phone app we used for door-to-door canvassing. I had heard that these investigations sometimes served as a pretext for gathering details on the inner workings of campaigns, and the barrage of questions about door-to-door canvassing and the phone app brought those rumors to mind.

I saw Joan Fleming write down "Andy ethical" when I told them we decided to hire our campaign consultant Andy Yates because he had impressed us with his sense of business ethics when we interviewed him twice before hiring him. She took few notes otherwise. At the end of the interview, Strach asked me if I had spoken to McCrae Dowless since certification was withheld. I recounted the conversation. I felt sure that investigators had heard a recording of this call, since by this time it was clear Dowless was the focus of a criminal investigation. I also knew that if they had heard my call with Dowless, they knew Mark and I were completely innocent. They knew that I believed it was the Bladen County Improvement Association who harvested ballots, and they knew that we had accepted Dowless's word, along with that of those who vouched for him, that he told his workers "never to touch a ballot."

The interview was over by around 1:00 p.m. I got in the car to head back to Charlotte. I tried to call Mark but didn't get an answer. I knew he was very interested in hearing about the interview. I had expected him to be sitting by his phone and to pick up on the first ring. I called my daughter, who was on her way to the house, and told her to give me a report as soon as she could. When she called me back, she said that Mark seemed very sleepy. She tried to give him soup, and he ate a few bites, but kept insisting that for the first time in days he felt like he could sleep, and he just wanted to lie on the couch and nap. My daughter was also concerned.

I raced home as fast as I could in the pouring rain and 4:00 p.m.

traffic around Charlotte. I was determined that when I got home, we were going to the hospital. When I got home, Mark was in bed. He told me the same thing he told our daughter, to please let him sleep. I told him if things were no better in the morning, we were definitely going to the hospital.

The shaking had stopped, and he didn't feel feverish. As I left the bedroom to head back downstairs, something odd happened. I can't remember if I asked him a question or if he spontaneously spoke to me, but in the sentence Mark spoke, he substituted a weird word for the word he meant to say. I don't even remember exactly what he said, but to illustrate the point, it was something like, "Can you bring me a glass of banana?" I called my daughter and asked if she could make arrangements for her kids in the morning. I needed her to come to the house and help me get Mark to the hospital.

I spent a restless night, and Mark did too. He was up and down several times, going to the bathroom. I had been making sure he drank both water and Gatorade. At last it was morning and my daughter arrived. We told Mark that he had to go to the hospital. He was starting to mix up words more and more but didn't demonstrate any visible signs of stroke. A stroke never occurred to me. All of his symptoms had been flu-like. In fact, the best way I can describe his appearance that Friday morning was that he not only looked like he had the flu, but he looked like a ninety-year-old man with the flu. Something the doctor said Monday came to mind. When we were back in the exam room, I mentioned that Mark kept complaining of a terrible headache, and I wanted to make certain he wasn't developing meningitis. The doctor ruled that out based on a physical test, and said, "If he had meningitis, he would just look bad. You would know because he would just look so bad, and he would get very sick rapidly." Well, this had taken five days, which wasn't rapid, but Mark's appearance certainly did look bad.

We left our house at around 8:30 a.m. and drove to the emergency room at Novant hospital in Matthews, North Carolina, which is closer to my south Charlotte home than the main hospital downtown.

They took Mark back quickly and began the usual tests, such as blood work. I answered their questions, describing Mark's condition throughout the week, especially the terrible shuddering of his body each night. I think at some point we may have moved to a bigger exam room. My daughter left to return home so that her husband could go to work.

Neither of us understood how gravely ill Mark was at that point. The pace of work in the room picked up and more doctors started coming in. At last, the main emergency room doctor came in and sat down. He looked very serious. He told me they weren't sure what was happening with Mark, but that his liver numbers were terrible. In fact, both his liver and kidneys were starting to shut down. I was stunned. I asked the doctor if he minded if I took a video of his comments on my phone, as I was so exhausted I wasn't sure if I would be able to process and remember everything he was saying. He told me he didn't want me to do that, for reasons I understand. I dug in my purse for paper and pencil.

He asked me if Mark could have taken too much Tylenol. I replied that because Mark was so sick I had been concerned about him taking his own medicine, and I had kept control of all the medicines, even taking them with me to Raleigh the day before. The doctor said that they actually had a pretty rapid test that would reveal a Tylenol overdose, since so many young people try to kill themselves that way. I remember commenting to a nurse in the room that I thought that was so sad.

The medical team didn't really understand what was going on with Mark. He appeared to have some type of infection, but they didn't know what. It would take up to 72 hours for cultures to grow. Because of his mental confusion, they needed to do a spinal tap, and I had to give consent, in order to see whether there was infection on the brain. Meningitis—exactly what I had feared on Monday. But that didn't make sense. Monday was five days ago. Meningitis develops rapidly into a life-threatening illness. Thoughts and questions raced through my mind. Of course, do the spinal tap. Do whatever you need to do, I told the doctors. They asked me to leave the room during the spinal tap. At 11:51 a.m., during the spinal tap, I texted our daughter Laura and asked if she could get her mother-in-law to watch her children and return to the hospital because I needed her there with me.

Laura later told me that when she got that text, she became terrified. I am generally extremely independent and very low drama. She knew things were not good if I was directly asking for emotional support. She got her mother-in-law to leave work and come to her house to watch her toddlers. The results from the spinal tap came back. The results were strange. There were white cells in the spinal fluid when there shouldn't be any present. Yet the quantity wasn't high enough to indicate meningitis. What was going on with Mark's brain? No one seemed sure.

Shortly after Laura arrived, they also told us Mark was severely dehydrated. I told them how much liquid he had consumed, and that I didn't see how that was possible, especially since he hadn't been throwing up or anything. That's when Laura and I actually began to understand the gravity of the situation. Mark had sepsis. An infection of unknown origin had entered his bloodstream. He was going into organ failure. Sepsis severely dehydrates, as the body tries to use all of its resources to fight off the infection.

Before I could make sense of that information, a neurology team came in. A neurologist began giving Mark the stroke test. He asked Mark to pull on his hands. It didn't look like Mark had weakness on one side. The neurologist did one or two more physical tests. He kept saying, "That's good." Laura and I were sitting in two chairs along the wall of the exam room. To my left was the equipment where a nurse kept working.

The neurologist was directly in front of me, talking to Mark as Mark lay in the hospital bed. He asked Mark to count backward by sevens. Mark started that operation correctly but faltered quickly. Then the neurologist asked him to name the president who preceded the current president of the United States. Mark looked totally confused. He stuttered and stammered, and then finally said he couldn't come up with the name. I burst into tears. We had lived and breathed nothing but politics for the past two years. Something was dreadfully wrong. Laura took my hand. Mark would later joke that his amnesia about the Obama presidency was the only good thing to come out of his illness.

I can't remember everything that happened in the next few minutes, but I believe Laura went out into the hall to make some phone calls. I was alone in the room with the neurologist. Mark had closed his eyes and was resting, it appeared. I stood next to the neurologist beside Mark's bed. He explained that Mark's symptoms seemed confusing and contradictory. On the one hand, he had white cells in his spinal fluid, which could indicate some type of infection had taken hold in the brain. On the other hand, he presented more like he had experienced a stroke, but not completely. One side of his body didn't seem weaker than the other side. He had no drooping of his facial muscles. Yet he had failed the cognitive portion of the stroke test.

There was also something going on with Mark's liver. This was turning into a complicated medical picture. All of the medical team at Novant was competent and kind, but I especially remember the two neurologists we worked with, Doctors Toqeer and Taqui. Both of these doctors stand out to me for their direct truthfulness, delivered with compassion. Both took huge amounts of time with me to explain each new discovery related to Mark's condition.

In those first few hours in the ER, I believe it was Dr. Toqeer who was on duty. He looked over at me and said, "We have to find out what is going on with Mark's brain. Depending on what it is, the prognosis could be very bad, even death." Time stopped. My mind was reeling. I couldn't believe the words he had just spoken to me. We had been in the doctor's office at the beginning of the week. We had spoken to the doctor's office on the phone two days before. Mark had been taking antibiotics for five days.

Yet another doctor came in. He was from the intensive care unit and would be on duty all weekend. I recall him being tall, kind, and funny. He told us that they were admitting Mark into intensive care. Mark told the doctor that I had pushed for an emergency room visit the previous day. The doctor joked back with Mark, "Remember, she's always right." Laura went into the hall to call her brothers and Mark's sister Sheila. Sheila had just been in our home Monday night and Tuesday. Today was Friday. She was incredulous on the phone. Laura related that Sheila kept saying over and over, "Mark? Mark? They are putting *Mark* into intensive care?" Sheila decided that she had to come down. She ended up being a godsend to us over the next ten days. The medical team decided they were just going to "throw everything they had" at the infection, meaning various powerful antibiotics would be started intravenously. Once they had the source of the infection nailed down, they would tailor the antibiotics to the infection.

Laura stayed by my side during the process of getting Mark into intensive care. They were giving him huge amounts of fluid intravenously, and he was starting to improve. The test for the Tylenol overdose came back negative at some point. Whatever was happening in his liver must be related to the overall infection. Once we were in intensive care, the infectious disease team started with us. It felt like at least ten times I told one doctor or another that we had not traveled out of the country in the past six months.

Novant hospital also realized that Mark was "the" Mark Harris, the Congressman-elect for the Ninth District embroiled in a controversy, and began, without my knowledge, but with my everlasting appreciation, taking steps to ensure our security and privacy during the period of Mark's hospitalization. They put him under a protocol called something like "breaking the glass," which meant that employees had to "break glass" figuratively to get to Mark's details. Employees unrelated to his case could not see his chart. They assigned us a nurse for the weekend who had been in the military. She was amazing.

Receptionists would truthfully tell reporters who might call that they didn't see a Mark Harris listed as a patient at Novant hospital. Unless we gave family members our room number, they would not be able to find us. I found out later that they even assigned an extra security person just to patrol our floor in the intensive care unit.

By late afternoon, Mark's condition was considered stable. He didn't appear to be deteriorating toward death. It might be days before we had a clearer picture of his illness, because of the time it took to grow cultures from his blood. Our son Matthew came over and our daughter Laura left at some point to return to her own family. Mark's sister Sheila arrived with her bags, ready to stay with me and be of whatever help I needed. Although she is seventeen years older than Mark, they are very close, talking on the phone almost daily. She also has a very nurturing personality and would make trips out for little things to make Mark more comfortable, like lip balm for his dry lips, and dry shampoo so he could wash his hair while in intensive care, where he could not take showers.

I don't remember much of that evening, except that by around 10:00 p.m. I could not hold my eyes open. Sheila is retired and a bit of a night owl, so she told me to go ahead and sleep, she would take care of Mark. He was alternating between periods of sleep and wakefulness and was often uncomfortable. At 2:00 a.m. I was awakened by the sound of his voice. He sounded completely normal. I sat up on the banquette where I had been sleeping. Mark was talking to his nurse. Sheila woke up as well. I pulled a chair next to the bed. It was like he had been in a coma and suddenly awakened. He was speaking normally and asking me what had happened. Later we would realize that while Mark had day-to-day memory for the period he was in intensive care over that weekend, when he recovered, he didn't remember anything that happened from Friday to Monday. I was so happy and relieved when we had a normal conversation at 2:00 that morning. After about thirty minutes, I went back to sleep and slept soundly until approximately 6:30 a.m.

By Sunday Mark was getting strong enough to have additional tests, and his blood was growing a culture. The same tall, funny doctor who had been on duty all weekend in the intensive care unit brought me the news, but with a word of caution. The culture was a bacterium in the streptococcus family. What they didn't understand was why. Strep has common forms and less common forms. It usually is found in the mouth and the throat. Some forms can live in the intestinal tract, but those were rarer. In fact, strep was so far off from Mark's symptoms that they feared they had a contaminated sample of blood, so they were going to do more labs.

Just to be safe, they wanted to do a special kind of scan of Mark's heart. Certain infections apparently "like" certain organs better than others, and strep can easily attach to the heart valves. If that happened, we could be back in life-threatening territory again. To see the valves, they would have to look behind the heart with a test called a transesophageal echocardiogram.

Mark's brother had come down to visit and his sister Sheila was still camped out at the hospital with me. While Mark was out having the heart valve scan, Sheila, Steve, and I visited. A neurologist, I believe it Dr. Taqui, came in the room with the results of an MRI taken earlier that morning. He pulled up a picture of Mark's brain on the computer screen at the little station the nurses used to record their observations and vital signs. The best way I can describe the picture is that it looked like a dark-colored shower cap with white pin-prick-sized polka dots all over it.

The neurologist looked at me and then at the screen as he pointed to the white polka dots. Each dot represented a bit of infection that had somehow traveled to Mark's brain. It didn't appear that the infection had taken hold in the brain, which was good news. Instead, bits of infection had showered over it, miraculously landing in an almost perfectly even pattern. These are called septic emboli, he explained. I asked him to repeat the term so I could try to remember it. Septic emboli. Then he told me more stunning news. Every white dot represented what he called "small strokes." The bits of infection had hit the brain the same way a blood clot does in a "normal" stroke.

When the doctor said "small strokes," I thought he meant mini-strokes. I had heard about those, knew quite a few people who had experienced them, and knew that mini-strokes didn't leave lasting impacts. "Do you mean mini-strokes?" I asked. He looked at me very directly and said, "No, I mean strokes." He went on to explain that these were true strokes. Their damage would be permanent, but they were very small in size and the brain would adapt. Because they were so evenly spaced, there wasn't concentrated damage on one side of the body.

I had a million questions. When the doctor finally left, Mark's brother Steve came over to me. "Do you realize he stood on his feet and answered your questions for one hour?" Steve asked. It felt like five minutes to me. "Not every doctor would do that," Steve continued. My appreciation for Doctors Taqui and Toqeer kept growing.

By Sunday night, the entire picture was coming together. The culture had been positively identified as a form of strep called streptococcus intermedius. It was a form of strep that could live in the GI tract. Furthermore, CT scans of Mark's abdominal area showed that he had a seven-centimeter abscess on his liver, and his hepatic vein, the large vein behind his liver, had an infected blood clot in it. It was clear to the doctors that the liver infection was a secondary infection.

The doctor asked me about some previous bouts Mark had experienced with diverticulitis, and if he had complained of stomach pain. I told them he had not complained of stomach pain. Mark would later tell me that his stomach had hurt every day since the day he resigned from First Baptist Charlotte to embark on the huge risk of the campaign, so it was hard to tell the difference.

Once the transesophageal echocardiogram was read, all the puzzle pieces finally fell into place. The tall, funny doctor came into the room just after dark Sunday evening. For the first time he had some degree of confidence in what we were dealing with. Mark apparently had a perforation in his colon due to diverticulitis. Infection had been released into his bloodstream. The awful shuddering of his body as he lay in bed each night was his body trying to throw off the toxins entering his bloodstream. As the days went by, he was taking an antibiotic that had absolutely no effect on streptococcus intermedius. A secondary infection set up on his liver and created an abscess. The transesophageal echocardiogram, with its unique view of the heart from behind, showed a birth defect Mark never knew he had, something known as a PFO: a small hole between the chambers of his heart.

The doctor moved his hand horizontally across his chest as he explained that normally, infection could not travel from a person's liver through the heart and into the head. Because of the PFO, in Mark's body, that was possible, and had occurred, showering his brain with the septic emboli and causing the multiple small strokes. He did not have meningitis, a full-blown infection of the brain, which explained why the white cells in his spinal fluid were not in quantities normally seen in meningitis patients.

The most urgent medical need was to drain the infected liver abscess. So much infection had overwhelmed Mark's bloodstream that he had gone into sepsis, one step short of lethal septic shock. Approximately one-third of people who find themselves at the early stages of organ failure due to sepsis, as Mark was, do not survive.

There was a debate amongst the doctors as to whether to try to do surgery on the liver or to try to drain the abscess through a procedure that uses a CT scan to insert a tube with something called a Jackson-Pratt drain. To do whichever of the two procedures doctors determined was best, Mark had to be transferred by ambulance to the main hospital downtown. He would go the next day, Monday January 21, the Martin Luther King, Jr. holiday.

That same Sunday night, our son John came from Raleigh. I had not seen him since December 21 at the annual Harris extended family Christmas party, as it had been our turn to have his family for Thanksgiving, but his in-laws turn to have them for Christmas. Due to his self-imposed ban on communicating with us, I had not spoken with him since then either, although I had started texting him updates about his dad once it became clear how bad things were. When John arrived, he was shocked at both of our appearances. Mark looked terrible because he was deathly ill. I looked terrible because of worry and lack of sleep. John insisted that Sheila and I go back to my house and get showers and a good night's sleep while he stayed at the hospital overnight. Now that Mark was improving, a diagnosis was in place, and a plan for treatment was in process, I welcomed the chance to sleep soundly in my own bed.

The next morning, Sheila and I arrived at the hospital very early. I did not want to miss doctor's rounds, especially since the question of surgery was still up in the air. The entire medical team was different Monday morning. Male and female surgeons came to Mark's room at different times trying to decide the question about whether to operate on the liver or drain it.

At one point I remember the male doctor pushed on Mark's abdominal area and asked him if it hurt. When Mark said that it did not, the doctor stepped back from the bed, threw his hands into the air, and said, "That's just unbelievable." The only remaining mystery from the illness is why Mark did not experience severe abdominal pain.

Finally, Mark was scheduled to leave by ambulance for Novant's main hospital near downtown Charlotte. It was bitterly cold. John was preparing to leave and return to Raleigh. We spoke briefly out in the hall. He urged me to find some way to prevent Mark from having to attend the State Board of Elections hearing. I told him that we had investigated that possibility but couldn't get a straight answer on the potential consequences of failing to appear. The "Order of Proceedings" indicated that a failure to appear would produce an adverse ruling. But what did that mean?

We were dealing with the notion of "taint" and a massive propaganda war against us. Would board members be certain to order a new election if we got an adverse ruling? No one seemed to know. John, who is an attorney himself, told me that healthy individuals get confused under examination and cross-examination, and that Marc Elias would be trying to confuse Mark. He said that there was no way his dad would be ready for that in four weeks.

I didn't know what to do, and frankly all I could think about was getting Mark up to the main hospital and the next medical step. I promised John that I would talk to our attorneys about it and have them evaluate Mark before the hearing. What I did not say to him was that he could not imagine the stress of the cloud hanging over us, and the agony of the uncertainty of it all.

Mark was supposed to have been sworn in to the 116th Congress on January 3, 2019. The hearing had already been pushed from December to January, and now to February. Would we have to ask for some kind of medical continuance? I couldn't imagine another postponement, mentally and emotionally. We already knew we weren't going to be adequately prepared, because the first high-powered attorney we had consulted told us after looking at the subpoena issued by the North Carolina State Board of Elections and Ethics Enforcement that it would take his firm four months just to prepare documents, and a million dollars to adequately represent us at the hearing.

I was getting sick of people telling me what I needed to do when I felt powerless to do any of it, and my husband had a life-threatening illness on top of it all. I made a mental note to be sure our attorneys saw Mark in person and to make sure they understood how sick he was, but I did not decide to keep Mark away from the hearing, which was my biggest mistake in the entire process.

Mark's sister also departed Monday morning. Monday afternoon, the drain was inserted into the abscess in Mark's liver and Mark returned to our new room in intensive care at the main hospital. I was watching his vitals very closely. His blood pressure kept going up. His head was hurting again. I grew alarmed. I became so insistent that something was wrong that the nurse finally called down to the radiologist who had done the procedure and let me speak to him.

In my heart of hearts, I knew what a second MRI would later confirm. Mark was having another stroke. With the acute nature of Mark's issues, there was nothing they could do. For some time they experimented with trying to get a blood thinner barely to therapeutic levels to dissolve the blood clot in his liver, but there were indications that he could have a brain bleed, so they stopped that. Bits of infection had apparently become dislodged as the tube was inserted into the liver and traveled once more to the brain. Everything was connected to everything else. Mark's body had barely started to get over the infection in the bloodstream, now that it had been identified and

IV antibiotics tailored to the particular strep bacteria. We were not leaving the hospital anytime soon.

I had been communicating with several people I felt close to about the seriousness of Mark's condition, but I did not want the world at large to know anything about it. Although I would only learn the full extent of certain Republicans' participation in the PR war against Mark later, everyone involved with our campaign had been shocked at the speed and viciousness with which many Republicans joined the rumor mill against Mark.

I feared that false rumors would start that I was lying about what was wrong with him, or that he had tried to commit suicide. I was realizing that people were capable of saying absolutely any cruel and ridiculous thing. I kept emailing and texting folks cancelling meetings and appearances he was supposed to make, trying to be as vague as possible.

There was one meeting Mark did not want to cancel but wanted me to attend in his stead. Saturday night, January 26, Mark was scheduled to be the keynote speaker for the Cumberland County Republican Party's Lincoln-Reagan Day Dinner. I talked to the chairman of the Cumberland County Republican Party and explained the situation, and that Mark was in the hospital, but that he would like for me to come in his place. The chairman was very kind and agreeable to that suggestion.

I asked a Novant doctor in intensive care if it might be appropriate for them to issue a statement about Mark's condition. The doctor I spoke with said that he would not do that under any circumstances. It would be up to us to determine how to disclose Mark's illness.

While Mark was in intensive care at the main hospital, to go to the bathroom I had to go to the intensive care waiting room. It was Monday, January 21, 2019, the Martin Luther King, Jr. holiday. In the waiting room someone had put up a poster with one of Dr. King's quotes. "If you can't fly, then run. If you can't run, then walk. If you can't walk, then crawl. But whatever you do, you have to keep moving forward." I started saying that to myself. It felt like I was crawling.

But I had to keep going. Our children who lived closer to Charlotte, Laura and Matthew, came and went, taking as much time as they could to be at the hospital with us.

The next day, we watched news coverage of our motion to ask the courts to certify Mark. Our motion was rejected. Our only hope of being seated was to stop a vote for a new election by the State Elections Board at the February hearing and then to survive an investigation which Democrats in the House had already vowed to launch before seating Mark. How long would that take? How much would that cost? How would we live in the meantime?

Thursday January 24, we left intensive care. I will never forget entering Mark's new room. Because of a lack of bed space, our "step-down" room was in the newer cardio wing of the hospital. It felt like walking into the Ritz Carlton after all the days in intensive care. Now instead of a chair I would once again have a banquette to sleep on, as had been the case at the Matthews hospital, and even sheets at night to put over the little mini mattress. There was a large window, too, with plentiful sunshine spilling into the room. Things should have been looking up, but for some reason once Mark was settled in the room and dozing, I sat on the banquette, put my feet up, and started sinking into despair.

I was tremendously concerned about our finances. I took my phone and started perusing job postings. I was kicking myself for being basically unemployed for a decade. My part-time job at a historic house museum paid very little. I did a lot of helpful things for people for free, but that wasn't going to pay the bills. What if Mark couldn't work? He was alternating between passing and failing the cognitive part of the stroke test. Although the medical team was optimistic and Mark was improving very rapidly, I just didn't know what the future held. How could I take care of Mark and start a new full-time job at the same time? What about the hearing? If Mark obtained certification and was sworn in, would he be able to serve? It was one of the lowest moments of my life.

Over the next few days, friends were finally able to come by and visit. That cheered us both, but life in the hospital was taking a toll. Mark started asking when he could go home. We had a phenomenal Christian nurse while in the step-down unit, a man named Patrick. He kept encouraging us to focus only on getting well and on our love for each other. We took laps around the unit daily and tried not to watch the news. Patrick tried to keep our spirits up.

On Saturday January 26, a week and one day into Mark's hospital stay, one of our campaign staff kindly offered to drive me to Fayetteville so that I could substitute for Mark at the GOP dinner. Sheila once again came down to stay with Mark Saturday afternoon. I left the hospital and returned home to get dressed up for the dinner. In Fayetteville I got up in front of the crowd and said something that I think sounded intelligible. Everyone was kind and encouraging. A reporter for the *Fayetteville Observer* was in the back of the room. I was learning to hate the media and would hate them even more before it was all said and done. *God knows what he will print*, I thought. I tried to choose my words carefully. We had already decided that Sheila would stay with Mark at the hospital that night and I would just go home since it would be midnight or after when I returned from Fayetteville. Having another night in my own bed was a wonderful luxury.

By Sunday we were told that Mark would probably go home the next day, Monday January 28. Streptococcus intermedius requires weeks of IV antibiotics, but home health could come to the house, deliver supplies, and I could administer the twice-a-day dosage through the PICC line. Mark was still taking IV antibiotics twice a day the week of the State Elections Board's "evidentiary hearing." We were now walking the halls several times a day. Mark was eating and getting stronger.

He looked better, although he had lost seventeen pounds through the ordeal. That night, Sunday night, was to be our last in the hospital. We decided to watch *Life, Liberty, and Levin* that evening. That night Mark Levin's guest was attorney Sidney Powell, talking about her book *Licensed to Lie*, about prosecutorial misconduct in the US

Justice Department. It was a fascinating and terrifying hour. Powell made the point in great detail that if the government wants you, it will find a way to get you.

That night an unshakeable terror took hold of me. I am not naturally anxious, although I am naturally cautious and not a huge risk-taker. I have always believed in the words from the Bible, in the book of Proverbs, that the righteous will never be begging bread. I always believed that there would be a job; there would be at least *opportunity*, if not always success. Now I was filled with a sense of dread I couldn't seem to get over, a sense of dread that followed me to Raleigh and the "evidentiary hearing," or as North Carolina Conservative blogger Brant Clifton dubbed it, "The Mark Harris Show Trial."

CHAPTER 16

THE MARK HARRIS SHOW TRIAL

THE "EVIDENTIARY HEARING" of the State Board was scheduled to begin February 18, 2019, which was President's Day and also the birthday of one of our children. All subpoenas had been issued for three days: February 18, 19, and 20. We had booked hotel rooms and packed our IV antibiotics in a cooler to be prepared for three days in Raleigh, which is a three-hour drive from our home in Charlotte.

The Order of Proceedings issued by the agency granted that the outcome of the Harris-McCready race was not in doubt. Four races from the November 2018 election were actually part of this one hearing. Referencing the three other contests, the Order of Proceedings states: "…the apparent margin of victory in each race represents fewer votes than those under scrutiny in the State Board's investigation." For the Ninth Congressional District, the Board will consider "evidence…in connection with an investigation into irregularities and alleged misconduct in certain counties."[1] No statement is made about the number of votes or the outcome of the election with regard to the Ninth District. Why does this matter? Precedent had always been to certify victories that were certain and then allow the agency to investigate. This clear model, I believe, is the way North Carolina law is intended. North Carolina law gives the state elections agency one year after an election to investigate possible criminal activity and refer for prosecution. The agency by definition is not part of the attorney general's office. The agency's staff are not state prosecutors.

With its "hearing" into the Ninth District's ballot irregularities, the elections agency and the appointed State Elections Board set itself up as judge, jury, and executioner on Mark Harris without giving him any of the constitutional protections involved in an actual court case. The hearing was supposed to decide whether Mark Harris would be certified in his election victory, but instead of determining whether Mark Harris won, the hearing focused on whether McCrae Dowless collected ballots and whether the Bladen County Board of Elections had run a secure election. The hearing became just an extension of the Democrats' propaganda, and the cards were stacked against us impossibly by the structure of the proceedings.

Written briefs had to be no more than twenty pages long and address the application of an obscure court case from far western North Carolina in 1980. Joshua Malcolm had cited that court case as the reason the State Board could take jurisdiction over the Ninth District race after each county had already certified the results. Meanwhile, the state elections agency would be presenting evidence about Dowless's activities. There is no discovery for these bureaucratic "hearings," so our legal team had not seen one shred of the agency's evidence beforehand. Our team did not possess a list of witnesses the state would call, nor have an opportunity to interview anyone.

From the Evidentiary Standards section of the Order of Proceedings: "Hearsay evidence will likely be admitted if found reliable." Who tested the reliability? Who made that determination? More from the Order of Proceedings: "Media reports will be accepted." A huge portion of Dan McCready's exhibits involved media stories. As we have already seen, the media was often reporting things released by the Democrat Party of North Carolina; things that had no bearing on whether Mark Harris should be certified, such as Lucy Young's affidavit from District Seven.

As far as the state elections agency needing an evidentiary record, evidence had already been collected in interviews. The chief investigator for the state elections agency had interviewed Mark and me. The SBI and FBI were already investigating Dowless. Criminal charges against Dowless and some of his workers were on the horizon, just days away. The only thing unique that could come out of this "evidentiary hearing" as put on by the elections agency and the State Elections Board was a public spectacle in which cameras got to catch Mark Harris's reactions as each new witness took the stand.

Don't be misled by the name—an "evidentiary hearing" is not in any way, shape, or form a hearing in a court of law. It is an agency proceeding with the deck stacked to favor the agency. The "quasi-judicial" North Carolina State Board of Elections had control over the following evidence which was not provided to us in advance.

- The summaries of 142 voter interviews they claimed to have made for the 2018 general election.
- The summaries of the thirty subject and witness interviews.
- The list of the State's witnesses who would be called at the hearing.
- Any information shared with them by the SBI or FBI when Dowless was under surveillance and otherwise being investigated and when sealed search warrants were issued against him.
- The contents of any emails or texts outside of those under our control. We had no idea about anything that might be in an email from our consultant Andy Yates directly to McCrae Dowless or vice-versa.
- The contents of any emails or texts gathered from any suspects in the alleged ballot- harvesting operation.

In short, the agency held a trial to determine whether Mark Harris was worthy to take the seat they knew that he won, based on the agency's interpretation of events in Bladen County involving absentee-ballot irregularities. Somehow, preventing election irregularities in Bladen County became the job of Mark Harris, not of the agency that had been chasing down the sources of those irregularities for over two years, with law enforcement closing in and just about to make arrests.

In her opening comments, Strach stated that the hearing would focus on "three main areas...that we were looking at based on our investigation."[2] Strach then enumerated the three areas: absentee ballot irregularities, the possible disclosure of early-voting results, and security issues at the Bladen County Board of Elections.[3] Two-thirds of the presentation and "evidence" introduced by Kim Strach involved Bladen County election security issues totally beyond Mark Harris's control.

The possible disclosure of early-voting results in Bladen County had no tie to Mark Harris's campaign. The results allegedly viewed were not those of the congressional race. Office security at the Bladen County Board of Elections certainly was not under Mark Harris's control. I listened, flabbergasted, while Kim Strach questioned witnesses about a key possibly hanging out in the open in an office in Bladen County. I felt like standing up and screaming: "That's your job!! Why didn't you go down there! You knew there were problems. We didn't!" I wanted Strach to have to take the stand and answer some questions.

Dan McCready had not filed a protest and was owed no voice in the matter whatsoever if the proceeding was based on the State of North Carolina assuming jurisdiction over the election. McCready was nonetheless allowed to bring in Hillary Clinton campaign attorney Marc Elias, who was named by President Trump as one of the Dems' best election-stealing lawyers, and who contacted Fusion GPS to do opposition research on Trump, resulting in the infamous Steele dossier. As we shall see, Elias ruled the hearing. Meanwhile, Mark Harris would learn about the state election agency's evidence with the rest of the world while cameras were capturing his every move and facial expression. The chair of the State Elections Board was not a trained judge. He did not have to follow standard court procedure. That too is stated in the Order of Proceedings. Remember, the state elections agency is just a "quasi" judicial agency. The thought makes me shudder.

We went to Raleigh Sunday night with our campaign manager Jason Williams. I could not have survived that week without Jason. I was going into shut-down mode. He made our hotel arrangements and drove us down and back. He had as much a stake in the outcome as we did, because, like us, he had left his career to join our campaign. He wasn't a kid, either. He was a young man with a wife and six children. Jason ranks high on my list of people who actually live out their Christian beliefs, even when it is hard. He paid another price for being on the Mark Harris campaign when, like me, his emails were presented over live stream at the "hearing" with his personal information left unredacted. Within 24 hours, hackers gained control of his phone and cleaned him out. They even ordered products from Amazon and rides from Uber using his apps.

The State Elections Board had decided to hold this "evidentiary hearing" in a courtroom at the North Carolina Bar Association. They really know how to set the stage for a drama. Monday morning, we were to arrive early. There would be a holding room for us until time for the hearing. As we approached the building from the sidewalk, I saw media already congregated at the top of the set of steps that led to the entrance. They wanted to make sure they got footage of us entering the hearing. I could not believe that this was happening to me. Was I going to be on the news like those grim-faced wives you so often see standing by their husbands as they enter court? I guess I had the alternative of not attending, but with Mark just coming out of the hospital three weeks earlier, I didn't consider that an option. He needed me in every way: mentally, emotionally, and even physically, as I was still giving him his IV antibiotics twice a day. I tried to look cheerful.

Finally, it was time for the hearing to begin. Chairman Bob Cordle gave an incorrect history of the situation to start selling the idea that delaying certification had been necessary to conduct an investigation. Cordle said that the old nine-member board was notified by its staff of irregularities and complaints, and from "a very limited investigation in Bladen and in the 9th District, thus the Board took action to delay certification."[4] In fact, the staff and several of the people on the nine-member board, particularly Joshua Malcolm, were well aware of the issues in Bladen County. In 2016, an investigation had been conducted into those activities, which in her own words, Kim Strach defined as "lengthy."[5] The SBI launched an investigation in February 2018, and the state elections agency chief investigator Joan Fleming held a meeting with Jens Lutz to hear accusations against Dowless in spring 2018.

Kim Strach put on her best investigative stern face and said that they had evidence of a coordinated, widespread absentee-ballot-harvesting operation. She then talked about the 595 voters who did not return their absentee ballots in the 9th Congressional District in Bladen County.[6] She did not, however, clarify that over 200 of those voters cast their votes another way, explaining why they did not return the absentee-by-mail ballots. The number of votes in question in Bladen County was between 331 and 337, according to both my research and that of a Dan McCready expert. Then she said something that has totally gotten lost in the reporting of the events of the "evidentiary hearing." She said, "We do not believe that there is any issue with ballots being unaccounted for."[7] Ms. Strach repeated that point at a forum held at Davidson College after the hearing. At Davidson College she said, "What we did not find were ballots harvested but not returned."[8]

Apparently someone, somewhere, sometime, was smart enough to decide to number every ballot. Apparently the staff at the state elections agency knows how to count the ballots. In 2016, when over 300 voted ballots were missing from Durham County, the elections agency figured it out after a routine audit. In 2018, the elections agency said that ballots were not missing. "Over a Thousand Absentee Ballots Possibly Destroyed" screamed the headline in *The Hill*. Nope. Didn't happen.

The state's first witness was Lisa Britt. I did not know until this "hearing" that Britt was McCrae Dowless's stepdaughter. I had met her a time or two, once at the Peanut Festival and once at an event after the election was over. She always wore her Mark Harris for Congress t-shirt, and she had a cute little boy. It was time for Britt's testimony. Kim Strach opened her presentation by playing a clip from a TV interview in which WBTV investigative reporter Nick Ochsner interviewed Britt during the early days of the 9th District controversy. In the interview, Britt denied that Dowless ever asked her to collect ballots. Strach then began her dramatic questioning.

Strach: Do you recall that interview, Ms. Britt?

Britt: Yes, ma'am.

Strach: And where were you when you sat for that interview?

Britt: I was in Mr. Dowless's kitchen.

Strach: And who was present at Mr. Dowless's home while you were conducting that interview—or sitting for that interview?

Britt: Mr. Dowless, his girlfriend at the time, his grandson, his grandson's girlfriend, my son, and I think there was another person present, but I'm not 100 percent sure if there was anyone else present.

Strach: Did you know you were going to be interviewed prior to arriving at Mr. Dowless's home that day?

Britt: No, ma'am.

Strach: And do you recall why you were going to Mr. Dowless's home that day?

Britt: To go over some paperwork.

Strach: Did Mr. Dowless call you and ask you to come over?

Britt: I don't remember if he had called me or if I had actually called him, because I speak to him on a daily basis.

Strach: When you arrived at Mr. Dowless's home, what did he say that led to that interview?

Britt: I remember I had spoke with him for a few minutes. The interviewer pulled up. He explained that was a friend of his; that he had spoke with a few times, and that he would like for me to give Mr. Ochsner an interview.

Strach: After looking at that and recalling that interview, Ms. Britt, were all the statements you made during that interview truthful?

Britt: No, ma'am.

Strach: Is it true that you had spoken with Chief Investigator Fleming and myself prior to giving that interview?

Britt: Yes, ma'am.

Strach: And had you at that time provided statements to us that were not consistent with the statements you gave during that interview?

Britt: Yes, ma'am.

Strach: Can you tell the Board why you agreed to be interviewed, knowing that you had already told us a very different story than you provided during that interview?

Britt: As I told you and Ms. Fleming, that my mother was married to Mr. Dowless back in—I want to say it was around 1989, so Mr. Dowless has always been a father figure to me...[9]

The only thing missing from this scene is Andy Griffith in a white suit with the *Matlock* theme music playing. Britt's testimony continued and she described the ballot-harvesting plan employed by Dowless in which she and other workers were paid to collect ballots and not just request forms. Britt also testified that she saw a man and a woman she thought might have been Lola Wooten of the Democrat group BCIA making copies in the office rented by Mark Harris for Congress where McCrae worked.[10] Then came another *Matlock*-quality moment:

Strach: And as far as the other gentleman, do you see him in this room?

Britt: Yes, ma'am.

Strach: Can you point him out?

Britt: He's sitting here in a chair.

Chairman Cordle: Would that gentleman please stand?

Director Strach: Would you stand please, sir?

(Male in the audience stands up)

Strach: That's the person you saw that would deliver requests to your office which you made copies?

Britt: Yes, ma'am.

[cut to close up on Horace Munn, cue music, fade to black]

Horace Munn, the president of the BCIA, was the man Britt identified. Munn never testified during the hearing, except to answer one question posed to him by Bob Cordle. For that, Munn wasn't sworn in as a witness, but rather spoke from his seat as a spectator. Munn later told WBTV he felt like a piece of meat for being subpoenaed as a witness and driving two hours from his home just to provide this dramatic moment for the show trial.[11] He also claimed that Chief Investigator Joan Fleming had duped him by telling him he was going to testify about her conversation with him regarding the 2018 investigation.[12]

During all of this testimony, I was furiously taking notes while simultaneously having my mind blown. I was particularly stunned by the insinuation that somehow McCrae was sharing office space with BCIA operatives, and even splitting turf with them over absentee ballots. That infuriated me, as I knew that the Mark Harris campaign paid the rent on that office. I immediately jumped to the conclusion that Dowless had lied to us and was a con artist.

Emma Shipman's affidavit, one of the first affidavits brought out by the Democrat Party of North Carolina in its propaganda campaign, was part of Britt's questioning, yet curiously Emma Shipman was not called as a witness. Britt indicated that she was the woman who had gone to Emma Shipman's house, but that she had left with Shipman's ballot sealed and signed by Mrs. Shipman.[13] One thing was consistent in both Britt's testimony and Shipman's affidavit. Britt had come to Shipman's home on a Sunday. Shipman indicated that it was the Sunday after Hurricane Florence. Britt indicated that Shipman was still at church when she arrived at the house with her four-year-old son. Twice, Britt asserted that her four-year-old son was with her.

Then something interesting happened a little later in Britt's testimony. As she was being questioned by Kim Strach about collecting ballots with other Dowless employees, Britt was finally allowed to talk beyond answering questions with "yes, ma'am," and "no, ma'am." Britt stated that she collected ballots with Jennifer Boyd in Robeson County right after the storm (Hurricane Florence) on Sunday.

Kim Strach questioned her, "So the Sunday you worked in Robeson County with Jennifer Boyd…what did you do with those ballots once you collected them?" Britt described how they took the ballots back with them to Bladen County. Britt stated that Jennifer Boyd had to take her home because "at that time I didn't have a vehicle."[14]

Hiding in plain sight in this account is a contradiction of the Shipman affidavit. How could Lisa Britt be in Robeson County all afternoon collecting ballots with Jennifer Boyd and also be in Bladen County at Emma Shipman's house waiting for her to come home from church the same Sunday? How could Lisa Britt have her four-year-old with her at Shipman's house if she didn't have a vehicle?

Our friend Stony Rushing drove to Emma Shipman's house and described the long dirt road she lived on as "full of huge holes and ruts." Rushing points out that "you had to really want to go down that road" to get to Shipman's house. In other words, Shipman's home likely wasn't on a normal door-to-door canvas route Boyd and Britt would have been completing.

Britt and a four-year-old could not have walked from one town in Robeson County over to another town in Bladen County where Emma Shipman lived down a remote dirt road. It's possible that someone was simply confused on dates, but it is interesting that no one noticed this contradiction and asked about it, especially in light of Jennifer Boyd's insistence that Dowless never asked her to collect ballots. Boyd has not been charged, nor was she called as a witness to offer support to Britt's assertions about their alleged activities.

After Strach led Britt through what certainly in hindsight seems like a rehearsed testimony, Marc Elias cross-examined her, and then our attorney, David Freedman, cross-examined her. I have heard people offer criticism of our attorneys, but I always reject that criticism. There is no one that could go into a setting so unfair as this hearing and be successful. Re-reading Freedman's cross-examination of Lisa Britt, Mark and I were impressed with his knowledge of the absentee-ballot request form logs, the affidavits, and the general timeline of events.

During the cross-examinations, the pattern began which continued throughout the hearing. Marc Elias was allowed to go on and on and on with whatever line of questioning he chose to pursue, while our attorney was constantly shut down. It also became apparent that the BCIA would be protected at all costs.

During Elias's cross-examination of Britt, he led her straight to the conclusion he desired: "Reflecting back on the activities that you were involved in and Mr. Dowless directed, I assume from your testimony you regret participating in it."

Britt replied, "Yes, sir."

Elias continued, "Do you think it was fair to the candidates involved?"

Britt: No, sir, I do not.

Elias: Can you understand why it casts doubt in the minds of voters?

Britt: Yes, sir.

Elias: On the fairness of the election?

Britt: Yes, sir, I do.

Elias: And I assume you agree that the activity of collecting the ballots and filling them out and everything else you talked about was improper.

Britt: Yes, sir.

Elias: And irregular.

Britt: Yes, sir.

Elias: Highly irregular.

Britt: Are you asking me was it irregular or is it something that happens regularly?

Elias: Irregular.

Britt: Yes, sir, it was irregular.[15]

In this exchange, Elias talked the witness through the entire conclusion that forms the basis for one of the reasons an election can be overturned under North Carolina law: taint that casts doubt on the election's fairness. He led the witness to say that the election was unfair to the candidates involved, and that highly irregular things occurred that cast doubt on the election.

In our attorney's cross-examination, a similar question from a different perspective evoked a different reaction from Democrat State Elections Board chair Bob Cordle.

Freedman: Do you think it would be fair to him [Dr. Harris] to not seat him in the 9th Congressional District?

Chairman Cordle: I'm going to object to that and move to strike it. That's not a proper question for this witness.

Republican State Board member Ken Raymond interjected that Mr. McCready's counsel asked about fairness. Freedman tried to rephrase the question and three times met objections and interjections from Chairman Cordle and Marc Elias. Finally, our attorney, David Freedman, asked his question. "Do you think it would be fair to Dr. Harris to punish him for your conduct?"

Britt answered meekly, "No, sir.[16]

Before the lunch recess on the first day of the hearing, Director Kim Strach was about to dismiss Britt when Britt asked if she could say one more thing. Strach replied, "Yes."

Britt stated, "I think you've got one innocent person in this whole thing who had no clue as to what was going on, and he's the one getting the really bad end of the deal here, and that's Mr. Mark Harris."[17]

Other witnesses were called during the rest of the first day of the hearing. They were mostly young women who testified that they had worked for the Dowless ballot-harvesting operation. I began to feel that the whole thing was creepy. A second young woman declared that Dowless was like a father figure. The state elections agency presented its case like McCrae Dowless groomed these young women to work for him. I was feeling sick.

McCrae never for a moment gave me the creeps in person. He was not a hair-sniffer like Joe Biden. Like me, he wasn't even that much of a hugger. Mostly when I was around him he was focused on the business at hand, and making sure we were making connections with the people around us, be it at the Peanut Festival, Beast Fest, a fundraiser, or a poll. Jason Williams told me at a break that reporter

Nick Ochsner had been very angry with Britt's testimony about the circumstances of their interview and had tweeted that she was lying about it. I was back to square one. I didn't know what to think.

The very last witness of the first day of the "hearing" was a young black woman named Precious Hall. Ms. Hall testified that she received an unsolicited absentee ballot in the mail, the same irregularity Lucy Young of District Seven swore to in her affidavit submitted by the Democrat Party of North Carolina with the demand for an investigation into the Ninth District. As it turned out, according to Ms. Hall's sworn testimony, Lola Wooten and Sandra Goins[18] of the Democrat BCIA then showed up to collect her ballot.[19]

According to state election records, Precious Hall's request to vote by mail was received on 8/24/18 and her absentee ballot was mailed on 9/11/18 in the first batch of ballots mailed out.[20] Hall's absentee-ballot container envelope shows that it was signed and witnessed on 10/03/18 by Lola Wooten and Sandra Guions.[21] On 10/10/18 Precious Hall's absentee-by-mail ballot was accepted at the Bladen County Board of Elections.[22]

To connect a few dots between propaganda and reality, the Dems presented an affidavit from a black female voter living outside of the Ninth District who claimed she received an unsolicited absentee ballot. The Dems used this District Seven voter's affidavit to demand a do-over for their candidate, Dan McCready, in the Ninth District.

At the hearing, we discover that a black female voter living in the Ninth District also received an unsolicited absentee ballot, which was followed by a visit from paid Democrat operatives to collect her ballot. We know that Lola Wooten turned in over 100 absentee-ballot request forms just prior to the first mail out of absentee ballots. Is it possible that one or more Democrat operatives turned in absentee ballot request forms for Bladen County relatives and neighbors without their knowledge?

According to the 2016 state elections agency investigation, that is quite possible. The 2016 investigation revealed instances in which voter signatures on absentee-ballot request forms turned in by BCIA operatives did not match voter signatures on ballots. Marc Elias did not grill Precious as he did other witnesses. He asked her eight simple questions about her intent as a voter, because in Elias's world, if Democrats collect ballots, voter intent is what matters when determining election results. On the other hand, if Republicans are accused of collecting ballots, the law against collecting ballots is what matters when determining election results. This is the Democrat alternate universe that the State Elections Board beamed into when they withheld Mark Harris's certification.

McCrae Dowless was called to the stand just before the 5:44 p.m. recess. He was present at the hearing with his attorney, Cynthia Singletary. Because the State Elections Board has subpoena power, but not really, they can't charge you with contempt like a court of law. If you are subpoenaed, when you show up you are technically "released" from your subpoena and then you are faced with a couple of options that are still under the control of the State Board. You can say that you are not going to testify, but only if they give you that option. If they force you to testify, you are granted some type of immunity from criminal prosecution. It is all very convoluted and confusing. The State Elections Board did not want to give Dowless immunity, so he was released from his subpoena. His attorney pointed out that he appeared as commanded but was not going to testify. While the cameras rolled and photos flashed, McCrae Dowless's appearance at the hearing was a spectacle, but provided nothing of substance.

CHAPTER 17

ON ICE

THE SECOND DAY of the hearing brought both the most maddening domination of the proceedings by Marc Elias as well as the funniest moment of the week when Elias got a smack-down from Bladen County affiant Agnes Willis. The entire morning of the second day, Marc Elias ran out the clock like Dean Smith playing four corners by tying up the proceedings over a roll of tape that looked a lot like the old cash register tape of days gone by. The entire morning of the second day had nothing to do with the Mark Harris campaign. For that matter, it had nothing to do with McCrae Dowless. Our witnesses were closed up for a second day in the witness room, with no hope that they would testify anytime soon. Chairman Cordle had stated at the end of the day Monday that he hoped the hearing could be finished the next day by early evening.[1] It soon became apparent there was no way that was going to happen.

The proceedings opened with questioning of Bladen County chief polling place judge Michele Maultsby by state elections agency Executive Director Kim Strach. Maultsby was questioned about whether anyone viewed the early-voting tape from a voting machine on Saturday, the last day of early voting. If someone knew the results, that would give them an unfair advantage going into Election Day. They would know exactly how many voters they needed to turn out for their candidate. The Democrat Party had not just implied, they had stated that Republicans had been let in on the early-voting results while Democrats had not.[2] Maultsby testified under oath that she had not seen anyone looking at the early-voting results or talking about the early-voting results. When asked about instructions she would give as a site supervisor to her workers about looking at results, Ms. Maultsby replied in a strong and firm voice, "Not on my watch."[3]

Next came Coy Mitchell Edwards, who served as a judge at the polling place under Chief Judge Maultsby. Strach walked Edwards through a detailed description of how he prints out the tape, signs it, and then Agnes Willis, another judge, signs it, followed last by Michele Maultsby, the chief judge. Edwards testified that as he signed the early vote tape, his eyes landed on the Bladen County sheriff's race and he saw the machine's results. He testified that he did not see the results in the Ninth District congressional race.[4]

Strach shifted gears and asked Mr. Edwards about his training and the Bladen County practice of running the early vote tape. Then Strach asked, "Has it been your practice in every election you've worked to run that tape at the end of the night?" After Mitchell responded affirmatively, Strach asked, "And you recognize now that that is not how we do it; that we don't run the results at the end of the night?"

Mr. Mitchell responded like a chastised child to Strach's motherly, yet condescending, tone. "I haven't been told that until you just--"

Strach cut Mr. Mitchell off. "I think you will be."[5]

My phone started buzzing with texts from friends saying: "Watch your facial expressions—the camera is on you all the time." Facial expressions? It was all I could do to stay in my seat. In fact, in hindsight, I should have left the room and taken Mark with me right then. Our subpoenas would have expired, and the State Elections Board could have figured out what to do with that. I was about to jump out of my skin. In a hearing to determine my husband's fate, after a three-month smear campaign against him which had robbed him of the right to be sworn in with the rest of the freshmen of the 116th Congress, did Kim Strach actually just indicate that somehow *her own lack of supervision and proper training of elections officials was*

part of this decision? Mr. Mitchell will be informed of proper procedure? He ***will be?*** The state elections agency had just conducted what it called a "lengthy" investigation into irregularities and improprieties in Bladen County in 2016. They had sent their investigation findings to prosecutors.

I can promise you, if my job were to secure the 2018 election in North Carolina, my behind would have been in Bladen County once a week. I would have taken the most updated training manual I possessed, and I would have gone down to Bladen County in April of 2018 as soon as the new County Board of Elections was sworn in. I would have signatures on file indicating that everyone who had anything to do with Bladen County elections had been trained according to most recent best practices.

I would have required Board of Elections Director Cynthia Shaw to email me the absentee-ballot request form turn-in log daily. When hundreds of absentee-ballot requests were turned in at one time by political operatives, I would have delegated one or two investigators to call at least twenty or so of those requesters to spot check and make sure that they ordered their ballots.

I would have visited that office and made sure its every specification was up to snuff for election security. And I most certainly would not have allowed the convicted cop impersonator Jens Lutz to camp out up at the Board of Elections office, even if Lutz had been appointed to the Bladen County Board of Elections.

Every time the slightest question is raised about the competence of the state elections agency, members of the agency get mumped up. Investigators blame prosecutors for inaction, yet when the US Attorney reached out to the agency in summer of 2018 to prevent document destruction, the agency's response was to ignore its subpoena.

Furthermore, only the agency knew the detailed results of its own investigation. No one involved with the Mark Harris campaign could have possibly known those results. The 2016 investigation summary was not shared as part of any public meeting of the State Board of Elections from the time it was written in January 2018 until after the

November 2018 midterm election. All the public knew was that the McCrory protests alleged malfeasance by Democrats in 2016.

Two-thirds of the evidentiary hearing had nothing to do with absentee ballots. Two-thirds of the hearing was about the Bladen County Board of Elections office and improper procedures that may have allowed someone to view early-voting results. Neither district attorneys nor federal prosecutors were in charge of securing the Bladen County Board of Elections. The Mark Harris campaign certainly was not in charge of election security. That job belonged exclusively to the state elections agency, yet here I sat in a courtroom listening to Kim Strach question a precinct judge about viewing the sheriff's race on an early-voting tape while the media circus swirled around me.

After this brief exchange, Marc Elias decided that he needed the actual early-voting tape brought into the courtroom. The copies weren't good enough. The transcript does not do justice to the glee with which Marc Elias made this request. He was in his element with strategy, and he knew it. He even glanced our way. He was icing us by dragging out the proceedings. Coy Mitchell Edwards started his testimony at 10:21 a.m. At 11:12 a.m., the tape finally arrived in the courtroom.

The third witness that day for the state elections agency was Agnes Willis. Willis had signed an affidavit during the blitzkrieg by the Democrat Party in the days between Malcolm's motion to pull Mark's certification and the State Elections Board's final decision to hold an "evidentiary hearing." During the wait for the tape, Willis was sworn in and her questioning by Kim Strach began. Ms. Willis indicated that her role at the polling place for the final day of early voting was that of a greeter. Mrs. Willis went on to describe that all of the workers, regardless of their roles at the poll that day, helped gather ballots from the voting machines and separate them by precinct for delivery to the Bladen County Board of Elections office. Ms. Willis also indicated that she had not personally witnessed Mr. Mitchell run the tape.[6]

As Kim Strach's questioning continued, Ms. Willis's testimony brought out new information. Willis stated that she saw the early-voting tape on a table. When directly asked by Kim Strach whether the tape was rolled up on the table or spread out, Ms. Willis did not directly answer the question. Instead, she explained that she was seated with her back to the table where the tape had been placed when she heard the words, "Oh my God."[7] Willis then indicated that another elections worker named Tojie King was looking at the tape. Willis said she approached the table with the tape and described King as having his finger on the sheriff's race. Willis indicated that several other people came over to look at the tape when King commented, "I thought the black guy had it."[8] Ms. Willis asserted that the only race viewed by the poll workers was the sheriff's race.

After Kim Strach's questioning wrapped up, Chairman Cordle asked Ms. Willis, "Did anybody ask you, or did you hear any rumors or otherwise about a leak of the information from the early voting?"[9]

Ms. Willis's reply, in her own words, is significant. "No. I did not, until an attorney called me, and I was baffled. Couldn't even understand why he was calling me. You know, what he was even about."[10] That attorney was Matthew Dixon, who brought over the affidavit for Ms. Willis to sign. The affidavit was part of the Democrat Party of North Carolina's press conference demanding an investigation into Ninth District irregularities. It was used a second time by the Democrat Party to mislead the public into thinking McCrae Dowless had seen the early voting tape.

Her testimony reveals that Ms. Willis did not initiate any type of complaint about early-voting results being viewed or given to McCrae Dowless or any other Republican. In her own words under oath, Ms. Willis demonstrated that she was not an active participant in any type of protest alleging that anything about the election had been compromised. In fact, she was "baffled" that an attorney would want to speak with her. The only person Ms. Willis indicated speaking to about the viewing of the sheriff's results was her own daughter. [11]

As the hearing continued, certain aspects of Ms. Willis's testimony started becoming problematic for Democrats. Ms. Willis testified that Deborah Monroe, one of three suspects interviewed by the state elections agency in its investigation of voter fraud by the BCIA in 2016, was her cousin.[12] She also testified that another relative, niece Wanda Monroe, who turned in 106 absentee-ballot request forms for the 2018 general election, would sometimes ask her to go back with her to homes to witness ballots, which is perfectly legal.[13] Director Kim Strach questioned Ms. Willis about a particular ballot she had witnessed with her niece, Wanda Monroe.

Strach: Do you know Joseph Barr?

Willis: Yes.

Strach: And did you visit his residence to assist him with completing his absentee ballot?

Willis: Yes.

Strach: And were you accompanied by Wanda Monroe?

Willis: Yes.

Strach: And did you in fact witness his ballot?

Willis: Yes.

Strach: And at the end of that...did you take his ballot with you?

Willis: No, ma'am.

Strach: What did you do with his ballot?

Willis: We left it with him.

Director Strach finally arrived at her main point when she asked Ms. Willis a hypothetical question indicating that Barr had told investigators his ballot was harvested. Strach asked, "If Mr. Barr told investigators that you took his ballot, collected his ballot after it was witnessed, why do you think he would tell investigators that?"

At this point Willis doubled down that she did not collect Mr. Barr's ballot, but she elaborated on the story and the timeline grew more confusing. After Strach basically dropped this line of questioning, despite the fact that Mr. Barr's ballot cover was an exhibit in the "evidentiary hearing," it was time for Marc Elias to have his second shot at cross-examination. Elias immediately played the race card, asking "Is Ms. Monroe African-American?" and "were the majority of voters she was registering...African-American?"[14] Elias's next question brought forth an objection from our attorney David Freedman.

Elias asked, "Are you familiar that North Carolina has a history of discrimination in voting against African-Americans?"

Freedman objected on the grounds of relevance. (Remember, this is not a real court of law.) After some direct bickering back and forth between our attorney Freedman and Marc Elias, Chairman Cordle, as usual, said, "Let's go forward with this."[15]

Then came the smack down. You had to be there to appreciate how hilarious this was. Marc Elias had just pulled out the bloody glove and asked Agnes Willis to put it on. He was about to nullify the illegality of Democrats taking Mr. Barr's ballot by pointing to past discrimination. In fact, Elias had just given a little political speech about "Jim Crow in this state." He was allowed to push forward with asking Agnes Willis a question so that he could glorify her motives.

Elias: Are you aware that North Carolina has a history of discrimination of voting against African-Americans?

Willis: To be honest and give you an honest answer, no.

David Freedman: I withdraw my objection.

(Laughter)

So reads the transcript.[16] Willis's facial expression made it clear that she was not interested into being baited into this game. She had resisted speculation and had answered a number of questions about various poll workers and her own relatives by saying she did not know their party affiliations.

After more back-and-forth about the early-voting tape, it was time for lunch, and afterward our consultant, Andy Yates would testify. One of the pieces of "evidence," if you can call it that, put forth by the state elections agency was a monetary figure they had derived from documents Andy Yates sent in response to their subpoena. In the lengthy examination of Andy Yates, the money paid to McCrae Dowless by Red Dome, Yates's political consulting firm, played a major role. Marc Elias also attempted to create the belief in the public's mind that Yates and Harris had ample opportunity to know all about Dowless's activities from 2016 board meetings and the 2016 investigation, which is false.

Many folks have a very simplistic view of the justice system that boils down to the central idea that if you haven't done anything wrong, you have nothing to worry about. From that belief, they extrapolate another belief: if you just show up and tell the truth, you'll be fine. There's too much evidence to the contrary. In our case, we weren't even dealing with the justice system. We were dealing with an agency that got to make up its own rules as it went along, which was overseen by a politically appointed board.

Because there were possible criminal charges coming against McCrae Dowless, we could not communicate with him. We did not communicate with Andy Yates, either. Attorneys (rightfully so) put the fear of God into their clients that any communication with anyone involved might earn an obstruction of justice charge. Obstruction of justice charges are handed out like candy as a result of such proceedings. McCrae Dowless earned himself an obstruction of justice charge for having his workers over to his house and telling them to stick together and plead the Fifth Amendment at the hearing.

Furthermore, because the proceedings had no requirement of discovery, we did not see any material that might have passed between just Yates and Dowless. This played a huge role in our inability to prepare to answer questions about the figures the state put forth about total dollars paid to Dowless by the Mark Harris campaign. We had invoices and sometimes clarifying emails that accompanied them, but we couldn't just pick up the phone and ask Andy to go over those charges with us. We couldn't ask McCrae about a charge noted as "grassroots" on an invoice and get clarification as to whether that was poll workers, his absentee-ballot request program, or something else.

Right out of the chute on the first day of the hearing, state elections agency Executive Director Strach introduced a figure and then immediately noted that it might not be the correct one. Marc Elias harped on this figure over and over and over in his examination of various witnesses. As part of her opening presentation, Strach stated that $131,375 was paid to McCrae Dowless by Red Dome consulting between July 3, 2017 (when the Harris campaign was organized) and the 2018 general election.[17] Strach immediately continued with her apology for the accuracy of the numbers, which naturally Marc Elias was never going to reference. He referenced only the $131,375. After introducing the $131,375 figure, Strach went on to say, "...we have not been able to interview Mr. Yates prior to this hearing, and so some of those payments may not be for the absentee program." She continued, "They may be for other things Red Dome was paying him [Dowless] for, including paying him for other candidates."[18] What? Strach introduced a figure for its gasp value and then stated that it might not be what Harris paid Dowless through Red Dome at all?

When thinking about the money, it is vital to note that we had two major elections during the seventeen-month campaign. One of those was a primary against a three-term incumbent, and the other was against a massively funded Democrat with national connections. We needed a district-wide ground game. A ground game never really changes. Whether in the primary or general election, it takes money to do grassroots campaigning with door-to -door canvassing, phone calls, getting people to the polls, and workers handing out campaign materials at the polls. All of that also takes organization. We had twelve precincts in Bladen County, all of Robeson County (which has the largest landmass of any county of North Carolina's 100 counties) and twenty precincts of Cumberland County. Dowless largely organized our ground game in those counties. The main campaign headquarters was 125 miles to the west in Union County, and all of our other campaign staff resided even farther west in Charlotte and its bedroom communities.

How did these numbers break down? Andy Yates testified on the second day of the "evidentiary hearing" that he estimated between $15,000 to $18,000 of the total he paid to McCrae came from candidates other than Mark Harris for contract GOTV work.[19] Deducting $18,000 from the figure presented by Kim Strach makes the "Mark Harris True Total" paid to McCrae Dowless $113, 375. Using Strach's numbers, Red Dome paid Dowless $47,682 for the primary and $65, 693 for the general election.

From both testimony and our invoices and emails, we know that McCrae Dowless received a salary from the campaign over a period of seventeen months. These numbers are crystal clear to us without consulting Yates or Dowless. Dowless was paid $1,200 dollars per month during the primary and $1,625 per month as salary during the general election. We literally had college students who made as much as this on the campaign. Our three professional full-time campaign staff members were paid more than twice this salary. This does not paint a picture of exorbitant spending. Our highest-paid professional staff member would have made less than $60,000 per year based on the salary he received for the campaign. Based on Yates's testimony, McCrae's salary over the seventeen months would equal $22,800.

For that salary, McCrae Dowless kept a campaign office open for the eastern counties of the district. When the drive time across this district as it was drawn in 2018 was more than three hours end-to-end, it was important to have offices in both the east and the west. Headquarters are places where copies can be run, signs can be stored for pick up and distribution, etc. We had the added expense during the general election that McCrae and whomever he hired to put out signs in the three eastern counties of the district had already put them up prior to Hurricane Florence. They had to be taken up and put back out again due to the hurricane and the massive flooding it caused in Cumberland, Bladen, and Robeson Counties.

What were the other expenses for which Red Dome reimbursed Dowless in addition to his GOTV program with absentee-ballot request forms? Per Yates's testimony, monthly rental on office space, plus a leased copier and one would assume anything that goes with making copies, like paper and toner. There were also other reimbursements as expected in a campaign: staffing, clerical work, setting up and staffing events, early-voting and election-day polls, plus the absentee-ballot request form program.[20] If poll workers were paid the $10-$12 per hour as indicated in one of Yates's emails, and there were two workers per poll, in Bladen County alone that would represent close to $10,000 for the two and a half weeks of early voting plus

Election Day. Poll work in eastern North Carolina is different than it is in other parts of the state. "Poll work" generally means standing outside a polling place and handing out campaign material. It is frankly shocking how many people come to vote without their minds made up about who they will choose when they cast their ballots inside the polling place.

In eastern North Carolina, possibly because in rural areas elections are bigger news and a bigger source of excitement, this poll work becomes a big production. People have tents for their candidates. The workers sit under the tents and often actually call out to people coming into the voting place with a kind of cadence. Sometimes there is lunch served to the poll volunteers/workers under the tent. Paid haulers pull up in rented vehicles and drop off voters at the polls. On Sundays, churches run "souls to the polls" with church buses and vans to encourage their members to go vote.

This hearing was not about finding evidence. It was about presenting evidence in a way that made the Harris-McCready race seem so tainted that the only remedy that would suffice would be a new election. Our expenditures were not anomalous for an eight-county congressional race. Even using the $131,375 figure given by Kim Strach followed by the immediate explanation that it was probably wrong, that made up only a small part of our $2.2 million campaign—approximately 5 % of the total campaign expenses.

Unfortunately we learned during Andy's testimony that he had not required documentation from McCrae. McCrae just itemized things over the phone to him. I could hear the whispering behind me as Andy Yates was questioned. One specific statement I heard was that the campaign had no accountability. That's not really true, and it certainly doesn't mean that anyone in our campaign thought McCrae Dowless was collecting ballots. Andy Yates, like a huge portion of the world, isn't always as attentive to details and deadlines as he should be. Yates did point out during his testimony that McCrae Dowless was in the budget for the campaign, and the campaign followed its budget, even cutting the budget, including McCrae's budget, as the primary approached.

In Marc Elias's cross-examination of Andy Yates, Elias tried to plant the idea that we had to be corrupt because no one could be stupid enough not to know certain evidence already existed about Dowless. We did not know, and could not have known, what investigators already knew about Dowless and the activities of Matthew Mathis and Caitlyn Croom, who claim Dowless paid them to collect ballots in 2016. An example of what I am talking about comes in an exchange between Elias and Andy Yates about what information was available about Dowless before we hired him.

Elias was grilling Andy Yates over his Google search of Dowless before he went down to meet with him for the first time.

Elias: Google in fact allows you to search the Google results of what Google result of search would have been at a given time.[21]

That is not a transcription error on my part, just confusing. What Elias is claiming is that he was able to go back and see the search results that would have popped up at the time when Andy Yates searched for McCrae Dowless. A big part of Andy's testimony had included that he had misspelled McCrae's name and did not know that McCrae's first name was Leslie. Elias began to show "Google results" claiming that the results he showed would have been available to Yates in spring 2017.

Almost instantly after Elias made his confusing statement about search results, a text popped up on my phone from a friend who owns a marketing firm. The text read, "Google search results are different for every user. This is garbage and prejudicious."

I responded, "Just copied to our lawyer."

Our attorneys began to offer objections because the things Elias was showing as available to Yates in 2017 had dates of 2018. Chairman Cordle as usual concluded, "Let's go on and see what he has."[22]

At another point, Elias spoke about the 2016 investigation results and the December 3, 2016 hearing. He pointed to a National Public Radio posting and also the state election agency's website.[23] Although

Yates said repeatedly he had not heard he NPR broadcast nor read the post, Elias was allowed to continue to question him about the contents over the objections of our attorneys.

I leaned forward at one point and asked one of the young assistant attorneys to go onto the elections agency website and find the date that the hearing transcript had been posted. He sent me back a sticky note. The "last modified" date for the December 3, 2016 hearing was December 3, 2018, two full years later.[24] This would not have been available to Andy Yates in July of 2017. There is no update on a transcript. There is no reason to modify it. The "last modified" date was the date the transcript had to have been posted, which was after the 2018 general election.

Even if Yates had read the transcript, he would have seen Dowless as the protestor claiming that the BCIA had fraudulently written in votes for Franklin Graham. No one without an inside knowledge of the 2016 investigation, which was also conveniently not made public until the Ninth District Investigation portal opened in December of 2018, would have understood that the 2016 hearing implicated Dowless in wrongdoing. My big takeaway from the 2016 transcript was that every protest was dismissed because it didn't alter the outcome. Poor Andy Yates just kept trying to answer the questions as best that he could without an understanding of the tactics Elias was using.

An assistant attorney for the state elections board, as well as Executive Director Strach, questioned Yates yet again about the money. In all, Andy Yates' testimony took the second half of the day Tuesday and the entire first half of the day Wednesday. Yates was on the witness stand in a proceeding to determine "evidence" held by unelected bureaucrats just thirteen minutes shy of eight hours—that's five hours longer than the O.J. Simpson jury took to arrive at its "not guilty" verdict in one of the most famous murder trials in history.

As we headed into the room provided for our campaign and attorneys to eat lunch, we were faced with solving two huge problems. In the order of proceedings, the state elections agency was designated to go first, followed by Marc Elias on behalf of Dan McCready, and then followed by us to present our case as to why Mark should be declared the winner of the election. We had a room full of witnesses who were subpoenaed only through Wednesday afternoon, and it was lunchtime Wednesday. People who had driven two hours each day from Bladen County and missed work to attend the hearing Monday, Tuesday, and Wednesday were telling us apologetically that they could not come back another day.

Our subpoenas also ran out Wednesday afternoon, and in hindsight the best course of action would have probably been for us to leave and not return. Jason was able to book his hotel room for another night, but we had to return to Charlotte. We had packed a cooler full of the large pre-filled syringes of antibiotics and supplies necessary to administer them twice a day. We had doses for Sunday night, Monday, Tuesday, and Wednesday, but not beyond. A cap had also broken off one of Mark's three PICC lines during the week. I had called his home health nurse about it and she directed us to get it replaced as soon as possible. Dallas Woodhouse kindly found a Raleigh resident who was willing to drive us all the way to Charlotte Wednesday evening and back Thursday morning. The way the hearing was dragging out was discouraging. We ate our box lunches as we did every day, unsure of what would happen next.

CHAPTER 18

SURPRISE APPEARANCE

A STRANGE THING happened the first day of the hearing when we were in our "attorney room." At lunch, Mark looked out the window and thought he saw our son John walking down the sidewalk. Mark called me over to the window. John was walking down the sidewalk away from the building with his back to us, so it was hard to tell, but that definitely looked like him. I didn't have a grasp on the geography of downtown Raleigh, so I asked if we were close to John's office. Was he walking to lunch? I would have loved to see him. Mark, however, pointed out that we were still not supposed to contact John. We had seen John's family at Thanksgiving, which was before Malcolm's motion. Other than that, we had seen him only at a big Christmas party for extended family and when Mark was hospitalized. We had no phone calls, texts, or emails other than my updates about Mark's condition during his illness.

Tuesday, the second day of the hearing, the same thing happened. Once again, we thought we saw John. We wondered if somehow he had come to watch the proceedings and we hadn't seen him in the courtroom. That night we were talking with our son Matthew by telephone at about 11:00 p.m., using Mark's cell phone. Mark mentioned to Matthew that he thought he saw John. Matthew couldn't bear what the state elections agency was about to do to Mark. He told Mark something that John had told him. John was under a subpoena to testify at the hearing. We later found out that John was subpoenaed at the last minute, Friday afternoon before the hearing started on Monday.

We also found out later that John thought he was there to testify about a text message exchange he had with me. Like Horace Munn, John did not realize he was being set up as one more dramatic element in Kim Strach's show trial. John was held in a special witness room one floor beneath the proceedings, instead of with the rest of the state elections agency witnesses. Mark called our attorney David Freedman to let him know that John had been subpoenaed by the state elections agency. Again, we did not have a list of the state's witnesses, so we did not know when John would be called or how many total witnesses the state would call. After lunch Wednesday, the third day of the hearing, John Harris was called to the stand.

After he was sworn in, Chairman Cordle asked John if he knew anything about the investigation. John replied, "…I have no idea what has happened, what is happening, or what will happen with respect to any investigation that may or may not exist. I simply know nothing about it."[1]

Kim Strach began to question John about communication with us. John stated that he had called attorneys he thought were representing the campaign to ask whether his communication before or during the period of the campaign was going to be considered privileged. Indicating that there had been some "back-and-forth" with attorneys for a couple of weeks without a clear answer, John stated that he contacted our personal attorney, David Freedman. According to John's testimony, Freedman "confirmed to me that they were not going to be asserting privilege" and "that they were not going to be asserting that they [emails] were confidential…"[2]

Strach then tried to lead John to state that he reached out to the state elections agency because of "uncertainty about whether emails had been turned over in the discovery process with the subpoena.[3] Strach's phrasing of this leading question is very significant. She is setting up our son to accuse us of being dishonest in the fulfillment of document production, which I find ironic in light of the fact that her response to a subpoena from the United States Justice Department was to simply reject it. I also find it hilarious that Strach used the phrase "discovery process." There was no discovery for us, only for the bureaucrats at the state elections agency. John responded, "Let me make sure I clarify as to the way that worked."[4]

John then went on to explain that on January 6, 2019 he had gotten a phone call from David Freedman telling him that his emails to us were going to be produced. John then explained his concern to Freedman over the emails in which he had shared his observations and speculation with us about Dowless's program. According to his sworn testimony, because of the fact that there had been "quite a media presence" in the case, John was concerned about the timing of when the state elections agency might post any evidence on the Ninth District portal.[5]

From the time Joshua Malcolm ordered the portal established, it was part of the propaganda. Everything to be used in the hearing was not posted. Things damaging to Dowless were posted. Interviews with subjects such as Lisa Britt and Sandra Dowless, both of whom actually lived in McCrae Dowless's home for a time, and both of whom stated under oath that Mark Harris did not know about the alleged ballot harvesting, were not posted. This was the substance of John's conversation with David Freedman: John wanted a heads-up before any of his emails went public on the Ninth District Portal set up by order of Democrat Board Chair Joshua Malcolm.

John went on to state that he called Josh Lawson, counsel for the state elections agency, and told him that he understood that there would be communications from him that would be produced by the Mark Harris campaign. He told Lawson that "in light of the fact that there was no sitting Board of Elections at that time, that I wasn't going to try to put up some kind of legal fight."[6]

John absolutely in no way, shape, or form, was concerned that his mom and dad would try to cover anything up. To use Kim Strach's words, "uncertainty" about whether the emails would be produced did not lead John to reach out to the agency. In John's own words, John was concerned about the publicity for himself, in his new role as an Assistant US Attorney. John was also giving clarity to his acquaintance Josh Lawson, whom he later said he called on a Sunday, meaning he had a personal contact number for Josh Lawson, that he wasn't going to try to use the confusion created by the replacement of the State Board in the middle of the "investigation" as the basis for any kind of legal fight.

In a nutshell, in this portion of his testimony John asserted that to the best of his understanding, documents were going to be produced that included emails from him, and so he touched base with an acquaintance at the state elections agency to let him know that despite the unseemly publicity, John was fine with his emails being on public display, and also fine with discussing them with the agency if necessary. That's it.

John went on to state, "Probably two and a half, three weeks later, Ms. Strach contacted me to come down for an interview."[7] That statement places Strach's request for an interview with John not long after he left the hospital in Charlotte on the Martin Luther King holiday January 21, 2019. The substance of John's testimony involved some observations and speculation he sent to both Mark and me after a conversation he had with Mark following Mark's first visit to Elizabethtown to meet McCrae Dowless. John, who was twenty-six when Mark ran for Congress the first time in 2016, indicated that he was "a sounding board" for his dad. John also described emails as continuations of he and his dad's political conversations. "We'd exchange emails. He'd send me poll results."[8] Our family loves to talk both politics and religion. In one's immediate family, there is no prohibition on those topics. We debated. As our children got married, their spouses joined in. All of us have a lot of passion about things we believe in. I am incredibly proud that all of our children can think and are substantive people, and that they have married substantive people.

Before discussing John's email, Kim Strach asked him if had ever talked to Andy Yates. John said that he had, and then recounted a conversation in which he shared two concerns with Andy. One was that they needed to be careful about running too far right in the primary because McCready would be formidable, and the campaign didn't need to alienate voters. The other concern John testified that he shared with Andy was about "McCrae."[9] John said that he asked Andy, "Are you sure that everything that he's saying he's going to do, he's actually going to do?" John said that Andy assured him that "we're going to make sure that, you know, that he does what he says he's going to do."[10]

John also said that Andy Yates gave him the impression of also being a little wary about McCrae. I found that interesting, since Andy Yates testified that Red Dome contracted with Mr. Dowless on behalf of several other candidates. When asked by Strach to list the ones he knew Dowless worked for in 2018, Yates indicated the Harris campaign, the Jim McVicker for Sheriff campaign, the Brenden Jones for North Carolina House campaign, and the Jody Greene for Sheriff campaign.[11] Representative Jones and Sheriff Greene were both candidates in Columbus County. The other candidates listed by Yates were certified and sworn into their offices. Seemingly, the only campaign targeted for a new election was the Harris campaign.

The next part of John's testimony concerned his analysis of the 2016 Republican primary election results. Everything that went wrong in the hearing boiled down to John's speculation about dates on an Excel sheet and the confusion over the production of an email containing this speculation. I later confirmed with John that all he looked at was the 2016 Republican Primary data sheet from the state elections agency website for absentee voting—he had not looked at postmarks, ballot containers, or anything else besides the Excel sheet. I wanted to be sure in my own conscience that I had not blown off something really concrete that John had shown me. It is helpful to understand the data in question, so I have included a table showing a portion of the data John saw without revealing voters' personal information. I added a row of column numbers at the top and a lettered column at the left for clarity but otherwise everything in the table is copied exactly as it appears on the state elections agency website for the 2016 congressional primary June 7. Each letter in the column at the left represents a voter in Bladen County.

John testified that he saw "higher than expected batches of ballots arriving on the same date" at the Bladen County Board of Elections. (Column 8.)[12] A more accurate wording of what John saw was that, in his view, he saw a higher than expected **number** of ballots arriving on the same date. A batch creates a visual picture that things were turned in together at a mailbox at once. This is why I called John right after the testimony. I wanted to be sure that he had not looked at ballot envelopes and seen ten mailed from the Elizabethtown Post Office at 2:00 p.m. on a particular date.

A "batch" is not discernable from the spreadsheet. To declare a group of ballots a "batch," one would have to look at the postmark dates and times on the envelopes. John also indicated that he sorted the data by race, age, and date. He did not indicate that he filtered out ballots marked "spoiled" that also had return dates. A spoiled ballot status (column 9) is typically an entry for someone who has voted in person at early voting. Ordering an absentee-by-mail ballot doesn't obligate you to vote that way. Also in 2016, because the congressional primary was a special election due to court-ordered redistricting, there were people who were automatically mailed absentee ballots because they had ordered them for the presidential primaries March 15, 2016. In column 7, the dates in January and February represent those ballots. Were those filtered out? I did not know.

John also made an assumption that was not supportable from the data he had at hand. John testified, "One would **expect** that if people are randomly sending in about 218 ballots, that they would be scattered over the course of days." John specifically said, "...**he expected there would be a kind of even distribution.**"[13] I have no expertise in patterns of absentee voting. Neither does John, as much as I love him. In my experience, generally people fall into two categories: they are either early or they run late. I would expect that the vast majority of absentee ballots come in either really early or just before Election Day as the election begins to take center stage in voters' minds. I do not in the least find the lack of an equal distribution of absentee ballot return dates to be problematic. In fact, a perfectly even distribution of dates might have appeared more suspicious to me. If Dowless is proven guilty, John basically made a lucky guess as to what was going on.

I realize this is tedious and in the weeds, but it is very important and speaks to why, when weighed against other factors, I dismissed John's speculation about ballot harvesting based on his interpretation of this spreadsheet. No matter the spin Democrat members of the State Board tried to put on this email, it represented just one opinion out of many opinions we were using to determine whether to hire Dowless, as John himself testified.

When we do a little reverse engineering on John's email, Mark's thinking does not seem so inadequate. If John's speculation based on one Excel sheet is correct, then a sheriff, a sitting judge, the administrator of the North Carolina Court System, a county commissioner who has been on the Board of Elections fifteen years, another county commissioner, a representative in the North Carolina House, and a North Carolina state senator are all either corrupt or Dowless was so skillful that he fooled them.

The other possibility is, of course, that Dowless did not collect ballots and will be exonerated when he comes to trial. Four of the officials I just named live in the same county as Dowless and vote in elections there. We lived three hours away in Charlotte. Perhaps if just one person had vouched for Dowless and others had been hesitant, I would not have been so quick to dismiss John's speculation.

In light of the information Mark was given by several highly credible officials, and in light of my own knowledge of the absentee-ballot database, I did not view John's conclusion as valid. Furthermore, if this conclusion was evident just from a spreadsheet, why hadn't the state elections agency picked up on it? By law, Mark Harris received an automatic recount of the 2016 Republican primary because the results were so close. Todd Johnson received an unusually high number of absentee-by-mail votes in Bladen County in 2016. Were we supposed to see red flags the elections agency didn't see, not even during a recount in a special election in which only North Carolina's congressional races and two judicial contests were on the ballot?

I was incensed when McClatchy News labeled John's analysis of this spreadsheet "foreknowledge" of Dowless's alleged activities. The McClatchy description got picked up on all the wire services and even ran across the ticker on the Fox News channel.

June 7, 2016 Congressional Primary Absentee by Mail Voters Bladen County (Partial)

	1	2	3	4	5	6	7	8	9
	Election date	voter-party	Voter precinct	District	Ballot request party	Ballot request date	Ballot send date	Ballot return date	Ballot status
A	6/7/16	UNA	BLADENBORO #2	CONGRESSIONAL DISTRICT 9	REP	5/4/16	5/4/16	5/18/16	ACCEPTED
B	6/7/16	UNA	BLADENBORO #2	CONGRESSIONAL DISTRICT 9	DEM	1/25/16	4/18/16		SPOILED
C	6/7/16	UNA	BLADENBORO #2	CONGRESSIONAL DISTRICT 9	DEM	1/25/16	4/18/16		SPOILED
D	6/7/16	UNA	BLADENBORO #2	CONGRESSIONAL DISTRICT 9	REP	5/4/16	5/4/16	5/23/16	ACCEPTED
E	6/7/16	UNA	BLADENBORO #2	CONGRESSIONAL DISTRICT 9	REP	5/9/16	5/10/16	5/23/16	ACCEPTED
F	6/7/16	UNA	ELIZABETHTOWN #1	CONGRESSIONAL DISTRICT 9	DEM	2/9/16	4/18/16	6/6/16	ACCEPTED
G	6/7/16	REP	BETHEL	CONGRESSIONAL DISTRICT 9	REP	5/31/16	5/31/16	6/6/16	ACCEPTED
H	6/7/16	UNA	BETHEL	CONGRESSIONAL DISTRICT 9	REP	5/31/16	5/31/16	6/6/16	ACCEPTED
I	6/7/16	UNA	BLADENBORO #1	CONGRESSIONAL DISTRICT 9	REP	5/11/16	5/11/16	5/23/16	ACCEPTED
J	6/7/16	UNA	BETHEL	CONGRESSIONAL DISTRICT 9	REP	5/11/16	5/11/16	5/23/16	ACCEPTED
K	6/7/16	UNA	BETHEL	CONGRESSIONAL DISTRICT 9	REP	5/5/16	5/9/16	5/18/16	ACCEPTED
L	6/7/16	UNA	ELIZABETHTOWN #1	CONGRESSIONAL DISTRICT 9	REP	5/9/16	5/10/16		

M	6/7/16	UNA	BETHEL	CONGRESSIONAL DISTRICT 9	REP	5/20/16	5/20/16		
N	6/7/16	UNA	BETHEL	CONGRESSIONAL DISTRICT 9	REP	4/26/16	4/27/16	4/27/16	SPOILED
O	6/7/16	UNA	BLADENBORO #2	CONGRESSIONAL DISTRICT 9	REP	5/12/16	5/12/16	6/6/16	ACCEPTED
P	6/7/16	UNA	BETHEL	CONGRESSIONAL DISTRICT 9	REP	5/5/16	5/9/16	5/18/16	ACCEPTED
Q	6/7/16	UNA	BETHEL	CONGRESSIONAL DISTRICT 9	REP	5/5/16	5/9/16	5/18/16	ACCEPTED
R	6/7/16	UNA	BROWN MARSH	CONGRESSIONAL DISTRICT 9	REP	2/10/16	4/18/16	4/27/16	ACCEPTED
S	6/7/16	UNA	ABBOTTS	CONGRESSIONAL DISTRICT 9	REP	5/5/16	5/9/16	5/23/16	ACCEPTED
T	6/7/16	UNA	BLADENBORO #2	CONGRESSIONAL DISTRICT 9	REP	5/6/16	5/9/16	5/13/16	ACCEPTED
U	6/7/16	UNA	BLADENBORO #1	CONGRESSIONAL DISTRICT 9	REP	1/25/16	4/18/16	4/18/16	SPOILED
V	6/7/16	UNA	BLADENBORO #1	CONGRESSIONAL DISTRICT 9	REP	4/18/16	4/18/16	5/3/16	ACCEPTED
W	6/7/16	REP	WHITE OAK	CONGRESSIONAL DISTRICT 9	REP	3/5/16	4/18/16		
X	6/7/16	UNA	BLADENBORO #2	CONGRESSIONAL DISTRICT 9	REP	5/9/16	5/10/16	5/23/16	ACCEPTED
Y	6/7/16	UNA	WHITE OAK	CONGRESSIONAL DISTRICT 9	REP	5/12/16	5/12/16	6/6/16	ACCEPTED
Z	6/7/16	UNA	BETHEL	CONGRESSIONAL DISTRICT 9	REP	4/18/16	4/18/16	5/2/16	ACCEPTED

At some point during John's testimony, we took a break. I approached him and laid my hand on his arm and told him I was praying for him. The fact that John was subpoenaed for that hearing was not John's fault. He had been told that his email containing speculation about possible ballot harvesting would be submitted with our documents. According to his testimony, he first called John Branch, attorney for the Mark Harris campaign on December 22, 2018. [14] When he did not get an answer from Branch, he called our personal attorney, David Freedman, on Friday January 4, 2019. Freedman returned John's call Sunday January 6 and told John that his emails would be submitted to the state elections agency.

John wasn't trying to rat us out. He did not think we had done anything wrong and he stated that he thought Dowless had deceived us, although he did say that he would have made a different choice when it came to hiring Dowless. It's worth pointing out that it wasn't just Mark Harris who agreed to use Dowless for GOTV. Andy Yates testified that he steered other clients to Dowless. Jim McVicker, sheriff of Bladen County, paid Dowless for GOTV in 2014 and in 2018. William Brisson and Brenden Jones, two members of the North Carolina House, also used Dowless at various times.

Most of the media, high on the haze of scandal in the air, didn't bother to report the rest of John's testimony. John also testified that he "absolutely believed that McCrae Dowless told them [Mark and me] that he never let anybody touch a ballot, and he gave them examples about where the legal lines were."[15] John also pointed out that these were "sounding board" conversations between parents and child, and that he and his dad had a lot of political conversations about all kinds of things. John reminded Kim Strach that he was not an on-the-ground staffer with the campaign.[16]

Strach asked John about whether Mark ever directly asked McCrae Dowless if he took ballots. "Did you think he [Mark] would go back and say, 'Hey, let me make sure…let me go and ask that question. And he's [John] really convinced this guy is collecting ballots. Let me go and ask him, just straight out ask him.' Do you think that ever happened?" Beyond the sheer stupidity of this question, because if Dowless is a lying con artist he would just lie in answer to a straight up question the same way he lied in his presentation, this is a very leading question. Strach is leading John to accuse his own dad of negligence in investigating and supervising Dowless. John did not take the bait. He simply answered, "I do not know."[17]

When Strach asked if at any time before, during, or after the election Mark or I had said anything that indicated we knew that Mr. Dowless was collecting ballots, John replied very firmly, "No. Absolutely not. I think they were lied to and they believed the person who lied to them."[18]

I find Strach's question interesting. She doesn't say "possibly collecting ballots." She doesn't say "allegedly collecting ballots." Dowless had not yet been charged with any crimes. There were no documents from law enforcement investigations produced as evidence at this hearing. But it is Strach's opinion that counts. She doesn't have to comply with subpoenas, but if she decides a man is guilty, and if she decides the man she is trying to rob of his congressional seat should have known about that man's guilt, Strach states that McCrae Dowless collected ballots as if it is a fact beyond all doubt. There are people who think that there is a lot of doubt about what Dowless actually did or did not do in the 2018 election.

All I can say about Marc Elias's cross-examination of John is that it reminded me of the moment the Grinch got out the door with all the Christmas presents. A lot of Elias's cross-examination focused on confusion over document production. The confusion and the dropped balls did look really bad. Marc Elias's praise for John made me sick to my stomach. Marc Elias is just about the last person on this earth I would want to praise my child. This was the most painful thing about John's testimony for me.

John is still young, at that time still in his twenties. He has a very strong love for God and all things that are right. He is smart enough to see that there was a political side to the proceedings, but at the time of the hearing no one knew about Malcolm's communication with Dan McCready. No one knew that Alaina Malcolm had been on the payroll of the Democrat Party of North Carolina during the election. I just kept imagining Elias sitting in a hotel bar somewhere having a beer while on the phone telling someone about what a piece of cake this hearing was turning out to be because of John. That thought made me want to cry.

John Harris and Lisa Britt were the dramatic bookends of the election agency's "testimony to develop an evidentiary record." Like Lisa Britt, John asserted Mark Harris's innocence in his testimony. At worst, we chose to listen to civic leaders in the county where Dowless lived, one of whom had served on the Bladen County Board of Elections for fifteen years, instead of rejecting Dowless just on the basis of John's analysis of a spreadsheet.

John let Chair Bob Cordle know that "in my view, this board... doesn't have the ability to conduct criminal investigations." He also let Cordle know that in advising us, John had told us to focus on the closed meeting in which Mark's certification had been withheld. In John's opinion, that was a violation of the state's open meetings laws.[19] John realized what it took me one year to realize—just how unprecedented Joshua Malcolm's maneuver at the November 27 State Elections Board meeting was. John also recognized that the lack of communication by the State Board to us was unforgivable. They went into closed session, came out with a decision, issued a subpoena to us a few days later, and then sprung evidence on us at a show trial.

Like Lisa Britt, before John Harris stepped down, he had something else to say. He talked about his love for us, and then John Harris took the State Elections Board to task.

> The thing about all of this and engaging in this process and watching it all unfold, I've thought a lot more probably about my own little ones than my parents, and the world that we're building for them. And I will be frank, Mr. Chairman, watching all this process unfold, we have got to come up with a way to transcend our partisan politics and the exploitation of processes like this for political gain. That goes for both parties, Democrats, and Republicans and Libertarians. And frankly, when I'm coming out of this process, I'm just left thinking that we can all do a lot better than this.[20]

Mark became emotional at this point, and of course cameras were constantly rolling and snapping. The McClatchy-owned *Charlotte Observer* continues to use a photograph snapped of Mark at this moment anytime they can scrape up the slightest excuse to talk about Mark. *The Daily Haymaker,* an independent blog/news source based in North Carolina, ran the real story under the headline, "North

Carolina-09: Shameful Driveby Scumbags and the Money-Bleeding Outlets that Employ Them." Brant Clifton wrote about how offensive McClatchy's coverage of the entire hearing was, and then talked about how the news service left the impression that "Harris was crying over accusations of criminality made by his son." Clifton went on to report that he had talked with his eyes and ears in the courtroom who had been there all week. This was the report of one of Clifton's eyewitnesses:

> The man was crying because his son had just said some very touching, moving things about his dad. Now I'm loaded with testosterone. But I found myself having to duck inside the men's room to wipe my eyes after hearing the words of young Mr. Harris. That was some touching stuff. The guy ought to be proud he has a son who cares so much about him."[21]

And so ended Day 3 of the Mark Harris Show Trial.

CHAPTER 19

THE IRON CALCULUS OF WAR

THE MAN WHO wrote a definitive text on warfare called *On War,* Carl Von Clausewitz, wrote: "War is a clash between major interests, which is resolved by bloodshed. That is the only way in which it differs from other conflicts."[1] Former Republican State Board of Elections Member John Lewis told me that he has basically disengaged from the political arena since his time on the North Carolina State Board of Elections ended. He said, "There was a time when our political leaders were statesmen. Politics has gotten really, really nasty. It is a blood sport. I'm glad to be out of it."[2]

Have elections become blood sport because the major interests of Democrats and Republicans cannot be reconciled? Are we headed once more toward civil war? Those in the Marxist, hard-left wing of the Democrat party don't seem interested in reconciliation or the process of peaceful change. They don't seem to believe the processes of the US government offer them any hope of attaining their goals. They must make new zones. They must become autonomous. They must tear down the old to usher in the new. They are not out to solve problems. They are out to destroy their perceived enemies. Their enemies are those who do not share their Marxist, destructive beliefs.

Our experience in the aftermath of the 2018 election certainly felt like war. Democrat Joshua Malcolm made it so by ignoring the means established by law and precedent to get at the problem of alleged ballot harvesting in Bladen County. Malcolm and the state elections agency did not want to wait for criminal prosecution of McCrae Dowless. Waiting for proper authorities, prevention, and following precedent: these options were removed from the equation.

Instead, Malcolm fired the first volley with his motion to pull Mark Harris from the winners' list and then the Democrats charged into battle. They struck at the very thing that made Mark Harris different from most political figures. They struck at the character of a man who has had nothing more than an occasional traffic ticket on his record for thirty years. Democrat Party propaganda led the way. The elections agency outmaneuvered him at the hearing. They did not spare even his family, issuing a subpoena to John Harris the Friday afternoon prior to the start of the Monday hearing. This was total war. It was mentally and emotionally damaging. The case could be made that it was physically damaging to Mark as well.

In war, there is a strategic equation called "the iron calculus of war." This concept is also credited to Carl Von Clausewitz. The equation goes like this: "resistance = means x will." War is generally not about annihilation. War is about obtaining an objective. It is about advancing a major interest. Democrats had a major interest in the Ninth District 2018 midterm. It was one interest with two sides, like a coin. Keep Mark Harris out of Congress and put Dan McCready in. It's as simple as that.

When Mark Harris ran out of both means and will, he would no longer be able to fight. Exhaust your opponent's means with endless investigations that require legal representation, and exhaust his will by smearing him and putting on a media circus. Part of the exhibits produced in the North Carolina-09 "evidentiary hearing" was a letter from the now-Democrat majority US House of Representatives stating that Mark would not be seated even if he was certified after the State Elections Board hearing. The Dems in Washington would need to run their own investigation. The Democrats employ this strategy over and over and over again. From President Donald Trump to Brett Kavanaugh to Congressman-elect Mark Harris, the strategy is the same. Wear down the means, wear down the will, and when both are running low, there will be little resistance. The tipping point will be reached at which the enemy simply cannot continue to fight. On Day 4 of the evidentiary hearing, over the technicality of document production, the tipping point came, and Mark Harris surrendered to the call for a new election.

I had never heard the term "document production" prior to undergoing this experience. Mark and I had never been placed under any type of a subpoena from a "quasi-judicial" body, or an actual judicial body for that matter. It is very important to understand the process of document production to understand what happened during the final day of the "evidentiary hearing" put on by the State Elections Board and the elections agency that answers to them.

A subpoena can request that an individual appear before a particular proceeding. Mark was subpoenaed individually to appear before the State Elections Baord for the "evidentiary hearing." A subpoena can also ask for documents that will be part of a grand jury investigation, or in this case, the State Elections Board investigation. The **Mark Harris for Congress campaign committee** was subpoenaed for documents with numerous search terms. The subpoena was issued to the **Mark Harris for Congress campaign committee.** Neither I nor Mark was individually subpoenaed for documents, yet we went above and beyond what was asked in a vague subpoena with more than 100 search terms, including first names and words like "stamp." We allowed our **personal** cell phones and emails to also be searched for terms responsive to the subpoena. If we were playing hardball with the State Elections Board and trying not to be cooperative, we would have searched only the business emails for Mark Harris for Congress, or fought the subpoena, as the agency did when it did not want to hand over its records to the US Attorney for a grand jury proceeding involving Immigration and Customs Enforcement.

It is also important to understand that there were three sets of attorneys involved in our case. The Mark Harris for Congress campaign committee, which was the entity technically involved in the hearing, had representation from two Raleigh, North Carolina law firms. Mark Harris individually also had a different attorney, David Freedman, from Winston-Salem, North Carolina. In other words, we had personal attorneys, and the campaign as an entity had different attorneys.

After the nine-member board that withheld Mark's certification was dissolved, there was no board for about one month. During that time, Mark Harris the individual filed a motion in court to get his certification via our personal attorney David Freedman. Meanwhile, a different law firm in a different city was preparing documents to submit to the elections agency on behalf of the Mark Harris for Congress campaign committee. All in all, there were three major law firms, none of them located where we lived in Charlotte, and not all in the same city with each other, who were involved with the preparation for this agency's evidentiary hearing. All had some experience with the State Elections Board. None had ever been involved in a situation where the elections agency put on a show trial like the one they rolled out against Mark.

There were lead attorneys and other attorneys assisting. There were attorneys doing document production and attorneys doing research. We as a team decided that our personal attorney, David Freedman, would actually argue our case for Mark's certification at the hearing. Since there would be examination and cross-examination of witnesses at the "hearing," our team thought David Freedman was the most experienced litigator in courtroom trials and was the best equipped to handle that task. That all made sense, but in another sense there were too many cooks in the kitchen and we were not in good shape to keep track of it all once Mark's severe illness put him in the hospital for the last two weeks of January prior to the February hearing.

One of the Mark Harris for Congress campaign committee attorneys stated at the "evidentiary hearing" that the subpoena for documents issued by the NCSBE would take four months to fulfill properly. The subpoena was issued December 1, 2018 for a hearing that was originally scheduled for December 11, 2018. Another Charlotte attorney whom we did not hire, but who looked at the subpoena, said exactly the same thing: it would take four months just to prepare documents.

Why would document production take four months? What is proper document production? In document production, your devices are searched for texts or emails that respond to the search terms in a subpoena. After the initial search, your attorneys go through the documents that respond to the query for the search terms and talk over things with you before submitting the documents to whomever has issued the subpoena. In our case, because of the time crunch, there was a three-step process. The law firm handling the document production for the campaign decided to use an E-discovery firm to speed the process. On December 6, 2018, a forensic computer company took data from our phones. They actually took my laptop for several days to get data from it, because I have had it for a number of years and it is a heavily encrypted MacBook Pro.

After data was captured, then the law firm had to print the documents and go through them with us as needed, followed by submission to the state elections agency. The act of submitting a document to the entity that issued the subpoena is called "producing" the document.

We submitted multiple productions of material to the state elections agency in a matter of about one month. In total, we submitted over 5,000 documents to the agency, but combed through many thousands more. According to an email from attorney John Branch, 130,000 documents responded to the query for all of the search terms. A sentence like "Andy, are you going to the Cumberland County GOP meeting?" would be pulled up based on the broad search terms of the subpoena the elections agency issued. That wasn't part of what actually needed to be produced, because it didn't have anything to do with the issue at hand.

In our case, the scope of the subpoena was a question as well. Since the Mark Harris for Congress campaign committee got the subpoena, we had discussions with our team about the time period of the subpoena. The agency wanted communication from January 1, 2016 to December 1, 2018. The Mark Harris for Congress campaign committee did not exist until July 4, 2017. You cannot produce documents for an entity that does not exist. The process of determining what documents will be produced also has legal considerations. One is attorney-client privilege. You are not expected to hand over documents involving communication with your attorneys.

In email exchanges with elections agency chief counsel Josh Lawson, John Branch of Shanahan-McDougal, PLLC in Raleigh expressed two concerns clearly and repeatedly. Representing the Mark Harris for Congress campaign committee, Branch twice expressed by email that document production would cover the dates that the campaign was in existence: July 4, 2017 to December 1, 2018, which was the date of the subpoena. At least two times Branch let Lawson know we were complying with the subpoena within the scope of the period of time that the Mark Harris for Congress Committee was in existence: July 4, 2017-Dec. 1, 2018. Branch also expressed concerns about the confidentiality of our documents, due to the portal that had been established for the public to access whatever documents the state elections board decided they wanted the public to see.

This was the same concern our son John had expressed to David Freedman. John wanted a heads up if his email was going to be produced to the agency, because that would mean it could possibly go public. He wanted to be prepared for that possibility.

Mark did not get the email thread between campaign attorney John Branch and elections agency attorney Josh Lawson about the document production until attorney Dudley Witt forwarded it to him Feb. 3, less than one week post-hospitalization for sepsis and two strokes. These are the emails in which Branch explains that the documents produced by his firm will cover the period July 4, 2017 to December 1, 2018. We had not been copied in on those emails initially.

Mark had previously had conversations with David Freedman about John's email and about two checks written to Patriots for Progress, the PAC started by Jeff Smith in 2014. Freedman's philosophy had been to submit everything. Somewhere there was a dropped ball and miscommunication between the attorneys, our son, Josh Lawson, and us. I don't think it is even clear that any one individual can be blamed for the fact that John's email was not produced, although attorney John Branch took the blame for it at the hearing, since Josh Lawson had sent him several emails asking him if document production was complete.

The most important fact about John's email was that if we wanted to hide it, we could have. There was a very simple way to do so, and that was to assert privilege. Our son was an attorney. John testified that if we had claimed that the document was privileged, he would not have ever spoken about it unless ordered to do so by a court. We had a perfectly legitimate and legal way to hide John's email forever. Instead, the miscommunication and confusion over the email's intended production led to a disastrous chain of events.

After John testified Wednesday afternoon, Mark and I had to get back to Charlotte. We had been told to prepare for a two-day hearing. We had prepared for three days. Now Marc Elias was talking about going into the following week. Exhaust the means, exhaust the will, and resistance gives way—the iron calculus of war. We did not have the option of staying in Raleigh, as our IV antibiotics were in the refrigerator at home. The pre-filled syringes were delivered about once a week to our home by the home health service Novant hospitals employs. Once a week, a nurse came out and checked the PICC lines and changed their tips. I flushed the lines twice a day, when I finished with the antibiotics. We got to Charlotte late and had to be up at 4:00 a.m. to be back in Raleigh for the hearing Thursday morning. I don't think either of us really slept.

We had no problem getting on the road early and arrived early at the North Carolina Bar Association. In the attorney room it felt like chaos. All of the attorneys were scrambling over producing additional documents. They were trying to explain what had happened. It was confusing and overwhelming. I understood that at some point a decision was made not to produce John's email because it was before the campaign existed. At some point in our conversation with our son Matthew on Tuesday night, Mark mentioned something about the email. He thinks he said to Matthew that John's email was not going to be an issue. I think I could have said over Mark's shoulder that John's email wasn't going to come up at the hearing, and Mark could have repeated that. It was late, and I don't really remember exactly what was said other than hearing from Matthew that John was going to testify.

When the hearing began, there was bickering between Mark Harris for Congress campaign committee attorney John Branch and elections agency attorney Josh Lawson. Branch accepted responsibility for mistakes in document production. Lawson was unforgiving. Branch was furious with Lawson. Marc Elias was pitching one of his fits over all of it. Immediately thereafter, Mark was sworn in to testify.

Agency Director Kim Strach began questioning Mark. Mark testified that in his decision to hire Dowless, "relationships said a lot." Mark believed that McCrae Dowless had built enough relationships within the county that people trusted him and trusted his GOTV program with absentee-ballot request forms.[3] Strach immediately began asking Mark leading questions based on her foregone conclusion that Dowless was guilty of a widespread ballot harvesting operation. She did it by throwing out quotes from John Harris's email.

Strach: Your son is sort of, when I read it I sort of—it sounds like to me a final pitch to you, to really think about this before you go forward. That's what it sounds like to me.

Mark: I would agree with that. That's exactly how I read it. That he said, "Good test is to see if you're comfortable with the full process he uses being broadcast on the news."

Strach: How do you feel about that sitting here today?

Mark: Well, sitting here four days into this meeting, my son was a good prophetic (sic) in his statement that day.[4]

The correct answer to Strach's question "How do you feel about that sitting here today?" is "I don't know, because McCrae Dowless has not been charged with anything criminal. I don't have all the facts. I wasn't given the opportunity to see evidence or witnesses presented this week ahead of time. My attorneys did not get to depose them to see if they are actually credible. My attorneys have barely been allowed to talk in this hearing. Their objections are shot down by a committee chair who is not a judge. This hearing does not follow standard courtroom procedure. Professional people have questioned the credibility of at least one of the witnesses already. I only know that in the past, elections have been certified based on the number of irregularities placed against the margin of victory, and you all have already demonstrated that you know that I won the election regardless of any of McCrae Dowless's activities. How do I feel sitting here today? That I should not even **be** sitting here, that's how I feel."

Mark cannot understand why I feel such anger toward the agency's 2018 Executive Director Kimberly Westbrook Strach. I know I shouldn't feel that way, but I do. I pray about it. I give assent in my head to the truth that she doesn't care what I think, and that my bitterness toward her harms only my own soul, but every day I still struggle to get past my angry feelings. I think this exchange helps me nail down why. The agency took Mark's trusting good nature and used it against him. He believed that things would work out, and he cooperated. We were warned by some familiar with processes such as these not to cooperate.

At first, Mark tried to speak cautiously or not speak at all, because he didn't know what might or might not have happened in Bladen County. He cooperated with their subpoena above and beyond what was required, the flub over John's email notwithstanding. He drove three hours to Raleigh and let them interview him. I let them interview me as well. Meanwhile the State Elections Board met behind closed doors; what they did produce publicly was designed to be damaging to Dowless and included no potentially exculpatory documents, for example the results of their 142 voter interviews. I'd like to see a chart that shows how many of those 142 voters said their ballots were taken. The agency used affidavits produced **by the Democrat Party of North Carolina** as evidence and even included an article from a left-leaning non-profit as part of an investigation report in the 2016 summary.

As Strach continued questioning Mark, she had to develop the only argument the agency could use to try to show that the election was "tainted." Since absolutely not one witness indicated that Mark Harris participated in or knew anything about ballot harvesting, the agency tried to show that somehow Mark Harris had missed some red flags. Somehow he didn't do enough homework. Somehow the whole thing was the fault of candidate Mark Harris who lived three hours away and had no idea about anything the agency had discovered during 2016. A full ten times Strach asked Mark about doing "due diligence." Thirteen times Strach or elections board members brought up "red flags" when questioning Mark. Michael Dickerson of the Mecklenburg County Board of Elections saw no red flags with the Dowless GOTV program **as described to him,** which was the same way it was described to us. John's email was the thin thread on which the board had to hang its supposition that somehow Mark should have known about alleged ballot harvesting.

Some of the questions were ridiculous. Strach once again asked Mark about 2016, when Dowless did GOTV for North Carolina State Senator Todd Johnson. "Did you call Todd Johnson and ask him what he knew about whether or not McCrae Dowless was collecting ballots as part of his program?"[5] What would Todd Johnson have said if Mark had asked him that? "Yeah, Mark... you know, I did know Dowless was doing illegal stuff but I used him anyway..."

Was she serious? Strach acted like normal daily life should be memorialized for a court case. That's not real life. When you are sitting on a sofa in a furniture store surrounded by several leading citizens of a town, you are not in a courtroom. The man you are there to meet is not on trial. If the guy has just described his GOTV program, and in that description he says explicitly that it is illegal to collect ballots and he doesn't do it, you are not going to turn around and ask, "Do you collect ballots?" The other men sitting on those sofas would think you had lost your mind. Yet these were the types of things Strach kept indicating Mark should have done if he were doing his due diligence.

At one point, Strach brought up Mark's checks to Patriots for Progress, which were written before the campaign started and attorneys for the campaign said could be considered donations to the Patriots for Progress PAC. Once the campaign opened, we paid Dowless directly and had zero dealings with the PAC. Strach asked Mark if he knew that Patriots for Progress was "non-compliant" at the time he wrote them checks in spring of 2017. She made it sound really dirty, as if Patriots for Progress was taking money under the table. Mark indicated that he did not know. When I turned over that rock, I found several worms writhing around in the dirt. If Mark Harris had checked the North Carolina campaign finance filings from Patriots for Progress in April of 2017 he would have seen:

- A letter from January 22, 2016 indicating Dowless was no longer a member of the PAC.
- A letter sent by the elections agency in March 2016 to Treasurer Crystal McLamb's home address instead of the business address for the PAC, a letter which never reached Crystal McLamb because she had been murdered in February 2016. The letter was returned with the word "deceased" written across the envelope.
- Another letter returned undeliverable because they used an incorrect home address for new treasurer Tabitha Joyce.
- An email response to an agency email from Tabitha Joyce providing her correct home address.
- More letters sent to the wrong address for Tabitha Joyce about missing reports.
- In April 2017 the PAC was still active. It was not terminated for failure to report until September of 2017. Not once did the agency get a non-compliance letter to the correct address for the PAC.

It was impossible for us, or anyone on our legal team, to be prepared for this type of commentary disguised as questioning without having some prior knowledge of what we would be facing. It has taken me two years to turn over all the rocks from board meetings, the 2016 investigation, news stories, Democrat propaganda, and testimony at the hearing.

Finally, Strach tried to lead Mark to the conclusion she was after all along—that he was somehow to blame for missing red flags about whatever ballot harvesting McCrae Dowless may have committed in Bladen County. For Mark to be made responsible, he had to conclude that Dowless collected ballots. Mark Harris had to pronounce McCrae Dowless, who had not yet been criminally charged with absolutely anything, guilty. Strach once again brought up our son's testimony to try to lead Mark to state her opinion as the answer to his question.

Strach: Your son said, "I think McCrae Dowless lied to them over and over and over." And my question for you is, do you believe that? [6]

Mark: Based on the testimony I've heard this week, absolutely.[7]

Our friend and Union County Commissioner Stony Rushing made an astute observation about this hearing. He said that the agency had to convince just one person that McCrae Dowless cheated, and that was Mark Harris. If Mark Harris could not believe that McCrae Dowless was possibly innocent of the allegations, Mark Harris would lose the will to keep fighting in the face of all the nastiness, the threat of further investigation by the US House, and all the media pressure, no matter how unfair the remedy of a new election was to him.

The State Elections Board changed its line of questioning after several board members questioned Mark about why he ignored "red flags," basically following the same line of questioning Kim Strach had just completed. Chairman Cordle testily asked, "Do you understand this investigation came from the staff of the State Board rather than from State Board members?"[8] Cordle was not on the nine-member board that withheld Mark's certification after Joshua Malcolm's motion, so I give him the benefit of the doubt, but the facts are clear. Mark's name was in the list of certified winners for 2018, which "staff" vouched for at the same meeting prior to Joshua Malcolm's motion to withhold certification.

Furthermore, the dogged work of WBTV's investigative team revealed that Joshua Malcolm had exchanged phone calls and texts with Democrat Dan McCready up to 48 hours prior to Malcolm's motion to pull Mark out of the list of certified winners. That was well after the SBI launched its investigation in early 2018. Chief Investigator Joan Fleming was aware that FBI and SBI agents were following up on allegations made by Jens Lutz eight months before Malcolm made his motion. Malcolm was also exchanging phone calls and texts with Lutz. A Republican member of that nine-member board has said on the record he had no idea that Joshua Malcolm was about to make that motion and he had received no briefings on any irregularities prior to the Board's entry into closed session on November 27. Those are facts.

Chairman Cordle now changed directions, asking Mark if he had been informed by anyone prior to John's testimony that John was going to testify. This question absolutely amazes me, as if the State Elections Board somehow had a right to keep all witnesses and evidence secret from our team and from Mark himself.

Mark answered that he found out in a conversation with his youngest son the night before John testified. Chairman Cordle asked if Mark knew at that time that John's emails had not been produced.

Mark answered, "I did not. It was my understanding—we had talked about those emails earlier; myself and Mr. Freedman had spoken about those emails back in December, and it was my understanding that, I mean that the documents were all going to be produced."

The hearing moved on and some other board members continued questioning Mark. Then Josh Lawson began to question Mark about the timeline of document production. I could see that Mark was getting a bit confused by the questioning. I was getting confused. It seemed to me that Lawson was being deliberately obscure.

Lawson asked, "So did you believe that those emails were part of the evidence in this case?"[9]

Mark answered, "I thought they were part of—I thought they were documents that would be discussed in this case."[10]

Lawson then asked, "Did you tell anyone throughout this past week that you believed that those documents were not part of the evidence in this case?"

Mark answered, "Did I tell anybody—excuse me. Clarify the question again."[11]

An exchange ensued between Lawson and Mark in which Mark repeatedly stated that he couldn't recall telling anyone that. Mark also clarified that he heard "this week" that they had not been produced yet. Mark was testifying on Thursday, and the phone call with Matthew was Tuesday. Many things were discussed about John and the documents over the course of those couple of days in between. Regarding what he may or may not have said to anyone about the documents, Mark did not take a firm stance. It is so clear from the transcript that he is not trying to deceive anyone. Josh Lawson continued asking him about the documents and what he may have said or not said about them, despite Mark's statements that he could not recall. Mark said, "I'm not denying that I could have said that... I just don't recall."[12] After a few more board members asked questions, Cordle said it was almost time for lunch. He asked Marc Elias if he wanted to get started or wait. Elias wanted to proceed.

Now it was Marc Elias's turn to cross-examine Mark. I was nervous about that. I remember another warning our son John had given. "Dad will not be in shape to face Marc Elias so soon after this illness." As Elias began his questioning, it was clear the avenue he would take. He was going to chase rabbits about a thousand things. He began to ask Mark about his educational background, and decision-making processes at the church. Shortly into Marc Elias's questioning, our attorney interrupted. He said that he would like a short recess and would like to meet with the Board in chambers. Cordle called for a lunch break.

We knew something was wrong, but we were not sure exactly what. I knew that somehow I had been made aware that the emails from John were not being produced, but I don't know when I got that piece of information. It might have been on the day of my interview with the agency investigator Joan Fleming and Director Kim Strach. We were supposed to have an attorney meeting that day in Raleigh, but Mark was too sick to go with me. I met alone with one of the campaign attorneys and one of our personal attorneys.

When the recess was called, we all went into our "attorney room" where we normally had lunch. My recollection of the approximately one hour we were in that room is like an impressionistic painting. Memories are thrown in thick, blurry strokes on a canvas of fear, anger, and pure exhaustion. I had now reached a point where I had no appetite at all and could not eat. Our son Matthew called me and said that Mark had told him that John's emails were not going to be part of the hearing. An attorney with Freedman's firm was on a laptop trying to prove that they had indeed told Mark the email from John would not be produced. That absolutely enraged me. We were fighting for our lives and Mark was falling into a state of a bit of confusion, but not intentional deception.

Voices were raised, including mine. I told them that I had expressed the concern that Mark would not be ready for this. Opinions were divided on what we should do. Some thought it was time to call for a new election; others thought not. At any rate, Mark would have to correct the record to say that he was wrong when he couldn't recall telling anyone that John's email would not be an issue. Matthew's call had indicated that Mark had told him that he didn't think John's email was going to come up.

Jason Williams came into the room. He was justifiably angry over the idea that we would have a new election. By that time, I was crying hysterically. After Jason became so upset, I tried to pull myself together and have a calm conversation about options. Our attorney was extremely concerned about potential perjury charges if Mark did not correct the record. Mark was more than ready and willing to correct the record.

Our attorney was also extremely concerned about the next-level investigation by the US House, which he assured us would be a thousand percent worse than this hearing. At some point we asked if everyone could leave us alone. Mark and I were seated next to one another at the large conference table. My resistance was gone. My will was exhausted. I didn't see how we could keep surviving on no income while we fought through another investigation. I said that maybe the fact that now both of our boys' names had been dragged into this thing was a sign that it was time to give up. We called everyone back in. One of the attorneys helped draft a statement that would accomplish correcting the record, and in which Mark would state that if it would restore public confidence, he was agreeing to a new election.

And so, in a 5-0 vote, after Mark Harris gave up, the State Board voted to overturn the 2018 congressional midterm for the Ninth District of North Carolina based on the fourth and most ambiguous legal standard available: "Irregularities or improprieties that occurred to such an extent that they taint the results of the entire election and cast doubt on its fairness." According to criminal charges filed against McCrae Dowless and others in Bladen County a few months later, the extent of the irregularities in the 2018 Harris-McCready race was ten ballots.

Could someone please define "cast doubt on its fairness" for me?" Perhaps fairness is judged by perfection. An election can be considered fair only if no irregularities occur. That would mean no one voted outside of his/her precinct, no voting machine issues occurred, no felons voted, and no illegal aliens voted. That would mean every audit came out perfectly in terms of numbers of ballots printed vs. numbers of ballots accounted for. According to Kim Strach's performance in the Mark Harris Show Trial, perfection would also mean that election security was perfect at every poll. It would mean that every election worker followed to the letter the most up-to-date procedures. Can that standard be proven for every race in North Carolina's 100 counties in every single election? Are candidates responsible for that?

Or perhaps fairness must be judged only in light of the sins of the past. Is it fair for certain groups of people who can point to historical oppression to break the law, but not fair for others? When a Democrat group allegedly collects ballots, it's about the intent of the voter. When McCrae Dowless allegedly collects ballots, it's about the law against collecting ballots. Perhaps that is the standard of fairness.

Or is fairness perhaps judged by numbers of irregularities? Is there some type of formula to determine where the threshold will be? 282,717 total votes were thrown out in the decision to order a new election in North Carolina's Ninth Congressional District. There are ten criminal charges of improper collection and mailing of absentee ballots in that election. Even the state's most damning witness against Dowless, Lisa Britt, testified that no votes were changed in the congressional race. Mark Harris won the election.

There used to be a clear standard to determine the fairness of an election. That standard was indeed based on the number of irregularities, and the threshold was enough affected votes to change the outcome of the election. Until Joshua Malcolm successfully convinced the rest of the North Carolina Board of Elections and Ethics Enforcement that Mark Harris should be removed from the list of county-certified victors awaiting the Board's final approval, the standard was the election results. Joshua Malcolm had preached that standard over and over. He made a motion against Governor Pat McCrory's election protests using that standard. Protests "should be dismissed because there was not substantial evidence of a violation of election law or other irregularity or misconduct sufficient to **cast doubt on the results of the election.**"[13] Those are Joshua Malcolm's words, not mine. Those are Joshua Malcolm's words, and McCrae Dowless is charged with collecting and mailing thirteen ballots across three election cycles.

When you hear the trivia that the 2018 North Carolina Ninth Congressional District midterm is unique because it was overturned... pause and think. There is a reason for that. The reason is not because it is the first time there have been allegations of impropriety, contract workers who allegedly didn't play by the rules, or mishandled absentee ballots improperly witnessed or mailed in North Carolina elections. The reason is the spectacular success with which Democrats with deep pockets played a propaganda game. The reason is that an agency set its eyes on targeting a political operator already under criminal investigation because they were so disgusted by both his alleged actions and his hubris in bringing a protest before them in 2016. The reason is that after over a year without income, coming off a two-week hospital stay and straight into a show trial, with his attorney panicking and talking about the US House investigation yet to come, and his wife beside him choking out a few words between heaving sobs about how Elias was going to try to destroy him and Chairman Cordle wouldn't stop it, and that their children were getting dragged into the mess, Mark Harris finally gave up. For the rest of our lives, both of us will regret that moment of weakness.

I wish I had taken John's speculation more seriously and sternly warned Mark not to pursue a relationship with McCrae Dowless. I regret not doing more to try to keep Mark from being at that hearing. It would have been better for him if he had just accepted an adverse ruling. But I don't hate McCrae Dowless. I don't even know if he is guilty or not. There are just too many questions. I will accept responsibility for any mistake that I made along the long journey that did not end well. But there is one thing I will not accept. There is one suggestion I very strongly resent, and that is the suggestion that somehow I should have held it together at the hearing because, while Mark had been quite ill, I had not been ill.

I endured everything from pornographic comments about me as a "servant lover" because of Dan McCready's attack ads on our Christian beliefs, to screaming college kids with phones shoved in my face, to being called the perfect example of white privilege. I did the long rides crammed in the back of a truck up and down highway 74. I did the kid recording me on his phone in his pocket and trying to bait me as I worked the polls. I downloaded the absentee list at 5:00 a.m. and very often was the first person at the campaign headquarters at 9:00 a.m. And when Mark was sick, I lost basically three weeks of sleep. I learned to clean out a bloody tube sticking out of his side, and I learned how to give antibiotics intravenously. And now I had to find full-time employment after being out of the classroom for a decade.

I was done. I am human. I had endured a lot, but I was not going to endure my son in a witness chair on a Dan McCready attack ad in the new election. It is a sign of how sick our society is that we tolerate that.

As we drove home, Stony Rushing called. Stony was our staunchest public supporter through the whole ordeal. He even drove to Raleigh to see the "hearing" in person. If Mark wasn't going to run, Stony would. But those decisions would have to be finalized soon. I had always said boldly that if there was a new election, of course Mark would run, and we would kick McCready's little you-know-what. That was all before I watched Mark in bed for a week in intensive care. Now I wasn't sure. He had been told he had to have surgery. Two surgeries, actually. Jason, although so hurt and angered by our decision to give up, quickly forgave us for that weakness and showed great kindness as we traveled in his car back to Charlotte.

When we got home, we took our stuff upstairs. I fell face down onto our bed with my head at the foot of the bed and started crying again. Mark sat slowly down in the rocking chair in the corner of the room. It had belonged to his parents. He asked me what I thought about him running in the new election. I sobbed while lying on our bed repeating over and over, "I can't go through another election...I can't do this again."

Mark sat very still. The rocker wasn't moving. He said with such kindness, "Now's not the time to talk about this." In the next couple of days, we made some rational decisions. We would call his personal physician to get his interpretation of how urgent the colon resection surgery was. We would talk to our children. We would do what we have always done in the thirty-three-year history of our family. We would make a decision together.

After hearing from his surgeon and physician that his colon surgery had to happen immediately or another life-threatening bout of infection could potentially occur, we made the painful decision not to run. We endorsed our friend Stony Rushing in the Republican primary. Immediately the pressure started from the GOP Establishment to go back on that endorsement. Mark has always been a man of his word and kept his commitments, and he was not going to go back on his endorsement. With a colon surgery four weeks away and a heart procedure a few weeks after that, it was clear our focus for 2019 would be on getting Mark back in shape for whatever God had in the future.

Mark signs the Values Voter Bus sponsored by Family Research Council's FRC-Action just before Election Day, 2018.

Dec. 2, 2018, Indian Trail NC Christmas Parade. We had nine events across the district within the first week after Mark's certification was withheld.

Congressman-Elect Mark Harris

Mark's Official Congressional Portrait was taken during orientation. We were in Washington for the second week of orientation when the North Carolina Elections Board voted to withhold his certification. An operative working for the campaign was later charged with improperly mailing 13 ballots to the Board of Elections.

CHAPTER 20

ALL THE GREAT THINGS

I WAS TRULY shocked to discover how many people watched the evidentiary hearing held by the State Board of Elections. More people than I ever would have imagined watched or listened to all of it, or almost all of it. And that brings me to my final point, and the reason I don't give up in despair.

The American people are still a good people.

I have been both humiliated and humbled by the events surrounding the 2018 midterms and their aftermath. Both feelings do their work in us spiritually, I suppose. The worst of it all was knowing that to calloused assassins like Marc Elias, the destruction of our lives was all in a day's work: amusing and gratifying. The end justifies the means. Dan McCready got a new election, and Mark Harris went down. Mission accomplished. Checkmate.

But the best far outweighs the worst.

So many of those who watched the hearing, so many of those who supported Mark, in fact so many we barely know or don't even know at all, have been so incredibly kind. These acts of kindness have been so numerous I cannot possibly name them all.

Before the "hearing," a GOP activist from another part of the state mailed me a book we had chatted about for no more than five minutes at the North Carolina GOP convention along with a very substantial check for Mark Harris for Congress and a kind note.

After we arrived home from the hearing exhausted and defeated, as I was preparing to give Mark his evening dose of intravenous antibiotics, one of the loveliest flower arrangements I have ever seen arrived at the house, a gift from my Republican Women's Club, the Mecklenburg Evening Republican Women. Our next-door neighbor brought a meal over.

The next day one of our major volunteers who became a good friend during the campaign, Mary Chapman, came to the house equipped with a plan she and two of my other dear friends had developed to take care of us in what they knew would be a rough few days. I cried as I hugged her. I felt absolutely helpless. We had let everyone down by not continuing to fight.

Food came, cards came…it was like a death had occurred, and truly it had. A dream that Mark and many others had worked incredibly hard for had died before our eyes. Our small Bible Study group from First Baptist Charlotte gave us a huge basket filled with grocery store gift cards, toiletries, and goodies. The gift cards from them and other family and friends got us through until we both started working full time again.

Pastor Mike Whitson of First Baptist Indian Trail, a church ridiculed by an arrogant young McClatchy reporter after Mark preached there, called nearly every day to talk through things. We would put the phone on speaker and Pastor Whitson would help us try to walk through and process what had happened. I'm still trying to process what happened. At one point I recall that Pastor Whitson took an almost stern tone with Mark and admonished him not to give in to despair.

A note came from the mother of a student I taught for one year over a decade ago. She remembered that I had been kind to her when her son was experiencing some troubles, and she let me know that she was thinking and praying for us, and that her son had become an aerospace engineer.

Our campaign staff stayed in touch. They had stayed with us through it all, despite the fact that the controversy had personally hurt and embarrassed them too, not to mention shutting off new career opportunities that should have come with the win. Even new staff we had planned to hire in DC hung in as long as they could through the drawn-out process of waiting for the hearing, despite not having paychecks at that point.

Getting through the hurdles of the first day back to work, first day back to church, first day back to a GOP event—all of these were made bearable because of the kindness and decency of others. Most tellingly, the kindness was not limited to those with whom we agree politically. Strangers approached Mark, sometimes even hugging him, expressing that though they disagreed with him politically they felt he had been royally screwed over. A work colleague who is 180 degrees from me on the abortion issue simply put her arms around me on my first day back after the hearing, saying, "I just have to hug you."

For the first time in our lives, we were facing a mountain of debt. We had Mark's $7,900 out of pocket maximum to pay for his hospitalization, which actually turned into almost $9,000 and counting, and two more medical procedures on the horizon, one of which would come under new insurance, since our COBRA expired March 31, 2019. Despite the National Republican Congressional Committee paying the legal bills of the team representing the campaign, we had acquired over $100,000 of personal legal bills, all at a time in which Mark had been unemployed for over one year and I was working a part-time job with minimal hours so that I could participate in the campaign.

A final slap in the face was the campaign debt Mark had ordered our consultant Andy Yates not to acquire. We would have to raise the money to pay that off, since that represented vendors who had performed legitimate services for us. Mark wrote a fundraising letter to try to help retire the campaign debt, which for him may have been the bitterest of the bitter pills he has had to swallow. To our amazement, people gave, again often enclosing beautiful personal notes with their checks.

The American people are still a good people.

While organizing files to write this book, I ran across a letter I wrote to our supporters on behalf of Mark's campaign around the end of 2017, just as we were packing up the last of Mark's office at First Baptist Church Charlotte. We had just seen the movie *Darkest Hour* over the Christmas holidays. *Darkest Hour* tells the story of Winston Churchill in the days leading up to the Battle of Britain, when Hitler would attempt to conquer the British Isles. In my darkest hour, an hour marked not by success but by failure, the sentiments I expressed during the scary-but-hopeful early days of the campaign just after Mark left his position at First Baptist Charlotte still hold true:

> A recent date night to see the new movie *Darkest Hour* prompted a flurry of Google-searches for Winston Churchill quotes. My favorite: "All the great things are simple, and many can be expressed in a single word: freedom, justice, honor, duty, hope."…

I continued:

> Challenges, change, and the wisdom required to navigate them help us clarify our thinking and we realize what Churchill meant. The great things are simple…We are already loving meeting the people of the 9th at football games, festivals, parades, and dinners. Your community-mindedness, creativity, work ethic, and patriotism inspire us.

I would add today, "and your kindness blesses us."

The American people are still a good people.

The American people deserve better that what they are currently getting from our public institutions. A hideous creature has replaced the constitutional operation of our republic through our elected officials. Like the mythical Greek Hydra, it has multiple heads, and when one is cut off, another seems to grow back in its place. A government bureaucracy so large that the people's elected representatives can't even understand, much less control it, selectively robs citizens of their civil liberties and is seldom held accountable for its actions. Congress is becoming an afterthought, its constitutionally assigned powers submerged in the swamp, as it increasingly exists simply to oversee the bureaucracy. People see no need to vote, because they intuitively understand that the real power lies with the bureaucracy. They deal on a daily basis with the Social Security Administration, the Veteran's Administration, the Internal Revenue Service, or the folks at Medicare/Medicaid. Most can't name their Congressman.

The American people are still a good people, but I fear that they do not adequately recognize the threats to our republic.

As for us, we are trying to move on with our lives. Mark had surgeries in March and June 2019, and was released by his neurologist in September 2019. We feel very blessed that he has made a full recovery. In the two and a half years since Election Day 2018, we have never been interviewed by anyone in law enforcement. Even at the "evidentiary hearing" no adverse ruling was found against Mark himself. There was the media circus, and the misleading McClatchy description of our son's guesswork based on an Excel sheet, but not an adverse ruling—just a new election for Dan McCready.

In July 2020, the district attorney who filed charges against McCrae Dowless and some of his GOTV workers took the rare step of issuing a press release declaring that her investigation was completed as far as Mark Harris was concerned, and that he would not be criminally charged. Usually district attorneys do not trouble themselves to make public announcements when charges are not filed. Amazingly, as only God could orchestrate it, the same day that District Attorney Lorrin Freeman issued her statement, WBTV in Charlotte broke the story that Joshua Malcolm had been in contact with Dan McCready just 48 hours prior to Malcolm's motion to deny Mark his certification.

Our campaign manager, Jason Williams, was chosen to be the North Carolina State Director for the Faith and Freedom Coalition.

In 2020, Jason was named "State Director of the Year" by the organization.

McCrae Dowless was indicted on several criminal counts stemming from 2016-2018 in two separate indictments in February 2019 and July 2019. All of his other clients are currently serving in their elected capacities. All. Of. Them. There is a spectrum of possibilities regarding the activities of McCrae Dowless in the 2018 midterms. Dowless has not been charged with fraudulently voting unsealed absentee ballots, nor has he been charged with destroying ballots. If he illegally mailed absentee ballots on a small scale, he is guilty of a crime, but seems to be one of very few people who have ever been charged for it.

No one from the Democrat Bladen County Improvement Association, which garnered over 600 absentee-by-mail votes for its candidates in 2016, and whom Lisa Britt testified shared office space with Dowless and had an informal "stick to your own turf" agreement with him, has ever been charged with possession of absentee ballots or any other crimes in connection with its GOTV program after being warned ahead of time to lie low in 2018.

North Carolina Board of Elections Executive Director Kim Strach was fired not long after the February hearing for focusing too much on investigations and not enough on securing elections up front, specifically in relation to security in Bladen County. She later got a cushy job as the "director" of the search process for the new president of the University of North Carolina system.

The appointed North Carolina Board of Elections as it stood when certification was withheld from Mark was dissolved by a judge in December 2018 and went their separate ways. Bob Cordle, who presided over the February 2019 "hearing" as the new chair of the new State Board, was forced out when he told an off-color joke at a public meeting.

Joe Bruno of WSOC TV in Charlotte won multiple journalism awards for serving as the mouthpiece for the propaganda and leaks fed to him by the Democrat Party of North Carolina.

Nick Ochsner, a twenty-nine-year-old reporter who lived in Bladen County for a time in order to investigate, become head of the investigative team at WBTV in Charlotte and has a book deal. He continues his pursuit of the truth as Democrats fight him every step of the way. WBTV has thus far been willing to pay for protracted court fights to get to the records that will shed light on what really happened with Jens Lutz, Joshua Malcolm, and Dan McCready.

Joshua Malcolm resigned his job as chief counsel at the University of North Carolina-Pembroke when investigative reporter Ochsner and WBTV sued the university and its president for its failure to hand over texts, emails, and phone logs showing communication between Malcolm and "Democrat operatives" in Bladen County in 2018. Malcolm stated that the resignation was unrelated to the lawsuit.

The leaders of the North Carolina Republican Party at the time of our crisis, Chairman Robin Hayes and Executive Director Dallas Woodhouse, went down in a much larger scandal involving pay-to-play donations reported to the FBI by the new Republican insurance commissioner of North Carolina, Mike Causey. Hayes, who was so insistent that a new primary was necessary for the Ninth District based on unverified false rumors, was indicted on five charges and pled guilty to one count of lying to the FBI. Woodhouse announced that he was stepping down after the North Carolina-GOP Convention that year.

Robert Pittenger still travels the globe holding "security conferences." He had to retract an email he sent containing lies about candidate Dan Bishop in the special election Republican primary after the threat of legal action by Bishop. Pittenger endorsed former Mecklenburg County Commissioner Matthew Ridenhour, who lost his 2018 re-election bid for county commissioner, in the special election primary instead of Bishop.

Dan McCready lost his do-over by an even wider margin than the original election. Up until Election Day in September 2019, he claimed votes were stolen from him. Once again the media was stunned at his loss, opining about what a great ground game he had. He immediately got an op-ed placed in the *New York Times* about how Dems could follow his strategy to win in 2020. News flash: he lost. Twice. The Bladen County Improvement Association stood down again, and McCready got twelve absentee-by-mail votes in Bladen County in the special election, compared to 258 in 2018. McCready continues to claim that he stood up to voter fraud.

And on Tuesday September 17, 2019 Dan Bishop, a former Republican state senator, was sworn into the 116th Congress as the Representative for North Carolina's Ninth Congressional District only one week after Election Day, two weeks before the process of certifying his election was completed under North Carolina law. Congress constitutionally controls its own members and can seat them whenever it wants.

What did the citizens of North Carolina get out of the new election? Fourteen million additional dollars spent, nine months without representation for the Ninth Congressional District, and 90,000 fewer votes cast, and yet the result was essentially the same. In Bladen County in 2016 Robert Pittenger got 58 % of the vote. In Bladen County in 2018, Mark Harris got 57 % of the vote. In the September 2019 special election, Dan Bishop got 59 % of the vote in Bladen County. In Bishop, the Ninth District got a Republican Congressman with views on public policy that are very similar to those of Mark Harris. The Ninth District as it existed in 2016 and 2018 is now gone, due to another court order to redraw district lines after lawsuits filed by Progressive groups.

I voted for Dan Bishop as soon as the polls opened at 6:30 a.m. the day of the Special Election and cried in the car on my way to work after I voted. I then vowed that those would be my last tears over this nightmare. Our daughter and her children and our youngest son, his wife, and his children came over for dinner on Election Day. The days were still just long enough to play outside after dinner, and even though it was hot and humid, we were all outside so that the toddlers could "play tennis," which for them means they stand there with rackets held up in front of them while an adult tosses a ball into the racket so they "hit it."

It was one of those moments when you stand outside of yourself. As I did so, I saw giggles and small running feet and the flowers in the front yard and two young adults with enough sensitivity to drive over and be with their dad on a tough day. Their lives are busy, their kids would get thrown off schedule on a weeknight, but they wanted to be with their dad.

I looked over at Mark taking it all in. The day before the election he had his final appointment with the neurologist. He was alive and he was healthy. I thought of the classic Christmas movie *It's a Wonderful Life*. Like George Bailey who never got to see the world, but remained forever stuck in Bedford Falls, Mark Harris had lost a dream. It was, and still is, a crushing blow. Mark Harris lost a lot, but not the great things that are simple. He did not lose his relationship with his Heavenly Father or his family. He did not lose his human decency, or the support of so many who wanted him to be their Congressman. Mark Harris did not lose the great things that can summed up in three words: faith, hope, and love. Mark Harris, with a mountain of bills still in front of him, and a lot of grieving still ahead, seemed to me at that moment to be like George Bailey, the richest man in town.

At the end of the day, I hope McCrae Dowless gets a fair trial, but the person I care about is my husband. I care about our supporters and the people who voted for Mark. I'm furious about the double standard. I'm furious that in 2016 the State Elections Board dismissed protests because the election's outcome was not in question, despite compelling evidence that the Bladen Improvement Association PAC harvested ballots and voted ballots instead of voters. Meanwhile, in 2018, a lame-duck appointed board caved to Joshua Malcolm and withheld Mark's certification despite clear evidence that the number of ballots in question did not swing the outcome of Mark's victory.

I'm furious that we have empowered bureaucratic agencies with powers like law enforcement and courts, without any of the accountability or constitutional protections for citizens that are built into the judicial system.

The events surrounding the 2018 midterms are starting to feel like a dream. They don't hurt as badly, and although I still feel angry when I talk about it, I don't feel the toxic kind of rage I used to feel. God doesn't owe me any explanations, because He is Sovereign, but I still pray for all the truth to come out.

The first week of October after the special election, my phone rang. Our son John called to say he would like to come for a visit the following weekend. I didn't ask any questions. One week later, on Saturday night October 12, 2019 our family sat around our big square farmhouse table eating pasta together. All six of my grandchildren were there—five scrunched on a bench and one still in a high chair.

Mark's brother called him a few days later to see how the visit had gone. I was listening from the kitchen, and I could tell Steve had asked Mark whether we had been able to clear any of the air with John on the hearing, or why he had decided it was the right time to resume communication with us. I heard Mark tell Steve that the only thing that mattered to him was that his entire family sat with their feet under our table. That made me happy. Very happy.

All the great things are simple.

And the greatest of these is love.

This seems to be the missing ingredient in our national discourse right now. You can label it "confirmation bias," you can label it "hate," you can label it with any other terms you want to put on it, but the truth is, we can't find the truth.

We are being manipulated by the political class, the people who make money from the political class, special interest groups, and the media. Those who have a financial stake into dividing us into our various tribes are using us for their own ends. And that has caused us to forget that we are all Americans.

Through debate and even bloodshed, over 200 years we have continued to reform ourselves to come ever closer to the great ideal expressed in our Declaration of Independence: "All men are created equal." All of us are endowed by our Creator with certain unalienable rights. Among these are life, liberty, and the pursuit of happiness.

In 2020 Marc Elias once again argued in court on behalf of leftist groups, seeking to change North Carolina's election procedure. In a stunning move that caused the Republicans on the State Elections Board to immediately resign, the State Board voted to settle the lawsuit with Elias by allowing changes in absentee-by-mail procedure. In other words, the appointed State Elections Board bypassed North Carolina's duly enacted statutes and created new election law all by itself.

Governor Roy Cooper won re-election after marching in the streets with Black Lives Matter and making a couple of fear-mongering commercials about wearing face masks. His wife had to publicly apologize for flipping off a family (including children) of Trump supporters and bragging about it on Facebook.

Donald Trump won North Carolina in 2020, just as he did in 2016.

As it did with North Carolina Governor Pat McCrory in 2016, the mainstream media dismissed allegations of election irregularities mounted by Donald Trump's campaign. This time, however, the tone was harsher. Those who even mentioned any of the alleged irregularities were dismissed as crazy and cancelled from the culture and social media platforms. *The Washington Post* took fake news to a new level when it claimed that Trump demanded that Republican officials in Georgia "find" votes for him.

On January 6, 2021 the nation was shaken when the United States Capitol was stormed. The images shocked and dismayed the world.

Faith, hope, and love are being replaced with rancor, hatred, violence and despair on all sides.

Those who are actively working to destroy the government that operates under our Constitution, the document that has given us the means to bring about peaceful change, don't want us to remember that we are all Americans. That means nothing to them. But it means something to me. I hope that it means something to you.

EPILOGUE: By Mark Harris

MORE THAN TWO years have passed since the unbelievable turn of events which would affect our lives forever. If I were to say that everything turned out rosy, and all is well that ends well, I would be less than truthful. It has been a journey filled with far more questions than answers, beginning on November 27, 2018 with the refusal of the North Carolina State Board of Elections to certify my election to the 116th Congress representing North Carolina's Ninth District. Throughout this book you have been invited into some of the most notable parts of this journey. But I have to confess; over these last two years I have asked repeatedly, how could this have played out differently? How should this have played out differently?

Even within the last few weeks, a stranger stopped me during a visit to a local restaurant. The person said to me, "You're Mark Harris, who ran for Congress?"

"Yes I am."

"Well sir, I'm probably as far to the left as you are far to the right on the political spectrum. But sir, I just want to say, I am sorry—you got ripped off."

Unfortunately, that was the scene played out over and over again, from the barber shop to the grocery store, to just about everywhere. Americans know injustice when they see it. They recognize right from wrong, and beyond political ideology, at the end of the day, the vast majority of Americans will stand for what is just and what is fair, given the opportunity. So, how could this whole situation have been handled in a far better way?

The passage of time has allowed me to reflect on so many things about this tragedy. The first stop I had to make was to reflect upon what I might have done differently. They say hindsight is 20/20. Some have asked me if I regretted ever going to Bladen County in the first place, meeting McCrae Dowless, and the other folks we have come to know there. So many politicians in a district like NC-09 would simply ignore a numerically insignificant county. Furthermore, they would point out that I only had part of the county's seventeen precincts in my district. Twelve of the seventeen precincts of Bladen County were in the Ninth District.

But truthfully, I have never regretted going to Bladen County, meeting McCrae Dowless, or getting to know many other folks throughout the county. Long before I ran for Congress I had ministered in Bladen County, preaching at First Baptist Church Dublin for revival and other special occasions. I have stated so many times over these last two years that more than anything, I really just want to know what happened. I know what the North Carolina Democratic Party claimed happened. I read the newspaper articles and listened with great pain to the media narratives that were being circulated. But what did McCrae Dowless do?

I have read the indictment and seen the charges that have been leveled against him by the state. I have heard him deny the charges. I have heard him through his attorney's statements maintain his innocence. For more than two years he has yet to receive his day in court to present his case. I only know what he told me his program involved, and that it did not involve taking ballots to mail. If Dowless is guilty then I believe it will be proven in time before a jury of his peers. If he is not guilty, and turns out to be a victim of a targeted attack that cost him his credibility, his work that he loved, and the embarrassment that no innocent man deserves, then the weight of this tragedy will be heavier than anyone ever imagined.

There cannot be proper reflection for myself about how this might have been handled better than to consider the conversations with my son John. I should have somehow listened and sought ways to have him more involved in the campaign. There were so many things that folks in the media were looking to pounce upon, and the relationship of a dad and his son, who happen to love each other very much, became a tremendous target. I am so grateful that the love and commitment to each other in our family runs deep enough to withstand whatever fiery darts some may try and launch at us.

The headline with the picture of me broken while my son John was on the witness stand was the low point of just how sick the game had become to those determined to get a new election. John had just said some incredibly gracious things about Beth and me, and his love for us in response to a question from David Freedman. At that emotional moment for me, the photographer for the *Charlotte Observer* shot the photograph. The headline was such a lie in that it implied that I had foreknowledge of what Dowless was being accused of doing. President Trump had it right when he calls them "Fake News."

John's advice to me in our email exchanges clearly indicated that he had concerns about me using Dowless, but those concerns were all based on spreadsheets and ways he thought ballots came into the Board of Elections. Marc Elias and Kim Strach wanted to make a big deal about John's position as an Assistant US Attorney for Eastern North Carolina. Surely, he must have known something. Surely, I would have done what he said, and not engaged Dowless's GOTV program.

It seems lost on the media that at the time we were discussing Dowless in April of 2017, John was not yet a US Attorney. He was an attorney with Smith-Anderson law firm in Raleigh. He did not even start the process of being recruited, interviewed, and brought on to the US Attorney's Office until late summer/early fall of 2018. He began his new job in October 2018, just one month before the November election. John has been very careful to keep himself out of the Dowless investigation, even breaking off communication with us for a time to prevent any conversation about the case.

To say that I am extremely proud of John Harris is an understatement. He is a phenomenal attorney, but an even more phenomenal husband, father, and son. He is a man who seeks to honor God and do what is right. For that I will always be grateful.

Another thing I wish I had done better would have been to speak to media more frequently. In the first few days following the State Board's decision to withhold my certification on November 27, 2018, I was in the midst of orientation for the 116th Congress. It was a very important time of learning how everything operated, and an important time of meeting with various members who might help with coveted committee assignments. Looking back, I should have caught the first plane back to Charlotte on that Tuesday evening, November 27th. I should have made my way down to Bladen County on Wednesday to find out what was going on.

Instead, we remained in DC for the remainder of orientation. This left Wednesday for the media to begin their efforts, Thursday for the North Carolina Democrat Party to come forth with their questionable affidavits, and Friday for the State Elections Board to meet again and make a final decision to withhold my certification of the elections victory, take jurisdiction and schedule an "evidentiary hearing" for December.

All these things transpired with me in Washington, getting updates by phone in between meetings. Even upon returning to Charlotte on Friday night, we were advised to avoid the media, and say nothing at all to them. Unfortunately, having little experience in this part of the political arena, I needed a public relations expert more than attorneys at this point. We had won the election by always being available, out front, leading, answering questions to the best of my ability. These decisions ultimately were mine to make, and in the moment where things were coming from all directions, I should have taken the leadership reins.

I think there are also a number of things the State Board of Elections should have handled differently. In fact, there are a number of questions some two years later that have not been answered, and may indicate a cover-up of great proportions. WBTV, the CBS affiliate in Charlotte, has invested a great deal in legal fees simply trying to get documents released that involve some key players in this whole saga. These documents are being held by public institutions who are subject to Freedom of Information Act requests. They involve Josh Malcolm, the State Elections Board member that began this whole turn of events on November 27, 2018 with his motion to withhold my certification as Congressman for NC-09.

While Malcolm resigned his post as chief legal counsel for UNC-Pembroke, the university, the State Board of Elections, and Democrat Attorney General Josh Stein's office are fighting desperately to keep certain documents out of the hands of WBTV. They have already had to turn over records that proved that Joshua Malcolm and Dan McCready communicated by texts and phone five times in the days before Malcolm made his motion.

What did McCready know, and when did he know it? Again, questions no one in the media other than WBTV has been willing to ask. Most in the "fake news" realm would just as soon ignore stories about Malcolm's communications, which likely violate NC General Statutes concerning ethics for State Elections Board members.

But what should the State Board of Elections have done? How should they have handled this situation differently? First of all, we raise the question that if McCrae Dowless was some kind of suspect in the State Board's investigation by spring 2018, why was my campaign never notified? Furthermore, if the concerns dated back to November 2016, why did the same board that included Joshua Malcolm certify my primary election victory?

Following the General Election held on November 6, 2018, not one single formal complaint was filed in Bladen County, or any of the other seven counties of NC-09, or to the State Board of Elections. So again, why would the Board of Elections not simply notify the Harris campaign and give us opportunity to deal with any questionable behavior being alleged? Unfortunately, no one was made aware of potential issues until Malcolm's motion to withhold my certification blind-sided us November 27th.

Another critical way that the State Board of Elections should have handled things differently would have been to follow its own precedent by certifying the race, and allowing me to be sworn in to the 116th Congress. They could have then turned over all their information and evidence to law enforcement. Law enforcement must actually bring charges. Officers of the courts are actually the ones who put a person on trial. The Constitution guarantees certain things such as due process and equal protection under the law.

The production put on by the State Board of Election was one of the best examples of bureaucratic overreach with the absolute worst of results. Without due process, without protection of basic rights, an unaccountable agency is able to play prosecutor, judge, and jury, while anyone they choose to go after has no right or ability to even know any evidence or witnesses that may be presented. To any thinking person who saw the production created by Kim Strach, State Board members, and Marc Elias and the Perkins Coie team, the proceedings brought new meaning to the phrase "Kangaroo Court."

Why should they have followed through on certification on November 27, 2018 and turned over evidence they had already gathered, or would gather in the weeks to come, to prosecutors? That was the way the State Board had always tended to operate. If there was evidence of mishandled ballots, or ballots improperly mailed by someone other than the voter's relative or guardian, the question had always been, and should always be, "were there enough mishandled ballots to change the outcome of the election?" The answer in my case was overwhelmingly no. In fact, when the indictment against McCrae Dowless was issued, his charges of taking possession of thirteen ballots over three elections included only two in my race with Dan McCready. Really? For two ballots, which he has pled not guilty to taking, 282,717 voters had their ballots thrown out so that there could be a new election. If McCrae Dowless is guilty of any criminal action, I trust in a court of law, he will be proven as such. He will be held accountable. But there is simply not evidence that his alleged actions could have changed the outcome of the election.

What would have happened had the State Board of Elections followed its own precedent in the 2018 midterms? I would have been sworn in on January 3, 2019, as a member of the 116th Congress. The State Board staff would have continued their investigation, turning over evidence to the Wake County District Attorney and the US Attorney's office. It is likely that indictments handed down by the Wake County District Attorney's office in February 2019 and July 2019 charging Dowless and his associates would have been handed down either way.

It is also very important to mention that in July 2020 the Wake County District Attorney, a Democrat I might add, actually put out a press release to media outlets across North Carolina stating that after a year and a half of investigation at federal, state, and local levels, there was no evidence to support any criminal charges against Mark Harris concerning the Ninth District Congressional race in 2018. Thus, all the speculation, accusations, and gossip were abruptly ended. Had the process been followed, I have no doubt investigations of me would have continued, as a sitting Congressman. But I had nothing to hide, and in July 2020 I would have been in my first re-election campaign when the news came that I had been cleared and nothing found.

I often wonder if Dan McCready ever regrets the way he played the game. McCready had no problems raising campaign cash, and had he only conceded defeat in 2018, and not pursued a new election, thus disenfranchising so many voters, he likely could have brought a challenge for a rematch in 2020. It would have been another epic battle. As fate would have it, between a severe illness that was no doubt affected by the character assassination I was undergoing, and the board's decision to vote for a new election, Dan McCready lost to Dan Bishop in the special election of September 2019. In less than a year, rising Democrat star McCready became a two-time loser.

While things could have been handled differently by me, by the State Board of Elections, and even by my opponent Dan McCready, we cannot go back and change the events as they unfolded. We can, however, learn from events that turn our lives upside down. In fact, it was in the balance of the year 2019 when God used a very unusual book to help me reflect on what I had just come through.

Beth and our children knew the disappointment in my heart and soul. It wasn't difficult to detect. I knew they were worried about me physically following my illness of January 2019 and subsequent surgeries. I knew they were worried about me emotionally. They had seen their husband and father put it all out there, give it everything he had to fulfill a dream. They had celebrated with me, and how grateful we were together for all that God was doing. Then, they saw it all evaporate, and along with it personal attacks and accusations which they knew didn't describe me. To watch what it was doing to their husband and dad was disconcerting.

I knew they were also worried about me spiritually. I make no bones about it, I trusted God with all my heart, but frankly, I was wondering where He was in all this. Surely, at any moment, something was going to break, and God was going to step in and clear the deck, making sense out of all this. But it wasn't happening, or at least I wasn't seeing it.

It was in the midst of this time that my youngest son, Matthew, and his family came over to our home. Matthew shared a book with me by an author I didn't know. It was a study of the book of Lamentations in the Bible. I had never really studied Lamentations. The book was entitled *Dark Clouds, Deep Mercy*, authored by Mark Vroegop. The book is filled with great insights. Vroegop takes you inside the personal family struggle that he walked through. The way he describes what it means to "lament" and to open up and pour your heart out to God was extremely helpful and freeing for me at this critical juncture.

But it was when I came to the chapter in the book covering Lamentations 3:22-33 that God opened the windows of my heart and blew a fresh breeze of new air into my life. In fact, weeks after reading this section, I appeared on a radio program with pastor, author, and speaker Dr. David Chadwick. I told David during the interview how this third chapter of Lamentations had been used of God to speak to me so clearly in the midst of my storm. I explained that Vroegop in Lamentations 3:22-33 reminded me of four of the most important things I nearly forgot in my storm.

First, God's mercy never ends. We are reminded in the great hymn "Great is Thy Faithfulness," of these verses from Lamentations 3:22-33. "Through the Lord's mercies we are not consumed. Because His compassions fail not, they are new every morning; Great is Your faithfulness." This phenomenal description of God's love is such a reminder of this covenant love, this gracious love.

Secondly, I was reminded that waiting is not a waste. In other words, I desperately wanted to understand what had happened. I desperately felt I needed to know why this had happened. And yet, I was getting no answers, and I was becoming impatient. But in Lamentations 3: 25-27, we are told that the Lord is good to those who wait for Him, and to souls who seek Him. He even reminds us in verse 27 that the discipline of God in our youth only trains us and equips us, just as it did the prophet Jeremiah in his youth. So, I would come to understand that I just needed to wait on the Lord and place my hope in Him.

Thirdly, I learned in verses 31-32 that the final word has not been spoken. For me personally, this was something I truly needed to know in my heart. You see, I had sought to walk with God, and to submit to His will and His plan for my life. Entering the political arena was not really what I had planned on doing from the time I surrendered to God's call to preach in June 1987. Up until that point, I was headed to law school, and was very interested in public policy. But from that time in 1987, I had never looked back, and running for political office was not in my list of things to do. But in 2012 through a series of events not the least of which was the Marriage Amendment and Family Research Council's Watchmen on the Wall Conference, God began a work in my heart, shaping me for leadership in the public policy arena.

I knew it in my heart. Others recognized it, and began encouraging me. Beth and I entered the arena truly seeking God's guidance and desiring to fulfill His plans and purposes. To see it all build to the moment of victory and then crash before our eyes, I needed to hear Lamentations 3: 31-32: "For the Lord will not cast off forever. Though He causes grief, yet He will show compassion according to the multitude of His mercies." Mark Vroegop reminded me that at some point in the future the final word will be spoken. God will intervene in His time, and He always makes things right.

The fourth and final lesson I learned from this study on Lamentations was that God is always good. Lamentations 3:33 states, "For He does not afflict willingly, nor grieve the children of men." It really is true. God is always good. And when my clouds seemed the darkest, it was true that I discovered God's deepest mercy.

Reflecting on life's troubling experiences can create some of the richest moments in a person's life. I can tell you with all certainty that even two years and some months after the events discussed in this book, I am unable to say I wouldn't trade this experience for anything. Sometime in the future, perhaps God will bring me to that place. I am just not there yet. I still believe I was rightfully elected in November 2018 and should have served in the 116th Congress. Coming to fully understand what, and who, was behind the plan to keep me from representing the people of NC-09, God Himself knows, and only in His will and His time will that truth be revealed.

What I recognize and know today is that God is always good. He has blessed me with restored health beyond anything I could have hoped for or imagined. He has blessed me with Beth, three incredible children and their spouses, and now nine of the most beautiful grandchildren God ever created. Welcoming new babies Charlie, Harris, and Virginia in 2020 and 2021 has been a reminder that God's mercies are always new.

He has blessed me with an incredible church family to pastor and shepherd at Trinity Baptist Church in Mooresville. In the midst of all of that, He has blessed me with a national leadership role, serving as Vice-President for Association of Churches and Ministries of the

Family Research Council in Washington, DC. Instead of one of 435 members of Congress, God has seen fit to use me to help raise up pastors and believers across the nation to bring our country face to face with the founding vision of the nation born out of the foundational principles for life and liberty found in the Word of God.

Years ago in the midst of a different life challenge, I was introduced to a song written by Babbie Mason and Eddie Carswell that sums up our journey.[1]

> God is too wise to be mistaken
> God is too good to be unkind
> So when you can't see His plan
> When you don't understand
> When you can't trace His hand
> Trust His heart.

NOTES

Chapter 1: Leap of Faith

1. Rick Klein, "Obama: 'I think same sex couples should be able to get married'," ABC News, May 9, 2012, https://abcnews.go.com/blogs/politics/2012/05/obama-comes-out-i-think-same-sex-couples-should-be-able-to-get-married.

Chapter 2: Swing State

1. Chris Cillizza, "The Nine Swing States of 2020," *Washington Post,* Web Edition, April 16, 2012. https://www.washingtonpost.com/blogs/the-fix/post/the-9-swing-states-of-2012/2012/04/16/gIQA-BuXaLT_blog.html.
2. Scott Horsely, "Obama Tries to Charm Youth Vote with College Stops," *National Public Radio*, April 24, 2012. https://www.npr.org/2012/04/24/151258192/obama-tries-to-charm-youth-vote-with-college-stops.
3. Billy Ball, "Director of State Board of Elections Married to Lawyer Defending Controversial Voting Reforms," *Indy Week*, Oct 15, 2014, https://indyweek.com/news/director-state-board-elections-married-lawyer-defending-controversial-voting-reforms/.
4. Ball, "Director."

Chapter 3: The 2014 Senate Race

1. All voter statistics are from the North Carolina State Board of Elections. Election and voter data can be accessed at http://www.ncsbe.gov.
2. Greg Hernandez, "Obama: Rainbow White House was 'One of the most special moments of my presidency'," *Gaystar News*, June 10,2016, https://www.gaystarnews.com/article/obama-rainbow-white-house-one-of-the-most-special-moments-of-my-presidency/#gs.LVrqeYg.
3. Michael Gordon, "Federal Judge Overturns NC Same-sex Marriage Ban," *Charlotte Observer*, October 10, 2014, https://www.charlotteobserver.com/news/local/article9200495.html.

Chapter 4: A Fateful Phone Call

1. "What you need to know about voting in the 2016 primary," WRAL.com, last modified July 13, 2018, https://www.wral.com/voting-in-the-2016-primary/15233649/. According to the article, absentee ballots would be mailed starting January 25, which was three weeks prior to the ruling.
2. "28270," United States Zip Codes, accessed June 21, 2019, https://www.unitedstateszipcodes.org/28270/.
3. "Quick Facts: Bladen County North Carolina," United States Census Bureau, accessed June 21, 2019, https://www.census.gov/quickfacts/bladencountynorthcarolina.
4. Observer Editorial Board, "Robert Pittenger's No Good, Very Bad Endorsement Day," *Charlotte Observer*, June 7, 2016, https://www.charlotteobserver.com/opinion/op-ed/article82098422.html.

Chapter 5: We Will Destroy You and Your State

1. Minutes of the Charlotte City Council, Charlotte City Council, February 22,2016, Charlotte.

2. NC House Bill 2, NCGS Chapter 115-C, Article 37, Chapter 143, article 81 (2016) (repealed 2017), accessed December 29, 2018, https://ncleg.net/sessions/2015e2/bills/house/html/h2v4.html.

3. Julia Marsh, "Bill de Blasio ships NYC homeless to North Carolina despite ban against state," *New York Post*, December 6, 2019, https://nypost.com/2019/12/06/bill-de-blasio-ships-nyc-homeless-to-north-carolina-despite-ban-against-state/. This was also reported in the *Fayetteville Observer*.

4. "North Carolina congressman: Charlotte protesters hate white people," wral.com, last modified July 12, 2018, https://www.wral.com/nc-congressman-charlotte-protesters-hate-white-people-/16039184/.

5. Hope Ford, "North Carolina Board of Elections vote to recount 94,000 votes in Durham County," WFMY.com, last modified November 30, 2016, https://www.wfmynews2.com/article/news/local/nc-board-of-elections-vote-to-recount-94000-votes-in-durham-county/83-359671688.

6. Elena Schneider, "North Carolina Governor Alleges Voter Fraud in Bid to Hang On," *Politico,* November 21, 2016. https://www.politico.com/story/2016/11/north-carolina-governor-alleges-voter-fraud-in-bid-to-hang-on-231728.

Chapter 6: The Pot Boils Over

1. Schneider, "North Carolina Governor."

2. Eliot C. McLaughlin, "NC Governor wants recount, though signs point to Cooper win," CNN.com, last modified November 22, 2016, https://www.cnn.com/2016/11/22/politics/north-carolina-governor-race-recount-pat-mccrory-roy-cooper/index.html.

3. Mark Binker, "State Board refers Durham election case to district attorney," WRAL.com, last modified October 13, 2016, https://www.wral.com/state-board-refers-durham-election-case-to-district-attorney-/16111651?.

4. Mark Binker, "Provisional Ballots Mishandled in Durham," WRAL. com, May 5, 2016, https://www.wral.com/provisional-ballots-mishandled-in-durham/15685134/.

5. Matthew Burns, "Durham Elections Worker Pleads Guilty to Altering Vote Counts in 2016 Primary," WRAL.com, Jan. 10, 2018, https://www.wral.com/durham-elections-worker-pleads-guilty-to-altering-vote-counts-in-2016-primary/17247689/.

6. Adam Entous, Devlin Barrett, and Rosalind Helderman, "Clinton Campaign, DNC Paid for Research that led to Russian Dossier," *Washington Post*, October 24, 2017, https://www.washingtonpost. com/world/national-security/clinton-campaign-dnc-paid-for-research-that-led-to-russia-dossier/2017/10/24/226fabf0-b8e4-11e7-a908-a3470754bbb9_story.html.

7. Schneider, "North Carolina Governor."

8. Lauren Horsch, "The Case of Missing Durham County Ballots Referred to SBI," *Indy Week,* November 9, 2016, https://indyweek.com/news/durham/case-missing-durham-county-ballots-referred-sbi/.

9. Kevin J. Hamilton, "Perkins-Coie letter," Board Book North Carolina State Board of Elections, November 20, 2016, 26. https://dl.ncsbe. gov/index.html?prefix=State_Board_Meeting_Docs/2016-11-19/.

10. Hamilton, "Perkins-Coie letter," 26.

11. Hamilton, "Perkins-Coie letter," 22.

12. "Minutes of the North Carolina State Board of Elections," North Carolina State Board of Elections Emergency Meeting, November 20, 2016. Raleigh, https://dl.ncsbe.gov/index.html?prefix=State_Board_Meeting_Docs/State_Board_Meeting_Minutes/2016%20SBOE%20Minutes/.

13. Ibid.

14. Secretary of State, North Carolina, "Business Listing for Politico Management Services, LLC," accessed November 16, 2019. http://www.sosnc.gov. PDF of the filing shows Dowless as a member.

15. "Patriots for Progress Campaign Finance Reports 2014 Organizational Report," July 14, 2014, https://cf.ncsbe.gov/CFOrgLkup/. Keywords: Patriots for Progress.

16. "Patriots for Progress Campaign Finance Reports: Third and Fourth Quarters 2014," https://cf.ncsbe.gov/CFOrgLkup/. Keywords: Patriots for Progress. Politico Management Services donated $2,347.32 to Patriots for Progress on 10-15-14.

17. "Statement of Organization 1-23-2016," Patriots for Progress Campaign Finance Reports, https://cf.ncsbe.gov/CFOrgLkup/. Keywords: Patriots for Progress.

18. Voter Look-Up Leslie McCrae Dowless, https://vt.ncsbe.gov/RegLkup/.

19. "In Re: Protest of Election of Leslie McCrae Dowless, Jr. before the State Board of Elections," North Carolina State Board of Elections, Dec. 3, 2016, Raleigh, 184, lines 19-20. https://dl.ncsbe.gov/index.html?prefix=State_Board_Meeting_Docs/2016-12-03/. Transcript_of_hearing.pdf.

20. Todd Johnson, 2015-2016 Campaign Finance Report, Disbursements, Federal Elections Commission, Washington, accessed March 15, 2021, 2. https://www.fec.gov/data/disbursements/?committee_id=C00613232&two_year_transaction_period=2016&data_type=processed.

21. All election results are from the NCSBE's official election results archive. http://www.ncsbe.gov. Search election results by year and county.

22. Eliza Castile, "Ralph Nader got the most Write-In Votes for President Ever," *Bustle*, Oct. 19, 2016. https://www.bustle.com/articles/190417-ralph-nader-got-the-most-write-in-votes-for-president-ever-but-election-write-ins-have-a-long.

23. "1996 Popular Vote Summary," Federal Elections Commission, accessed June 19, 2020, https://transition.fec.gov/pubrec/fe1996/summ.htm.

24. "Election Protest McCrae Dowless," Board Book, North Carolina State Board of Elections, December 3, 2016, 3 https://dl.ncsbe.gov/index.html?prefix=State_Board_Meeting_Docs/2016-12-03/. BoardBook_2016_12_03.pdf.

25. Brian Hehl, "Brian Hehl letter," Board Book North Carolina State Board of Elections, December 3, 2016, 7, https://dl.ncsbe.gov/index.html?prefix=State_Board_Meeting_Docs/2016-12-03/.BoardBook_2016_12_03.pdf.

26. Rick Henderson," Democrat Absentee Ballot Mill Alleged in Bladen County," *Carolina Journal* November 16, 2016. https://www.carolinajournal.com/news-article/democrat-absentee-ballot-mill-alleged-in-bladen-county/.

27. "In re: Protest of Election of Leslie McCrae Dowless, Jr.," 12-13.

28. "In re: Protest of Election of Leslie McCrae Dowless, Jr.," 216.

29. "In re: Protest of Election of Leslie McCrae Dowless," 241, lines 23-25.

30. "In re: Protest of Election of Leslie McCrae Dowless," 247, lines 9-11.

31. All election results are the official North Carolina State Board of Elections results as posted at https://er.ncsbe.gov/. Search by County: Bladen, Search by year: 2016.

32. "Bladen County Improvement Association-PAC finance reports 2016," https://cf.ncsbe.gov/CFOrgLkup/. Keywords "Bladen CTY IMPROV."

33. Ibid.

Chapter 8: Uncharted Territory

1. "Minutes of the North Carolina State Board of Elections and Ethics Enforcement," North Carolina State Board of Elections, Raleigh, March 27, 2018, 5, https://dl.ncsbe.gov/index.html?prefix=State_Board_Meeting_Docs/2018-03-27/.

2. Richard Fausset, "North Carolina's Guru of Elections: Can-Do Operator Who May Have Done Too Much," *New York Times*, December 8, 2018, accessed at https://www.wral.com/north-carolina-s-guru-of-elections-can-do-operator-who-may-have-done-too-much/18049309/.

3. "Affidavit of Bobby R. Ludlum," Exhibit 7.1.1.2, January 10, 2019, https://dl.ncsbe.gov/index.html?prefix=State_Board_Meeting_Docs/Congressional_District_9_Portal/.

4. David Hodges, "Bladen County Improvement Association President Says He was Tipped Off About Absentee Ballot Investigation," *News,* WBTV, February 26, 2019, https://www.wbtv.com/2019/02/26/bladen-county-improvement-association-president-says-he-was-tipped-off-about-absentee-ballot-investigation/.

5. "Bladen County Improvement Association-PAC finance reports 2018," https://cf.ncsbe.gov/CFOrgLkup/. Keywords "Bladen CTY IMPROV."

6. In 2016, the total of all contributions (individual and political party) to the BCIA PAC was $21,048. In 2018, the total of all contributions (individual and political party) to the BCIA-PAC was $10,400. Summary data for these reports was not available, so I totaled all contributions from individual quarterly reports.

7. I accessed the search warrants issued for McCrae Dowless at https://games-cdn.washingtonpost.com/notes/prod/default/documents/d1bedbcb-6a52-41c1-b380-14ab7003b763/note/a74e7cdc-7eeb-4f1e-9367-ed6606225f5f.pdf. Last accessed March 15, 2021.

8. "In the Matter of in re: Clark, in re: Cochran, Review of Emergency Motion to Stay Certification Pending Appeal in re: Bowen Transcript," Bipartisan State Board of Elections and Ethics Enforcement, Raleigh, May 3, 2018, 83, lines 10-12. https://dl.ncsbe.gov/index.html?prefix=State_Board_Meeting_Docs/2018-05-03/. SBE_Transcript_2018-05-03.pdf.

Chapter 9: Harris Stuns Pittenger

1. "Transcript in the matter of in re: Clark, in re Cochran, Review of Emergency Motion to Stay Certification Pending Motion to Stay Certification Pending Appeal in re Bowen, Before the State Board of Elections," North Carolina State Board of Elections, Raleigh, 74, lines 7-10, https://dl.ncsbe.gov/

index.html?prefix=State_Board_Meeting_Docs/2018-05-03/
SBE_Transcript_2018_05_03.pdf.

Chapter 10: Taking Down Goliath: The 2018 General Election

1. Katie Glueck, "A Democrat Who Talks Like a Republican Could Steal a Major North Carolina Race from the GOP,"*mcclatchydc. com*, June 5, 2018, https://www.mcclatchydc.com/news/politics-government/election/article212479684.html.
2. Ibid.
3. G. Scott Thomas, "How North Carolina's Job Growth Stacks Up to National Stats," Charlotte Business Journal," November 18, 2016, https://www.bizjournals.com/charlotte/news/2016/11/18/north-carolina-job-growth-unemployment-october2016.html.
4. Opposition research on Dan McCready performed for the Harris campaign estimated his net worth at $32 million in 2018. McCready's financial disclosure to Congress indicated that his total yearly income from his company fell in the $1-5 million range.
5. http://vt.ncsbe.gov. This is a search-by-name voter look-up tool on the official elections board website for the state of North Carolina.

Chapter 11: We Will Not Consent

1. "Sebastian Kielmanovich, Assistant US Attorney letter," North Carolina State Board of Elections and Ethics Enforcement, Raleigh, September 7, 2018, https://dl.ncsbe.gov/index.html?prefix=State_Board_Meeting_Docs/2018-09-07/ EDNC Letter 09062018.pdf.
2. "State Subpoenas," North Carolina State Board of Elections and Ethics Enforcement, Raleigh, September 7, 2018, https://dl.ncsbe.gov/index.html?prefix=State_Board_Meeting_Docs/2018-09-07/. State_Subpoenas_[PUBLIC]_pdf.
3. Executive Director Kim Strach, "Numbered Memo 2018-09," North Carolina State Board of Elections and Ethics Enforcement, Raleigh, September 7, 2018, https://dl.ncsbe.

gov/index.html?prefix=State_Board_Meeting_Docs/2018-09-07/ numberedmemo2018-09.pdf.

4. "Board Meeting North Carolina State Board of Elections and Ethics Enforcement Audio File pt. 1," North Carolina State Board of Elections and Ethics Enforcement, Raleigh, MP3, 05:09, September 7, 2018, https://dl.ncsbe.gov/index.html?prefix=State_Board_Meeting_Docs/2018-09-07/ State Board of Elections and Ethics Enforcement, 9-7-18 MP3 Pt. 1.

5. "Board Meeting North Carolina State Board of Elections and Ethics Enforcement, Audio File pt. 1," 06:00.

6. "Board Meeting North Carolina State Board of Elections and Ethics Enforcement Audio File pt. 1," 09:12.

7. "Malcolm Motions Transcript," North Carolina State Board of Elections and Ethics Enforcement, Raleigh, September 7, 2018, https://dl.ncsbe.gov/index.html?prefix=State_Board_Meeting_Docs/2018-09-07/. Malcolm_Motions_Transcript_09072018.pdf.

8. Brant Clifton, "North Carolina-09: The Cover-Up Comes to a Crescendo," *The Daily Haymaker*, March 4, 2019, https://daily-haymaker.com/nc-09-the-cover-up-comes-to-a-crescendo/.

Chapter 12: Sprint to the Finish

1. Michael Kruse, "They're Angry, Disgusted, and Out for Revenge. But Do They Exist?" *Politico*, October 25, 2018, https://www.politico.com/magazine/story/2018/10/25/north-carolina-ninth-district-mcready-harris-2018-221914/.

2. Nick Ochsner, "Prosecutor Won't File Charges Against Harris in North Carolina-9 Probe," *NC District 9 Investigation*, WBTV, July 15, 2020. https://www.wbtv.com/2020/07/15/prosecutor-wont-file-charges-against-harris-nc-probe/.

3. "Board Meeting North Carolina State Board of Elections and Ethics Enforcement Audio File pt. 1," North Carolina State Board of Elections and Ethics Enforcement, Raleigh, MP3, 13:45, November 27, 2018 https://dl.ncsbe.gov/index.

html?prefix=State_Board_Meeting_Docs/2018-11-27/State Board Meeting 2018_11_27_pt1.mp3.

4. John Lewis telephone interview with author, June 18, 2020.

Chapter 13: Freeze the Target

1. "In Re: Investigation of Election Irregularities Affecting Counties Within the 9th Congressional District Before the North Carolina State Board of Elections and Ethics Enforcement 2019," Exhibit 7.1.2.2 Affidavit of Emma Shipman, October 29, 2018, 13, https://dl.ncsbe.gov/index.html?prefix=State_Board_Meeting_Docs/Congressional_District_9_Portal/.

2. "In Re: Investigation of Election Irregularities Affecting Counties Within the 9th Congressional District Before the North Carolina State Board of Elections and Ethics Enforcement, 2019." Evidentiary Hearing Transcript Day 2, North Carolina State Board of Elections and Ethics Enforcement, February 19, 2019, 329-334, https://dl.ncsbe.gov/index.html?prefix=State_Board_Meeting_Docs/Congressional_District_9_Portal/.

3. *Bladen Journal Online* staff writers, "Election Board Members Face Complaints for Third Time." *BladenJournal.com*, January 21, 2020. https://www.bladenjournal.com/news/29578/election-board-members-face-complaints-for-third-time.

4. Steve Harrison, "North Carolina Democratic Party Submits Affidavits of Bladen County Voters who Claim Wrongdoing," *National Public Radio.* November 29, 2018, https://www.wfae.org/post/nc-democratic-party-submits-affidavits-bladen-county-voters-who-claim-wrongdoing#stream/0.

5. The Democrat Party's letter, the five affidavits, and Lucy M. Young's ballot container were all in the submission from Wallace and Nordan LLP on behalf of the Democrat Party of North Carolina to the North Carolina State Board of Elections and Ethics Enforcement, November 29, 2018. I accessed them at "The Democratic Party's Letter,"WRAL.com, https://wwwcache.wral.

com/asset/news/state/nccapitol/2018/11/29/18029262/NCDP_
Letter_to_Penry-DMID1-5gywvc30z.pdf.

6. The Democrat Party's Letter, WRAL.com.

7. Elections and Ethics Enforcement Act, North Carolina General Statute 163 A-1181. Re-recodified as Chapters 120C, 138A, and 163 by Session Laws 2018-146, s.3.1.(a),(b). https://www.ncleg. gov/Laws/GeneralStatuteSections/Chapter163A.

8. There was also a Libertarian on the ballot. The numbers used reflect the percentages of votes cast only for either Mark Harris or Dan McCready.

9. http://er.ncsbe.gov.

10. Travis Fain, "Bladen Town Hall Sparks Passion over 9th District Results, Little New evidence of Fraud," WRAL.com, Raleigh, December 12, 2018. This article was submitted as exhibit 123 in the Dan McCready Campaign Exhibits for the Evidentiary Hearing held by the North Carolina State Board of Elections. https://dl.ncsbe.gov/index.html?prefix=State_Board_Meeting_Docs/Congressional_District_9_Portal/.

11. Ibid.

12. "In Re: Investigation of Election Irregularities Affecting Counties Within the 9th Congressional District Before the North Carolina State Board of Elections and Ethics Enforcement, 2019, Evidentiary hearing transcript Day 1" North Carolina State Board of Elections and Ethics Enforcement, Raleigh, 222. https://dl.ncsbe.gov/index.html?prefix=State_Board_Meeting_Docs/Congressional_District_9_Portal/.

Chapter 14: Malcolm Takes Charge

1. "In Re: Investigation of Election Irregularities Affecting Counties Within the 9th Congressional District Before the North Carolina State Board of Elections and Ethics Enforcement, 2019," Exhibit 2.2.2.1, North Carolina State Board of Elections and Ethics Enforcement, Raleigh, December 19, 2018, https://

dl.ncsbe.gov/index.html?prefix=State_Board_Meeting_Docs/
Congressional_District_9_Portal/.

2. "Cindy Lewis, hand-written letter accompanying Patriots for
   Progress 2016 4th Quarter campaign finance filing," The date on
   the letter is Jan. 22, 2016. Investigation documents by the state
   elections agency incorrectly give the date March 21, 2016. https://
   cf.ncsbe.gov/CFOrgLkup/. Keywords: Patriots for Progress.

3. Joan Fleming, Summary of the investigation into Patriots for
   Progress IE PAC and BCIA IEPAC, Exhibit 2.2.2.1, North Carolina
   State Board of Elections and Ethics Enforcement, Raleigh,
   January 23, 2018. The summary is dated January 23, 2018, but
   was not publicly available until December 19, 2018. https://
   dl.ncsbe.gov/index.html?prefix=State_Board_Meeting_Docs/
   Congressional_District_9_Portal/.

4. Marshall Tudor Memo November 29,2016," Summary of the
   Investigation into Patriots for Progress, Exhibit 2.2.2.1,, North
   Carolina State Board of Elections and Ethics Enforcement,
   Raleigh, January 23,2018, 53. The summary was post-
   ed on the 9th District portal December 19, 2018. https://
   dl.ncsbe.gov/index.html?prefix=State_Board_Meeting_Docs/
   Congressional_District_9_Portal/.

5. "Complaint of Brenda M. Register October 20, 2016,"
   Summary of the Investigation into Patriots for Progress, Exhibit
   2.2.2.1, North Carolina State Board of Elections and Ethics
   Enforcement, Raleigh, January 23, 2018, 55. The summary was
   posted on the 9th District Portal December 19, 2018. https://
   dl.ncsbe.gov/index.html?prefix=State_Board_Meeting_Docs/
   Congressional_District_9_Portal/.

6. "Bladen County Improvement Association-PAC finance reports
   2016"

7. "Linda Johnson-Baldwin Letter October 4, 2016," Summary
   of the Investigation into Patriots for Progress, Exhibit
   2.2.2.1, North Carolina State Board of Elections and Ethics
   Enforcement, Raleigh, January 23, 2018, 58. The summary was

posted on the 9th District Portal December 19, 2018. https://dl.ncsbe.gov/index.html?prefix=State_Board_Meeting_Docs/Congressional_District_9_Portal/.

8. "Joan Fleming/Marshall Tutor, Interview of Linda F. Johnson-Baldwin November 15, 2016," Summary of the Investigation into Patriots for Progress, Exhibit 2.2.2.1, North Carolina State Board of Elections and Ethics Enforcement, Raleigh, January 23, 2018, 63. The summary was posted on the 9th District Portal December 19, 2018. https://dl.ncsbe.gov/index.html?prefix=State_Board_Meeting_Docs/Congressional_District_9_Portal/.

9. "Joan Fleming/Marshall Tutor, Interview of Michael Cogdell November 14, 2016," Summary of the Investigation into Patriots for Progress, Exhibit 2.2.2.1, North Carolina State Board of Elections and Ethics Enforcement, Raleigh, January 23, 2018, 15. The summary was posted on the 9th District Portal December 19, 2018. https://dl.ncsbe.gov/index.html?prefix=State_Board_Meeting_Docs/Congressional_District_9_Portal/.

10. "Fleming/Tutor Interview of Michael Cogdell," Summary, 16.

11. "Fleming/Tutor Interview of Michael Cogdell," Summary, 16.

12. Bladen County Improvement Association –PAC finance reports, Quarters 1-4 2016.

13. Fleming, Summary, 5.

14. Ibid.

15. Ibid.

16. Ibid.

17. Ibid.

18. Fleming, "Summary," 3.

19. Fleming, "Summary," 6.

20. "Joan Fleming/Marshall Tutor Interview of Michael Cogdell," Summary, 15.

21. "Forensic Laboratory Report," Summary of the Investigation into Patriots for Progress, Exhibit 2.2.2.1, 168. Charlotte Ware, forensic handwriting specialist, positively identified 167 write in votes in no more than 7 different handwritings.

22. Alaina Malcolm resides at the same address as Joshua D. Malcolm, who in December 2018 was named chair of the North Carolina State Board of Elections and Ethics Enforcement. From August-November 2018 Alaina Malcolm was on the payroll of the North Carolina Democratic Party Federal Account and was paid a total of $2,537.56 during those months. Campaign Finance Report, Democratic Party of North Carolina Federal Account, Federal Elections Commission, Washington, 2017-2018, last accessed March 15, 2021. https://www.fec.gov/data/disbursements/?committee_id=C00165688&two_year_transaction_period=2018&data_type=processed.

Chapter 16: The Mark Harris Show Trial

1. North Carolina State Board of Elections and Ethics Enforcement, Order of Proceedings in the matter of investigation of election irregularities affecting counties within the 9th Congressional District.
2. "In re: Investigation of Election Irregularities Affecting Counties Within the Ninth Congressional District Day 1," 16-17.
3. Ibid.
4. "In Re: Investigation of Election Irregularities, Day 1," 7, lines 10-14.
5. "Strach letter to acting U. S. Attorney John Stuart Bruce," Exhibit 2. 2. 2. 1.1, North Carolina State Board of Elections, Raleigh, North Carolina, January 30, 2018, https://s3.amazonaws.com/dl.ncsbe.gov/State_Board_Meeting_Docs/Congressional_District_9_Portal/.
6. "In Re: Investigation of Election Irregularities, Day 1," 15, line 25.
7. "In Re: Investigation of Election Irregularities, Day 1," 26, lines 4-5.
8. Davidson College Facebook page, accessed 4-9-2019.
9. "In Re: Investigation of Election Irregularities, Day 1," 30-32.
10. "In Re: Investigation of Election Irregularities, Day 1," 43-44.
11. David Hodges, "Bladen County Improvement Association President Says He was Tipped Off about Investigation," February 26, 2019.
12. Ibid.

13. "In Re: Investigation of Election Irregularities, Day 1," 54.
14. "In Re: Investigation of Election Irregularities, Day 1," 82, lines 19-24.
15. "In re: Election Irregularities, Day 1," 138-139.
16. "In Re: Investigation of Election Irregularities, Day 1,"160-162.
17. "In Re: Investigation of Election Irregularities, Day 1," 91.
18. "In re: Investigation of Election Irregularities" transcript uses the spelling "Goins." From her signature and BCIA financial records the spelling is "Guions."
19. "In Re: Investigation of Election Irregularities, Day 1," 221.
20. Ncsbe.gov/absentee data file 2018 general election, November 6, 2018, entry for Precious Nicole Hall.
21. "In Re: Investigation of Election Irregularities, Day 1," Exhibit 17, Absentee Ballot Container Envelope for Precious Nicole Hall.
22. Absentee data file entry for Precious Nicole Hall.

Chapter 17: On Ice

1. "In Re: Investigation of Election Irregularities, Day 1," 185.
2. "The Democrat Party's Letter," WRAL.com.
3. "In Re: Investigation of Election Irregularities, Day 2," 255.
4. "In Re: Investigation of Election Irregularities, Day 2," 282.
5. "In Re: Investigation of Election Irregularities, Day 2," 286
6. "In Re: Investigation of Election Irregularities, Day 2," 303-308.
7. "In Re: Investigation of Election Irregularities, Day 2," 308, line 18.
8. "In Re: Investigation of Election Irregularities, Day 2," 309, lines 4-25.
9. "In Re: Investigation of Election Irregularities, Day 2," 318, lines 13-15.
10. "In Re: Investigation of Election Irregularities, Day 2," 318, lines 16-19.
11. "In Re: Investigation of Election Irregularities, Day 2," 315, line 7.
12. "In Re: Investigation of Election Irregularities, Day 2," 361, lines 1-6.
13. "In Re: Investigation of Election Irregularities, Day 2," 361, lines 14-17.

14. "In Re: Investigation of Election Irregularities, Day 2," 353, lines 15-20.
15. "In Re: Investigation of Election Irregularities, Day 2," 353-354.
16. "In Re: Investigation of Election Irregularities, Day 2," 355.
17. "In re: Election Irregularities, Day 1," 22, line 17
18. "In re: Election Irregularities, Day 1," 22, lines 18-22.
19. "In re: Election Irregularities, Day 2" 417, line 6.
20. "In re Election Irregularities, Day 2," 391-392, 449.
21. "In Re: Investigation of Election Irregularities, Day 3," 658, lines 10-13.
22. "In Re: Investigation of Election Irregularities, Day 2," 659, lines 16-25.
23. "In Re: Investigation of Election Irregularities, Day 2," 545-548.
24. "In Re: Election Protest of Leslie McCrae Dowless." The date is posted next to the entry for the transcript.

Chapter 18: A Surprise Appearance

1. "In Re: Investigation of Election Irregularities, Day 3," 682, lines 5-8.
2. "In Re: Investigation of Election Irregularities, Day 3," 684, lines 1-8.
3. "In Re: Investigation of Election Irregularities, Day 3," 684, lines 13-19.
4. "In Re: Investigation of Election Irregularities, Day 3," 684, lines 20-21.
5. "In Re: Investigation of Election Irregularities, Day 3," 685, line 6.
6. "In Re: Investigation of Election Irregularities, Day 3," 685.
7. "In Re: Investigation of Election Irregularities, Day 3," 686, lines 2-4.
8. "In Re: Investigation of Election Irregularities, Day 3," 686, lines 13-17.
9. "In Re: Investigation of Election Irregularities, Day 3," 688.
10. "In Re: Investigation of Election Irregularities, Day 3," 688, Lines 17-19.
11. "In Re: Investigation of Election Irregularities, Day 3," 433-434

12. "In Re: Investigation of Election Irregularities, Day 3," 699, Lines 11-15.
13. "In Re: Investigation of Election Irregularities, Day 3," 699. Lines 18-19.
14. Evidentiary hearing transcript, pp. 776-777.
15. "In Re: Investigation of Election Irregularities, Day 3," 712, lines 7-9.
16. "In Re: Investigation of Election Irregularities, Day 3," 717, lines 1-5.
17. "In Re: Investigation of Election Irregularities, Day 3," 717, lines 11-16.
18. "In Re: Investigation of Election Irregularities, Day 3," 720, lines 6-7.
19. "In Re: Investigation of Election Irregularities, Day 3," 784, lines 5-18.
20. "In Re: Investigation of Election Irregularities, Day 3," 794.
21. Brant Clifton, "North Carolina-09: Shameful Drive-by Scumbags and the Money-Bleeding Outlets that Employ Them," *The Daily Haymaker,* Feb. 21, 2018, https://dailyhaymaker.com/nc-09-shameful-driveby-scumbags-and-the-money-bleeding-outlets-that-employ-them/.

Chapter 19: The Iron Calculus of War

1. Michael I. Handel "Who is Afraid of Carl Von Clausewitz," coursework, U. S. Naval War College, 1997 Clausewitz.com, accessed 7-3-20.
2. John Lewis Interview.
3. "In Re: Investigation of Election Irregularities, Day 4," 687.
4. "In Re: Investigation of Election Irregularities, Day 4," 867, lines 6-15.
5. "In Re: Investigation of Election Irregularities, Day 4," 870.
6. "In Re: Investigation of Election Irregularities, Day 4," 910, lines 3-5.
7. "In Re: Investigation of Election Irregularities, Day 4," 910, lines 6-7.
8. "In re: Investigation of Election Irregularities,"921.
9. "In Re: Investigation of Election Irregularities, Day 4," 929.
10. "In Re: Investigation of Election Irregularities, Day 4," 929.
11. "In Re: Investigation of Election Irregularities, Day 4," 929.

12. "In Re: Investigation of Election Irregularities, Day 4," 930, lines 1-2.
13. "In re Election Protest of Leslie McCrae Dowless," 216, lines 16-24.

Epilogue

1. Babbie Mason and Eddie Carswell, "Trust His Heart," Causing Change Music, Dayspring Music, LLC, May Sun Publishing, Word Music, LLC, 2001.

CPSIA information can be obtained
at www.ICGtesting.com
Printed in the USA
FSHW020706041021

9 781977 241917